Uncreated Timeless Self of Radiant Emptiness - Onliness Consciousness and Commentaries

Uncreated Timeless Self of Radiant Emptiness - Onliness Consciousness and Commentaries

Awakening to Self-as-Self Supreme Reality

Revised Second Edition

Martin Treon

Auroral Skies Press
Goodyear, Arizona USA
2016

Auroral Skies Press
Goodyear, Arizona
2016

Library of Congress PCN Control Number: 2016910631
ISBN: Softcover 13 digit 9780965574068
10 digit 0965574067
1. Consciousness. 2. I Ching. 3. Enlightenment.

This book was printed in the United States of America.

Passage quotations printed by arrangement with The Acorn Press, P.O. Box 3279, Durham, NC 27715-3279

Other book by Martin Treon

The Tao of Onliness: An I Ching Cosmology - The Awakening Years

Fires of Consciousness: The Tao of Onliness I Ching

Enlightenment Dialogues: A Journey of Post-metaphysical Onliness Awakening

Enlightenment's Awakening: An Onliness Path of Truth-consciousness Realization

To my Teacher Sri Nisargadatta Maharaj, whose words have been centrally important toward My Awakening to Supreme Nondual Self-as-Self Reality

To
my wonderful wife, Margot H. Treon
(How lucky can I get!)

To my marvelous children:
Annette, Jacqueline, Erik, Valerie, Areca and Orion

Also

In loving memory of my parents:
my mother, Ruth Clauson Treon Carlson
my father, Avery Treon
and my stepfather, Einar Carlson

And in loving memory of my brother
Dennis Treon

TABLE OF CONTENTS

PART ONE

"Q [Questioner]: I find being alive is a painful state.

M [Sri Nasargadatta Maharaj]: You cannot be alive for you are life itself. It is the person you imagine yourself to be that suffers, not you. Dissolve it in awareness. It is merely a bundle of memories and habits. From the awareness of the unreal to the awareness of your real nature there is a chasm which you will easily cross, once you have mastered the art of pure awareness.

Q: All I know is that I do not know myself.

M: But whatever can be described cannot be yourself, and what you are cannot be described. . . Once you have understood that you are nothing perceivable or conceivable, that whatever appears in the field of consciousness cannot be your self, you will apply yourself to the eradication of all self-identification, as the only way that can take you to a deeper realization of your self. . . To know that you are neither in the body nor the mind, though aware of both, is already self-knowledge.

Q: If I am neither the body nor mind, how am I aware of them?

M: 'Nothing is me,' is the first step. 'Everything is me,' is the next step. Both hang on the idea: 'there is a world'. When this too is given up, you remain what you are - nondual Self. You are *it* here and now, but your vision is obstructed by your false ideas about yourself.

Q: If I alone am and the world is merely a projection, then why is there disharmony?

M: You create disharmony and then complain! When you desire and fear and then identify yourself with your feelings, you create sorrow and bondage. When you create, with love and wisdom, and remain unattached to your creations, the result is harmony and peace. . . It is only your self-identification with your mind that makes you happy or unhappy. Rebel against your slavery to your mind, see your bonds as self-created and break the chains of attachment and revulsion. Keep in mind your goal of freedom, until it dawns on you that you are already free, that freedom is not something in the distant future to be earned with painful efforts, but perennially one's own, to be used! Liberation is not an acquisitions but a matter of courage, the courage to believe that you are free already and act on it."

-Sri Nisargadatta Marahaj
from *I Am That* (2012)

PREFACE

PRIMARILY THIS BOOK is a revision of the book I wrote in 2008-09 entitled *Uncreated Timeless Self of Radiant Emptiness: Onliness Consciousness and Commentaries.* However, this second edition of that book has now been extensively modified in content, and thus basically altered through further develop of its content, which pertains to transcendent Self Awakening and Self Realization.

Like the first edition of *Uncreated Timeless Self of Radiant Emptiness*, this revised second edition presents a transpersonally oriented theory and perspective called Tao of Onliness, or just Onliness. However, primarily due to the influence of Sri Nisargadatta Marharaj, this second edition reflects an important shift within, and development-evolvement of, My own Path of transcendent Nondual Self-as-Self Awakening, Remembrance and Realization. Thus, in this text there is more clearly recognized the limitations of relative, conditional and conditioned waking yet dream-based *personal-egoic* self and consciousness, and its related *mind-based* mental knowledge, comprehension and insight into the Awakening of *transpersonal, trans-egoic* and *trans-mental* transcendent Nondual Self-as-Self Reality and Realization.

The basic limitation of this relative, conditional and conditioned knowledge, comprehension and insight of *body-mind* centered and identified compound personal-egoic self's *pre-transcendental* consciousness is that it cannot, in and of itself, transcend itself. This is so precisely because the *relative* knowledge, comprehension and insight consciousness of pre-transcendental mind is predominantly self-referencing, conditioned and conditional, and thus is necessarily bounded by and engulfed within *personal-egoic* fear and desire. In this way, it is, of itself, unable to effectively engage and employ One's *transpersonal, trans-egoic* and *trans-mental* Awareness and Experience toward Awakening from the illusion of this *relative* waking yet dream-based realm-wave mind reality.

Self-contained and self-contracted within its pre-personal pre-egoic, personal-egoic, and conditioned social-cultural self identity and consciousness, it does not, *of itself*, have the capacity to *transcend* the partial, distorted and limited knowledge, comprehension and insight of this relative compound personal-egoic mind and self reality, this illusory waking-dream reality, and thus Awaken to *transcendent*, transpersonal, trans-mental and trans-egoic Self of Absolute Reality. That is, Awakening to this uncreated, causeless, unborn and undying Truth-consciousness Self-of-no-self that each and every Consciousness Being and Entity always and already is, has ever been and will ever be.

Nonetheless, within pre-transcendental personal-egoic consciousness, such relative, conditional and conditioned *conceptual* mind-based wisdom, knowledge and understanding can be very helpful and important as a *preliminary* pre-transcendental transitional foundation and facilitator for subsequent development-evolution toward *transpersonal, trans-egoic* and *trans-mental* Truth-consciousness Self Remembrance and Awakening. And this is one of the primary reasons that I have written this book. But understand, that although such compound personal-egoic self mind-based pre-transcendental *mental* wisdom, insight and understanding can be valid and useful *cognitive* ways of metaphorically suggesting and "pointing to" transcendent *trans-mental* and *transpersonal* Self-realization Consciousness Reality, *within* Nondual Self-as-Self Awakening *itself,* mind's waking dream-based reality of relative visions, knowledge and wisdom are indeed invalid and thus developmentally-evolutionarily misleading, and ultimately are incapable of *directly* Expressing the True Nature, Condition and Identity of such transpersonal Awakened Self-realization.

The True Nature, Condition and Identity of Awakened Self-as-Self Reality Enlightenment is mentally unfathomable, unknowable, unqualifable and unspeakable. The Supreme Nondual Self Reality of such Awakening, as conceptually expressed in the mind-based dream of relative pre-transcendental waking consciousness, is best conveyed and broadly characterized, and ultimately trans-mentally Realized, through One's developmental-evolutionary transcendent Ascent in Truth and Wisdom, and the One's immanent Descent of Unconditional and All-embracing Love, Care and Compassion, which I discuss in the following pages.

Part I of this book describes one of several possible conceptual (mind-based) developmental-evolutionary Paths or Ways of transcendental Awakening and Enlightenment, but from the point of view of the Path that I call transcendent Onliness, or, in relative self perception, Onliness theory and perspective. Part II is a *reference text*, and presents the 64 hexagram-symbolized *Tao of Onliness I Ching Commentaries*. These Onliness I Ching Commentaries *initially emerge* within, and comprise, the sixty-four "Faces" or Dimensions of Onliness theory's transpersonal developmental-evolutionary sub-realm-wave of *universive* Subtle Prim-istence Revelation. In turn, this sub-realm-wave is embedded within the broader realm-wave of Subtle Prim-istence Awakening and Realization (see Figures 3, 4 and 5). Both of these realm-waves of Truth-consciousness are described in Part I. In Onliness theory, these 64 *I Ching* hexagram-symbolized texts are the polaric "Faces" or Expressions of Spirit, of Self, that define and express the developmental-evolutionary Self Illumination content of *universive* Subtle Prim-istence Awakening and Realization.

In Onliness theory and perspective, *I Ching* and Onliness's *Tao of Onliness I Ching* consultation is intended to be used as an *early stage* form of *meditation* toward transcendental Self Awakening, Remembrance and Realization. As discussed in *Fires of Consciousness*, such consultation is *not* a "magic" fortune-teller game, but rather a quiet and mindful *preliminary* form of meditation. That is, it is an opportunity to more *deeply* and *intuitively* See into One's own Self-nature. There is nothing magical about it. In this way, the Part II content of these 64 hexagram-symbolized *Tao of Onliness I Ching* Commentaries are intended to mediate, facilitate and support Inquiry and Insight into One's Truth-consciousness Awakening to Self-as-Self Nondual Supreme Reality, through meditative consultation of the *Tao of Onliness I Ching*, in conjunction with consultation of the traditional *I Ching* itself.

It is important to note Ken Wilber's (1995) pre/trans fallacy warnings in this regard, but in this instance in relation to *I Ching* consultation since it has historically so often been seen and used in magic and mythic "fortune-teller" terms and context. That is, one must carefully avoid confusing and confounding *pre-rational* (i.e., pre-personal, pre-egoic and pre-mental) consciousness realm-wave levels of human development-evolution (e.g., of archaic, magic, and mythic realm-wave levels of consciousness) with transcendent *trans-rational* (i.e., trans-personal, trans-egoic and trans-mental) realm-wave levels of Intuitive Consciousness Realization, by misinterpreting, mis-identifying and thus mistaking *pre-rational* realm-waves of *relative* self and consciousness for *trans-rational* realm-waves of *transcendent* Self and Consciousness, with disastrous results.

PART 1

THE TAO OF ONLINESS:
AWAKENING TO NONDUAL SELF-AS-SELF
RECOGNITION, REMEMBRANCE AND REALIZATION

"When all things are seen as perfect expressions of Spirit, just as they are, all things become deeply, painfully beautiful."

-KEN WILBER (*ONE TASTE*, 2000)

IN ADDITION TO sleeping dream-state consciousness, Your mental waking-state consciousness experience and awareness is also a relative, conditional and conditioned mind-based *waking dream* reality, a waking consciousness *dream* of body-mind identity only and alone. None of these mentally constructed waking consciousness dreams include or unveil Ultimate Self Reality. None Reveals Supreme Self which alone is *Real*. All are merely attentionally-fleeting mental images, sensations, shadow-phantom memories and expectations of relative self reality. All are *unreal* transient projected or introjected ideational, sensory and emotional waking dream illusions, that we earth-centered humans agree to call "reality." These body-mind self-identity mentally formulated dream-based realities of waking consciousness are not of Reality or Truth at all.

This relative mind of polarity-within-unity waking consciousness experience and awareness creates a space-time bounded, conditioned and conditional temporal world. Again, this is a *waking yet dream-based* reality of mental consciousness toward which you self-identify, and in which you believe yourself, and appear to yourself, to be *of* and to live *within*. It is a mind-based relative reality of illusion, which sees Reality only through the distorting veil of personal-egoic transient pain and pleasure, fear and desire. But, ultimately, *all* of this ideational content is created by body-mind memory, expectation, imagination and illusion. However, this *illusory* mental waking-dream reality of body-mind creation is *not* Your True Nature, Condition and Identity. In Truth, You are *not* a body, and You are *not* a mind. It is *All-inclusive and All-embracing Self of Supreme Reality* that You Are, have ever been, and will ever be.

Self Is, and Is Not, and Is Neither. Ultimately, Self is ineffable, unfathomable, unknowable and unspeakable. Self is also this *completely* approachable, accessible, fathomable, knowable and speakable *gateless gate* of Self-remembrance and Self-realization. Self is the Watercourse Way of the Tao. It is this Transparent Everyday Self of Truth and Wisdom, and of Unconditional and All-inclusive Love, Care and Compassion. And You, and indeed each and every Being and Entity of Consciousness, are always and already this birthless and deathless Bliss-Divine Self of Nonduality; this uncreated, causeless, boundless and timeless Self of Radiant Emptiness; this Truth-consciousness of *Absolute* Self-as-Self Reality.

The Way of Onliness is simply *one Path*, among a vast number of other equally valid Paths, of Nondual Self-as-Self transcendent Awakening, Remembrance and Realization. As presented here, the Way or Path of Onliness theory and perspective is expressed from a pre-transcendental advanced vision-logic stage or realm-wave of developmental-evolutionary consciousness. There is here no claim that Onliness theory and perspective is in any sense absolute, ultimate, eternal or universal in any pre-given sense. The realm-waves of transcendent Self-recognition Truth-consciousness discussed in Onliness are developmental and evolutionary in nature, not pre-created pre-given, pre-destined or pre-ordained.

Onliness theory claims that, overall, the unfolding of these realm-wave stages of manifest Spirit's or Self's transcendent Self-remembering *emerge* and *evolve* over vast periods of time, and gradually establish themselves as patterned *tendencies* of realm-wave Consciousness Self Realization, as Pathway tendencies or "trails" so to speak. This *diverse beings* Reality Pathway emerges through sequences of commonly repeated developmental-evolutionary realm-waves (i.e., pathway and trail tendencies) taken by countless numbers of diverse manifest Consciousness Beings and Entities (human, human-like and non-human). And, of course, the diversity of Pathways is a function of the *greatly differing* evolutionary types, temperaments, experiences, physical environments and structural forms of these Beings and Entities. It has been postulated (Wilber, 2007) that, over the vast time periods of Self's or Spirit's developmental-evolutionary unfolding, each of these countlessly repeated realm-waves (Pathways) becomes established as Kosmic structural states and stages of Consciousness. That is, they become developmental-evolutionary realm-wave Self Recognition and Realization *structures* of "Kosmic habit," as Ken Wilber and others have suggested.

Onliness theory and perspective is a contextual and interpreted *mental-conceptual* construction. It is post-metaphysical in the sense that its proposed realm-waves, stages, states, pathways, trails etc. of developmental-evolutionary Truth-consciousness Self Revelation are open to experiential testing (i.e., are experientially evidence-based) through application of One's own personal and transpersonal Experiential evidence gathering toward its verification and validity, or its rejection and invalidity. However, such *necessary* personal and transpersonal Knowledge acquisition and subsequent testing is challenging and not easily accomplished. As Wilber (1995, 1997, 1998, 2007) points out, this evaluation and assessment requires three broad knowledge acquisition and testing strands or steps.

This first step entails *preparation*, through One's specification and enactment of an *injunction*. This injunction takes the form of a disciplined and sustained attention to, instruction in, and knowledge of what needs to be learned, known, practiced and done, *prior* to such testing, so as to fully and directly access the experiential Consciousness Realization of the particular Onliness realm-wave (stage, state etc.) under study and testing. *Potentially*, this may involve years of such attention, instruction, study and practice.

In the second required step, One acquires the developmental-evolutionary *experiential evidence data* (potential confirmation data) in the form of a transcendent Awakening and Illumination (i.e., a Prehension, Recognition, Awareness, Realization) as to the Nature of the particular Onliness realm-wave's proposed Revelations under consideration and testing. And the third strand or step in this process requires a communal confirmation or rejection, which involves conferring with and sharing One's Onliness realm-wave Experiential evidence data (One's experiential Recognition, Awakening, Awareness, Illumination, Realization) *with others,* who have also completed strands one and two of this Knowledge and Experiential acquisition and testing process in relation to either this Onliness realm-wave level, or to its equivalent transcendent Consciousness realm-wave level from a different but authentic Enlightenment Pathway. That is, with others who are thus adequately prepared to judge, and are thus able to affirm as valid or reject as invalid, One's experiential evidence data in relation to this proposed Onliness realm-wave Realization, in a kind of *peer review* of One's overall findings and interpretations.

Onliness is a *relative* mind-based theory and perspective of transcendent Spirit or Self Illumination and Realization that has progressively developmentally emerged in My own physically, socially-culturally, historically and environmentally embedded and contextualized personal and transpersonal Consciousness over many years. Onliness theory and perspective is not so much an answer as it is a question; not so much response as stimulus. Onliness perspective emphasizes the *integration* of *cognitive-epistemologic* awareness and insight in all domains of knowledge, and *meditative-contemplative-ontologic* experiential being and being-ness Recognition, Remembrance and Realization, all in the course of developmental-evolutionary transcendent Awakening.

The Onliness dimensions of Awakening and Revelation discussed here attempt to describe the realm-waves of Self's or Spirit's developmental-evolutionary *transcendent* Ascent of Wisdom and Truth, and its *immanent* Descent of Unconditional and All-embracing Love, Care and Compassion. The Dimensions of transcendent Truth-consciousness addressed in this text are what Ken Wilber (2007) calls 3rd Tier levels or stages of *transpersonal* Consciousness. Using the color spectrum of light, he visualizes and describes these sequentially as: *Indigo,* which is *Psychic* stage or level (i.e., Illuminated Mind, Para-Mind, Trans-global - World Soul); to *Violet,* which is *Subtle* stage or level (i.e., Intuitive Mind, Meta-Mind - Illuminated Vision Soul); to *Ultraviolet,* which is *Causal* stage or level (i.e., Overmind - Unmanifest Formless Spirit); to the trans-stage-and-state of *Clear Light,* which is *Supermind* or Nondual Spirit-as-Spirit Awakening and Realization.

In Onliness theory, the *final* two holon-poles and their *final* holon-polarity is of World- Soul *Being* (i.e., the open and abundant Fullness of Spirit's or Self's Abyss of eternal and ever-evolving Manifest Form), and *Nonbeing* (i.e., the open and abundant Freedom of Spirit's or Self's Abyss of timeless and changeless Unmanifest Emptiness) realm-wave Self Awakening and Revelation. In turn, this Realization ultimately unveils and reveals the realm-wave of Universal Spirit's or Universal Self's Causal Holistence *holon-only* (beyond polarity-duality) developmental-evolutionary transcendent Self Recognition and Awakening. And, in turn, such Causal Holistence Realization ultimately unveils and reveals the *trans-realm-wave* Awakening Transformation of Supreme Nondual Spirit-as-Spirit or Self-as-Self Enlightenment (see Figures 4 and 6).

Onliness theory recognizes that all pre-transcendental mind-based *conceptually* interpreted, formulated and proposed pathways, trails, states, levels, realm-waves and stages of Consciousness Awakening (including those described in this text) are relative, limited, conditional, as well as personally, socially-culturally and historically contextual and conditioned, ways of expressing One's developmental-evolutionary Realization *of* and *as* Self-as-Self or Spirit-as-Spirit Truth-consciousness Enlightenment. Ultimately, You and I are always and already Illuminated Supreme Self of Spirit *only*, are Unqualifable and Unassailable Enlightened Self-as-Self Reality *only*, beyond and prior to all such proposed pre-transcendental mental-conceptual illusory dream-based (i.e., I-am-my-body based) *relative reality* pathways, trails, states, realm-waves and stages of Enlightenment.

In this text, the *meaning* of phrases such as "Onliness asserts" or "Onliness theory and perspective claims, proposes, accepts, embrace or suggests" is that *I,* as a pre-egoic pre-personal, personal-egoic, and conditioned social-cultural person, so assert or claim, propose, accept, embrace or suggest. In this obvious sense, Onliness theory and perspective is my own *personal* conceptual formulation. However, its deeper and more profound ideas, concepts and insights are certainly *not* originally mine. Its underlying foundational ideas, concepts, knowledge and insights did not originate with me, but rather were formulated by, and derive from, *so many* others who, presently and over many centuries, have originated, developed and expressed these Onliness related ideas, concepts and insights, which I have here integrated and arranged as Onliness theory and perspective.

Onliness theory proposes that the *Path* of Onliness Awakening, which is put forward as one of eight broadly defined Enlightenment Realization Modes of transcendent Truth-consciousness Revelation, is commonly shared by countless numbers of quite different but related kinds or *types* of Consciousness Beings and Entities (i.e., and thus countless numbers of so called (i.e., relatively perceived) individual Beings and Entities within each type). In Onliness theory, these eight holon-polar *Enlightenment Realization Modes* (symbolized through the 64 *I Ching* hexagrams) begin to initially arise and emerge within developmental-evolutionary Consciousness at the *source* of sub-realm-wave *universive* Subtle Prim-istence Recognition and Awakening (see Figures 3, 5 and 7). Subsequently, these eight Modes of Enlightenment find Expression *throughout* transcendent World-Soul's realm-wave of Subtle Prim-istence Self Realization, and developmentally-evolutionarily flower to full Self Remembrance, Synthesis and Resolution within its final sub-realm-wave of *absolute* Subtle Holistent Prim-istence Awakening (see Figures 3, 4, 5 and 7).

The descriptions of developmental-evolutionary transcendent Consciousness Recognition and Illumination put forward in this text focuses primarily on *manifest* Consciousness Beings and Entities, of this and all possible worlds, dimensions and universes, who are on a transcendent Consciousness Path of Self-awakening and Self-realization. However, this focus is *not* intended to imply that such *relatively* developmentally-evolutionarily advanced Consciousness Beings and Entities are somehow more important or significant in relation to less developmentally advanced Beings and Entities. Onliness theory assert that in Ultimate Nondual Self-as-Self Realization all so called separate Consciousness Beings and Entities are of *One*

Buddha-mind. All are thus of *equal* and the *same* Buddha-nature, and are of exactly *equal* and *same* importance and significance.

In Self or Spirit, which is to say in Reality and Truth, there is *no* separateness or otherness whatsoever, and thus the existence of so called separate individual Beings and Entities is an illusions of relative, conditional and conditioned mental self and consciousness. *All* such perception is a polarity-based subject-versus-object perceived otherness and separateness *illusion* of compound personal-egoic self's mind-based discrimination. In Onliness theory, such Beings and Entities of Consciousness extend all the way from string, to quark, to atom, to grain of sand, to organic plant, to bacterium, to insect, to human being, and far beyond. At least for earth-centered human beings, it is only within this *relative, conditioned* and *conditional* compound personal-egoic self and consciousness of waking but dream-based reality that Consciousness Entities and Beings appear to differ in quality and degree of Awakening to transcendent Nondual Self-as-Self Reality.

The Tao or Way of Onliness is a transcendental Transformational Spiritual Path and perspective that certain human, human-like and non-human Beings and Entities tend to be *predisposed to* by virtue of their similar, and even shared, temperaments, manifest configurations, and environmental experiences. Indeed, the reason I speak of Tao of Onliness and Onliness theory is that the following content is *viewed* and *interpreted* from this Onliness perspective or point of view. That is, it is understood and formulated from, and written within, this Onliness frame of reference. However, it is *not* that Onliness transcendental perspective is *in any way* special or privileged in relation to other transcendental views or perspectives. It is merely *one* (hopefully) complementary view and interpretation within the context of many other equally important and valid transcendental views and interpretations. Onliness theory and perspective is intended and presented as an advanced vision-logic pre-transcendental *relative* consciousness mental formulation. It is a mind-based *conceptual formulation* of truth, and thus a *partial* truth, but certainly *not* Truth Itself.

In this way, Tao of Onliness is written *from* Onliness perspective for the simple reason that, by psychologic and genetic temperament, including factors of individual experience, cultural background, history, socioeconomic and physical environment, it happens to *My own* predominantly predisposing developmental relative point of view and frame of reference. And while the focus of this text tends to be primarily on a "positive note" of the evolution and development of transcendental Self or Spirit Recognition, Remembrance, Awakening and Realization (as viewed from Onliness perspective), such focus is *not* meant to imply that *relative* human evil, greed and cruelty, which variously derives from individual and collective desire, fear, ignorance and delusion, does not exist. In fact, it seems quite apparent that it is *presently* and *frequently* manifest in this transient and conditional and conditioned world of birth and death.

Onliness theory is an *integral* and *radically Transformative* spiritual perspective of the developmental-evolutionary transcendent Ascent of Wisdom and Truth, and the immanent Descent of Unconditional and All-encompassing Love, Care and Compassion. In this way, the witnessing and application in daily relative life of such Ascending-Descending Wisdom, Truth, Love, Care and Compassion through transpersonal Awareness and Experience is critically important from Onliness perspective. Also important in the Path of Onliness, is the necessity of One's engagement in a disciplined and sustained meditative practice. In Onliness, such a focused and ongoing meditation practice provides a fundamental "Means-whereby" through which One can *directly* Experience (and test for One's self) the *radical* transpersonal Revelations and Transformations of Self that occur in transcendental Self Recognition, Awakening, Remembrance and Realization.

There are many *Transformative* meditation practice options available that One may employ. I would encourage You to research, take instruction in and practice one or more of these that seem right for You. Such meditative and contemplation practices occur and are described in almost all of the great mystical-religious spiritual traditions of the world. The practice I primarily employ, the one I seem best suited to, is of the Soto Zen Buddhism tradition and is called serene reflection meditation or *zazen* (described elsewhere in this book). However, I would add that even *I Ching* and *Tao of Onliness I Ching* consultation which specifically addresses *transpersonal* levels of Self Reality, if approached and accomplished with a meditative-contemplative and quiet mind, can be considered an *early stage* form of contemplation-meditation.

However, from Onliness perspective, all meditation practices must *not* be viewed or understood as a means to an end, but rather as an end *in* and *of* itself. Also, it is *necessary* to integrate One's developing transpersonal Self Awareness, Experience, Insight, Compassion, Love, Care and Wisdom, which emerges through such meditation practice, into *application* and *implementation* in relation to other Beings and Entities within One's relative daily life activities. The Way of Tao of Onliness is certainly a "call to practice and application" as a *central* transpersonal Means-whereby of this Transformative Evolution and Revolution of Nondual Self-as-Self Awakening and Realization.

In Onliness theory, such ongoing and focused meditation is a basic developmental-evolutionary Way toward *radical* Transcendence of One's narcissistic and self-contracted life of compound personal-egoic waking dream-based self and consciousness, toward Realization of One's *True* Nature and Condition of Bliss-Divine Nondual Self Identity. Thus, the Path of Onliness *is not* in any way intended to bolster, pacify, nurture, prolong, support, enhance or sustain such compound personal-egoic (i.e., pre-personal pre-egoic, personal-egoic, and conditioned social-cultural) self of pre-transcendental consciousness. Rather, Onliness is a Spiritual Path of *radical* Transcendence, but inclusion within the context of such Transcendence, of such relative, conditional, and conditioned compound personal-egoic self identity and consciousness.

In the Way of Onliness then, it is important that the fruits of meditative practice's transpersonal Self Awakening be included with, and integrated into, One's day-to-day relative life and work. Thus, the spiritual life practice, of which such meditation is a part, which One subsequently develops and evolves should, as much as possible, be *integrated* and *continuous* with, and *expressed* throughout, One's everyday so called (i.e., relatively perceived) interior-individual and exterior-social-cultural-environmental life awareness and experience. This is an transpersonal Self Expression of Love, Care and Compassion. In this regard, as a part of One's integral spiritual life practice within pre-transcendental relative self and consciousness development, I would suggest that One could greatly benefit from careful study of, and insight into: the ancient world's spiritually oriented

Great Nest of Being's perennial philosophy and its related Eastern and Western World philosophies of *pre-modern* wisdoms and truths; as well as *modernity's* individual-centered, democratic, rational and scientifically oriented wisdoms and truths; and also *post-modernity's* contextual, interpretive, pluralistic, co-created and aperspectival wisdoms and truths.

However, in Onliness theory, this mind-based relative, conditioned and conditional waking dream-based knowledge, understanding and insight that is valid, relevant, meaningful and important to One's integral spiritual life practice throughout this pre-transcendental self and consciousness developmental realm-wave, is *much* less, to only marginally, relevant and meaningful within One's transcendental *World-Soul* Awakening of *trans-mental* Psychic Multi-istence and Subtle Prim-istence Self Realization (see Figures 4 and 6). And, indeed, is even less valid, relevant and meaningful, to very often invalid, within One's transcendental *Universal Spirit* Self Revelation and Realization of the *trans-mental* developmental realm-wave of Causal Holistence Awakening.

And ultimately, within the All-encompassing Ground that is the transpersonal, trans-egoic, trans-mental, trans-polaric and trans-realm-wave Supreme Self Reality of Awakened Nondual Self-as-Self Realization, *all* of this waking yet dream-based relative mental knowledge, understanding and insight of compound personal-egoic self and consciousness is no longer valid, relevant or meaningful *at all*. That is, such fear and desire mind-based *relative* knowledge, understanding and insight have *all* been transcended, but included within such transcendence, and are thus ultimately invalid, irrelevant and meaningless within Awakened Supreme Self Reality and Consciousness.

In Onliness theory, both the Unmanifest Emptiness and Manifest Form of transcendent *Wisdom, Compassion* and *Communion* together comprise the *three focal centers* or bases of an integral spiritual life practice throughout One's developmental transcendent Ascent of Wisdom and Truth, and One's immanent Descent of Unconditional and All-inclusive Love, Care and Compassion, which finds full Expression in Nondual Self-as-Self Enlightenment. See this configuration of *Compassion, Communion*, as well as *Knowledge* and *Meaning* which together comprise *Wisdom*, in Figures 5, 6 and 7. Embracing the causeless, timeless, uncreated and boundless Self Awakening of both changeless Emptiness and ever-changing Form, Onliness theory proposes that human Beings have two *basic* Ways or Paths by and through which each of *Wisdom, Compassion* and *Communion* can be Recognized, Mediated, Facilitated, Supported, Experienced, Revealed, and Developed in the context of One's everyday life of relative self reality.

First, in the Path of Onliness, and while still identified with conditioned and conditional pre-transcendental and transitional transcendental relative self and consciousness, One needs to develop an earnest, self-disciplined and sustained transpersonally focused integral *meditation practice*. And to do this, whenever possible, within the context of a supportive and similarly oriented spiritual community or group of others, and with supportive teaching and guidance from a recognized, trusted and experienced spiritual teacher(s).

Second, also still within this relative self reality of waking dream-based pre-transcendental and transitional transcendental self and consciousness awareness and experience identity, One needs to ongoingly develop an earnest, self-disciplined and sustained *integral* study-therapy-practice-exercise-application of at least the following awareness, experiential, knowledge, insight and comprehension dimensions of relative mind and consciousness: (a) cognitive (aesthetic, analytic, literary, philosophic, scientific, etc.), (b) affective-emotional-sexual, (c) physiologic-physical-bodily, (d) interpersonal-relational-social-cultural-environmental, (e) justice-ethics-morality and (f) relative mind-based awareness of transpersonal-spiritual Knowledge, Insight, Wisdom and Understanding.

THE IMPORTANCE OF KEN WILBER'S WORK IN ONLINESS THEORY FORMULATION

Ken Wilber's profound, inclusive and integral insights into the nature of Ultimate Reality have importantly influenced and informed Tao of Onliness theory and perspective. Fundamental to Wilber's philosophic spiritual perspective is that the development-evolution of Consciousness Beings and Entities is always *holonic* in nature. In this, *all* of manifest Beings' development-evolution occurs through the emergent sequence of *holons*, in which each newly emergent holon is a *new whole* in that it *transcends* but includes its preceding holons, which becomes a part of this new holon. And then, in turn, this new and more inclusive holon becomes a *part* of the *next* newly emergent holon after or above it. Additionally, however, throughout all of pre-transcendental and up through all transcendental World-Soul developmental realm-waves of Self Illumination and Awakening, Onliness theory asserts that polarity-within-unity *always* occurs within such *holonic* context of developmental manifest Beings and Entities. As described by Wilber (1995) then, the development-evolution of each Consciousness Being and Entity of manifest Form Reality is comprised of hierarchically (or more accurately holarchically) organized holons. This nested holon hierarchy is one of progressively greater depth (height) of pre-transcendental and transcendental Consciousness Awakening, Inclusion and Embrace.

Onliness theory acknowledges the validity and importance of scientifically based Darwinian evolutionary theory, and its evolutionary factors and forces, such as adaptation to environmental change and migration, as well as inter-life competition and defense survival, and so on. Additionally however, Onliness theory, in agreement with Wilber (1995, 1996, 1998, 2004), and others (e.g., Whitehead, 1967), asserts that there is *inherent* in transcendent Spirit's or Self's developmental-evolutionary Expression an underlying and fundamental *directional* motive-ground capacity for ever-emerging *creativity* and *novelty*. In Self or Spirit Awakening, Revelation, and Expression this underlying directional capacity of emergent novelty and creativity functions as a kind of telos "pull" of Eros toward Self-transcendence (i.e., Self-recognition, Self-remembrance and Self-realization), through which new developmental-evolutionary holons emerge and manifest in Form Reality. In this regard, the Sage Sri Nisargadatta Maharshi (2012) has said that in the heart of each human there is an inherent universal power that works toward Enlightenment and Liberation, which he calls *Sadashiva*.

As suggested, when successive holons emerge in development and evolution, each succeeding and more Consciousness inclusive (i.e., more Self-awakened and Self-realized) senior holon *transcends but includes* its immediately preceding, and less Consciousness inclusive, junior holon. That is, the preceding junior holon becomes a *component part* of its succeeding senior holon (i.e., the junior or lower holon is included within, and integrated into, the senior or higher holon as its sub-holon component part). This succeeding senior holon is a *new whole,* in that it recognizes and realizes new and greater depths of Truth-consciousness Self-realization inclusion (i.e., greater depths of Self-recognition and Self-revelation) than did its preceding junior holon. Thus, each successive senior holon creates its own distinctive and defining *expanded* depth (or height) of such Truth-consciousness inclusion; it creates a *new whole* that was *not* previously available at the level of its preceding junior holons.

It is in this sense that each and every holon is said to be a *whole/ part* (i.e., every holon is at once a *new whole* in relation to the preceding junior holons below it, and is *a part* in relation to the succeeding senior holons above it). All realm-wave development-evolution of Consciousness Beings and Entities within manifest Form Reality, all the way up and all the way down, up to Nondual Self Realization itself, is composed of such holarchically *nested* holons, one within the other, such that each lower (less Truth-consciousness inclusive) holon is contained within its next higher (more Truth-consciousness inclusive) holon. This is what Wilber (1995, 1996) calls the "nested holarchy of being."

Wilber (1995, 2000, 2007) asserts, and Onliness theory fully agrees, that manifest Spirit's or Self's evolutionary-developmental Remembrance and Realization of Its True Nature, Condition and Identity as Spirit *only,* occurs from matter, to life (body), to mind, to Soul, to Spirit. And in human life, from pre-egoic, to egoic, to trans-egoic; in moral development from pre-conventional (me), to conventional (we: my group, tribe, country), to post-conventional (we: all people universally); from pre-rational, to rational to, trans-rational; from pre-verbal, to verbal, to trans-verbal; from sub-conscious, to self-conscious, to super-conscious; from pre-personal, to personal, to trans-personal; from egocentric, to sociocentric/ethnocentric, to worldcentric.

Wilber (1995, 1996, 1997) describes the course of *evolution* as the developmental-evolutionary ascent of Spirit, from physical matter, to life (body), to mind, to Soul, to Spirit, and ultimately to the Realization of Spirit-as-Spirit (i.e., Nondual Self-as-Self Realization). Conversely, the course of *involution* is described as the return or reverse process. That is, the developmental-evolutionary descent of Spirit, from Spirit-as-Spirit (Nondual Self Realization), to Spirit, to Soul, to mind, to life (body), to physical matter. For Consciousness Beings and Entities, this process of involution is thought to begin at, and occurs within, death; while evolution begins at conception and *can* occur throughout life. As a working and viable *hypothesis*, Onliness theory includes this understanding of the developmental-evolutionary courses of transcendent Spirit's or Self's involution and evolution of into its perspective.

Also important in Onliness theory and perspective is Ken Wilber's (1995, 1999-2000, 2007) conception of the existence of multiple valid knowledge sources, which are described within the context of his formulation of the four quadrants. Recall, these four quadrants inherently arise within each and every sentient Being's holonic development. According to Wilber, these four quadrant sources of valid knowledge (or simply the Big Three of I, You-We-Thou, and It) occur at *each* and *every* stage and state of Consciousness. Wilber postulates that each of the four quadrants of every holon, of all sentient Beings, expresses itself as an equal, distinct and valid source of knowledge, which knowledge cannot be reduced or collapsed into any other quadrant of that holon.

Using a circle divided into four equal quadrants to visualize this, Wilber indicates that the upper and lower quadrants of the *right half* of the circle (the two right quadrants) are both the *objective and exterior* (e.g., physical, form, empirical, scientific, observable, quantifiable) manifestations of any given holon (the exterior dimensions of the holon), while the upper and lower quadrants of the *left half* of the circle (the two left quadrants) are both the *subjective and interior* (e.g., awareness, experience, meaning, values, consciousness, qualifiable) manifestations of any given holon (the interior dimensions of the holon).

Again using this circle, the right and left quadrants of the *upper half* of the circle, the two upper quadrants, are both the *singular individual* (e.g., intentional, behavioral) manifestations of any given holon, while the *lower half,* the two lower quadrants, are both the *plural collective* and *communal* (e.g., cultural, social system, worldspace, worldview) manifestations of any given holon. Thus, each holon of each and every sentient Being concurrently manifests as these four quadrants: upper-left Interior-Individual, lower-left Interior-Collective, upper-right Exterior-Individual, lower-right Exterior-Collective. Each of the four quadrants is a fundamental and equally important holon manifestation and source of knowledge. Furthermore, the valid knowledge of any one of the four quadrants cannot be reduced to any one of the other three.

For humans, the upper-left *subjective* Interior-Individual *intentional* quadrant (the "I" quadrant) centrally concerns *truthfulness* (e.g., sincerity, integrity, trustworthiness). The upper-right *objective* Exterior-Individual *behavioral* quadrant (the "it" quadrant) is centrally involved with *truth* (e.g., correspondence, representation, propositionality). The lower-left *intersubjective* Interior-Communal *cultural* quadrant (the "We" quadrant) is concerned with *justness* (e.g., cultural fit, mutual understanding, rightness). Finally, the lower-right *interobjective* Exterior-Communal *social system* quadrant (the "its" quadrant) is concerned with *functional fit* (e.g., systems theory, structural-functionalism, social systems mesh) (Wilber, 1995, 1996, 1998, 2007).

Wilber points out that the *knowledge* derived from the four quadrants of each and every human Being holon can be simplified into (summarized as) the language of "the Big Three": I, We and It. That is, a holon's upper-left quadrant's *knowledge* realm is expressed in interior-subjective *individual* "I" dialogical language, which involves truthfulness, sincerity, aesthetics, art, beauty, and *the Beautiful* (as in Plato's philosophy), as founded and expressed within *individual* consciousness, self, and the dignity of the individual; and in Buddhism, it is the Buddha.

A holon's lower-left quadrant's *knowledge* realm finds expression in interior-subjective *communal (collective)"You/Thou/We"* dialogical language, which involves intersubjective justness, culture, ethics, morals, worldviews, goodness, and *the Good* (as in Plato's philosophy), as founded and expressed within shared communal contexts, intersubjective communication and meaning, mutual understanding, appropriateness, and the dignity of community and culture; and in Buddhism, it is the Sangha.

A holon's *two* right quadrant's *knowledge* realms are respectively expressed in exterior-objective *individual* or *communal* and *collective* *"It"* and *"Its"* monological language, which includes science and technology, objective nature, objective truth, and *the True* (as in Plato's philosophy), as founded and expressed within *empirical* forms (including brain and social systems), propositional truth, the dignity of science and exterior objective truth; and in Buddhism, it is the Dharma.

Ken Wilber's profound and thoughtful insights into the nature of pre-transcendental and transcendent Nondual *Self Recognition and Realization*, as presented in his writings (1995, 1996,1999-2000, 2004, 2007), and as sketchily summarized above, have played an very important role throughout the formulation and development of Onliness theory and perspective. I consider Wilber's writings, especially those from 1995 to the present (2016), to be among the most accurate, integrated, comprehensive, and inclusive cognitive philosophic accounts of the nature of pre-transcendent and transcendent Consciousness Reality ever presented. When even partially integrated into Onliness theory, the wisdom of Wilber's insightful mind-based advanced vision-logic consciousness perspectives add immeasurably to the clarity, meaning and depth of Onliness theory and perspective, for which I am forever grateful to Ken Wilber.

TAO OF ONLINESS THEORY BACKGROUND AND FOUNDATIONS

Tao of Onliness mind-based conception-formulation is *primarily* rooted in *Mahayana Buddhism* (especially Zen Buddhism) and *Taoism*, with substantial contribution to its content and construction based on meditative consultation of the *I Ching*. However, Onliness also attempts to *honor* and *include* expressions of the mystical and transcendental Wisdom and Truth, as well as the Unconditional and All-pervading Love, Care and Compassion, that are variously presented and described in all of the major spiritual-religious traditions of the world.

In *The Tao of Onliness: An I Ching Cosmology - The Awakening Years* (Treon, 1989) and *Fires of Consciousness: The Tao of Onliness I Ching* (Treon, 1996), I broadly outlined Onliness theory and perspective, but only in a brief and limited way. Both books are written in a combined *play format* (involving three characters) which occurs within a narrative story format. In *Fires of Consciousness*, I also used a fixed number of syllables per line to create a kind of *verse* patterning. Because of the constraints of these format factors, there tended to be a limited amount of content elaboration put forward concerning the meanings and implications of the various Onliness realm-waves of transpersonal Self Awakening, Remembrance and Realization. Thus in the first edition of this book, and currently in this book's second edition revision, I am attempting to address this problem with a more detailed discussion and elaboration of such meanings and implications.

Also, over the past thirty-nine years since I initially began Tao of Onliness content formulation in 1977 (see Treon, 1981a and Treon, 1981b), My understanding of, and insight into, the meanings and implications of Onliness theory and perspective has evolved (see Treon, 1996, 2009, 2011 and 2015), together with my spiritual Self-awakening development and relative mind-based general knowledge and insight. In this way, I am now (in 2016) presenting a somewhat altered and significantly revised version of Onliness theory and perspective. And, hopefully, it reflects a clearer and more profound understanding of the nature and meaning of Tao of Onliness as a Path of transcendent Truth-consciousness Awakening, Illumination and Realization of Nondual Self-as-Self Absolute Reality, than previously was the case.

From the beginning, I *strongly* relied upon, and *extensively* used, consultation of the *I Ching* in formulating Tao of Onliness theory and perspective. In creating the Tao of Onliness I Ching in *Fires of Consciousness*, I especially used extensive *I Ching* consultation to aid in determining which of the sixty-four (a) primary name identities, (b) spiritual text quotations, and (c) photo images that I had taken and selected, were to be assigned to and associated with each of these 64 hexagrams. This is the way in which I determined how each of its sixty-four primary names, spiritual quotations, and photo images accorded and belonged with (needed to be placed with) each of the sixty-four *I Ching* hexagrams in *Fires of Consciousness: The Tao of Onliness I Ching*. As I've previously indicated, there is *nothing* at all magical or mysterious about the *I Ching,* or about its consultation. Used in a quiet meditative context, and at an advanced vision-logic realm-wave level of relative consciousness, I believe *I Ching* consultation can be, and is, a *early-stage* form of meditation which can facilitate and enhance One's *intuitive* vision-logic insight and awareness in to Self.

Indeed, I have always found such advanced vision-logic relative consciousness based *I Ching* consultation very useful and informative *if* approached with equanimity, in peaceful and quiet solitude, and especially in a meditative frame of mind. It was in this way that I approached and employed *I Ching* consultation in formulating Tao of Onliness theory and its Tao of Onliness I Ching content. The yin and yang polarity-within-unity patterned symbol-structure of the *I*

Ching made it uniquely suited to all aspect of such Onliness theory and perspective formulation.

Each of the following seven Onliness theory diagrams is intended to be interpreted as a *generalized, abstract* and *simplified* visual depiction of certain particular features and aspects of Onliness theory structure and content. These diagrams do not claim, and are not intended, to describe the *specific* course of Consciousness development-evolvement of any *given* so called individual Being and Entity. The course of development for an individual Being, as Wilber suggests (1999-2000, vol. 4; 2007), is perhaps better visualized as a spiral pattern, with sometimes progression and sometimes regression in the various developmental lines, stages and states of development, and with frequently erratic and irregular *rates* of development within each line, stage and state of Self Awakening and Realization.

Also, spiritual pathologies can and do occur within any developmental line, stage and state of Consciousness development-evolvement. Such pathologies can occur when higher stages and states (i.e., realm-waves) of Consciousness act to repress, suppress, deny or alienate lower realm-waves, instead of *transcending but including* the lower *within* the higher realm-wave stage and state, which is the *optimal* developmental sequence that should occur according to Wilber (2007) (Wilber, Engler and Brown, 1986).

As suggested, different *lines* of an individual's development (e.g., cognitive, moral, emotional-sexual, social, artistic, spiritual) often progress at differing rates, or even in different progression-regression directions, which can play a part in stage-specific realm-wave pathologies of Consciousness that can occur. As Wilber (1999-2000, vol. 4) and others have pointed out, it is the job of the ego or separate self-sense personal self, what I call One's relative, conditional and conditioned compound personal-egoic waking yet dream-based self and consciousness reality, to, hopefully, coordinate, associate and integrate the movement and course of all of these varied developmental lines.

The overall result is that development progresses, *if* it progresses at all - and it may not, in quite individually unique and often uneven and irregular ways. This kind of nonlinear and three-dimensional spiraling pattern is how each of the following abstract and generalized diagrams of Onliness theory should be visualized and interpreted in relation to a so called *individual* human Being's course of realm-wave development-evolvement.

Finally, what is written here is not intended to be the *final* truth or *ultimate* interpretation of Onliness theory and perspective. Quite the contrary, it is merely a *preliminary* interpretation, a sketchy and limited outline, of such theory and perspective. It is My hope that others will develop deeper, more profound and more complete interpretations and expressions (and corrections) of Tao of Onliness theory and perspective in future times. As the philosopher Ken Wilber (1995, 1996) reminds us, "We are all tomorrows food."

THE NATURE, STRUCTURE AND CONTEXT OF ONLINESS THEORY AND PERSPECTIVE

Tao of Onliness is an *Enlightenment Path* within which is described mind-based theoretical formulations and hypotheses concerning various transcendental developmental-evolutionary Self-realization realm-waves of Self Recognition, Remembrance and Revelation. Ultimately then, this is the Revelation of Invulnerable, Immutable, Unassailable and Absolute transcendent Nondual Self-as-Self Awakening and Realization, to which certain, but *diverse*, manifest sentient Beings and Entities are variously predominantly predisposed. Onliness theory is a relative expression, primarily from an advanced vision-logic realm-wave mental point of view, *of and beyond* the pre-modern stream of transpersonal Knowledge and Insight that is often called the *perennial philosophy* (i.e., the common core content and essence of the world's great spiritual and mystical Wisdom Traditions).

Onliness theory asserts that the *deep structure* and *essential meaning* of each of its realm-waves, and of its trans-realm-wave of Radiant Nondual Self-realization, is an Expression of one possible *Universal* transcendent developmental-evolutionary Pathway of Self Awakening. That is, a Pathway of Spirit itself and only. It is, then, within and through such developmental-evolutionary realm-waves, and their Ground and Source trans-realm-wave of Awakened Nondual Self-as-Self Reality, that advanced-consciousness Beings and Entities Ascend to transcendent Wisdom and Truth, and simultaneously immanently Descend in Unqualifable and All-containing Love, Care and Compassion.

Also, Onliness theory proposes that such developmental-evolutionary Ascent and Descent Awakening and Realization occurs *only* in the sequence in which these realm-waves are holarchically arranged, without by-passing or omitting any single holon-polar or holon-only realm-wave of Self Realization. However, it is fully recognized that the meaning and truth of this particular formulation and description of Onliness theory is primarily an expression of My own relative, conditioned and conditional mind-based pre-egoic, personal-egoic, and conditioned so-cial-cultural-historical waking yet dream-based self and consciousness.

Tao of Onliness theory accepts and incorporates many of the central tenants of the perennial philosophy's "Great Chain of Being" (or more aptly, *Great Holarchy or Great Nest of Being*), particularly in the Nondual Ground Spirit-as-Spirit or Self-as-Self Realization traditions. And, by way of moderately updating this Great Holarchy of Being's Wisdom and Insights, I have in the process of formulating Onliness theory and perspective, attempted to integrate some of Ken Wilber's *developmental* and *evolutionary* integral holonic Self-realization insights and perspectives into perennial philosophy's pre-modern perspective.

Wilber (1995) defines a "holarchy" as a developmentally-evolutionarily unfolding *nested* sequence of progressively deeper and more encompassing stages and levels (realm-waves) of Self-recognition Consciousness inclusion. Thus, holarchy, as a true holism, *necessarily* involves the ranking of increasingly whole, inclusive and embracing developmental-evolutionary levels of Self Realization. In this holarchic ranking of increasing depth of Self-awakening Consciousness inclusion, the senior level, with its embrace of expanded depths or wholeness of Self Revelation and Remembrance, transcends but includes, in a nested way, all of its junior levels, which are *less* inclusive in this way, less whole. Note that Onliness theory agrees with, and has incorporated, this manner of nested holoarchic ranking depth of Truth-consciousness inclusion into its perspective.

Onliness is mind-based pre-transcendental consciousness *theory*, and as such can be tested as to its relative validity. Recall Wilber's (1995, 1996, 1998) holonic four-quadrant formulation, in which each holon has it own unique and important knowledge domains: individual-interior (subjective-intentional), individual-exterior (objective-behavioral), collective-interior (intersubjective-cultural) and collective exterior (interobjective-social-structural). Each of these four domains has *different types* of knowledge that require *different validation protocols*, and thus yield *different types* of truth.

By way of brief review, *valid knowledge acquisition* in all four of Wilber's quadrant domains requires: *first*, a valid, specified and disciplined practice for generating and gathering data in a given worldspace Consciousness domain (i.e., a valid *instrumental injunction* or paradigm that brings forth a given data domain); *second*, a direct *data-apprehension* or interpretation-illumination of the data brought forth within that worldspace Consciousness domain (whether sensory, mental or spiritual experience); and *third*, the communal confirmation/rejection by others who have adequately completed these previous injunctive and apprehensive valid knowledge acquisition steps. This is a peer review and *knowledge-quest replication* of the injunction and apprehension data findings, so as to confirm or reject these findings. This step represents the falsifiability principle. Onliness theory can thus be experientially tested by using these broadly based and generally accepted validity-claim testing processes and criteria.

As a working hypothesis, Onliness theory tentatively accepts the involution-evolution concept of Spirit or Self which is embraced in certain formulations and expressions of the Great Holarchy of Being (Wilber, 1995). In this view, Spirit or Self utterly "throws forth" Itself, in what humans might call a "playful" way, *into* involutionary manifestation; from the One into the Many. Self "playfully" casts and abandons Itself into the manifest Form of time and space, thus creating the physical-material universes of space-time reality. There thus occurs developmental *involution* from Spirit-as-Spirit, *to* Spirit-as-Soul, *to* Spirit-as-mind, *to* Spirit-as-life, *to* Spirit-as-matter (i.e., Spirit's lowest level - and the *exterior* form of all levels of Self-realization and Consciousness). This is the *involution* of Spirit or Self, in which the One developmentally involutes and manifests as the Many (Wilber, 1995, 1996).

Conversely, and in this same "playful" way, manifest Spirit or Self casts and abandons Itself into Self-transcendent and Self-remembering developmental *evolution* from the Many to the One: starting *from* Spirit-as-matter, *to* Spirit-as-life, *to* Spirit-as-mind, *to* Spirit-as-Soul, *to*, once again, its full Self-realization of Spirit-as-Spirit or Self-as-Self, well beyond, and prior to, the stream of space-time reality. This is the *evolution* of Spirit or Self, in which the Many developmentally evolve and manifest as the One.

In the Way or Path of Onliness Self Awakening, equal balance and importance are given to the developmental-evolutionary Trans-gnostic transcendent *Ascent* of Wisdom and Truth, and the Pan-gnostic immanent *Descent* of Unconditional and All-pervading Love, Care and Compassion. And although in transcendent development-evolution this Ascent and Descent Self Recognition, Expression and Realization tends to be balanced, and to simultaneously and integrally occur together, Onliness theory asserts that such Ascent and Descent is not necessarily *equally* Expressed or Manifest in the *overall* course of any *given* developmental-evolutionary realm-wave of Spirit's or Self's Revelation. Nonetheless, in transcendent Self-as-Self Illumination and Realization Onliness theory stresses the developmental-evolutionary *equality, unity* and *synchrony* of Self's transcendent Ascent of Wisdom and Truth, *together with* its immanent Descent of Love, Care and Compassion.

It is important to understand that the holarchically nested developmental-evolutionary realm-waves proposed in Onliness theory are to be interpreted in broad, generalized and non-literal ways, and always within the context of transcendental Meaning and Implication. What this text attempts to present are the *deep-structure patterns* and *relationships* of Self's transcendental development-evolution, but from a mind-based advanced vision-logic Onliness consciousness point of view. Also, Onliness realm-waves of transcendent Consciousness are not intended to be strictly categorical or mutually exclusive of one another, but rather interpreted and understood *interactively* and *interdependently*, and especially in transpersonal, metaphoric, symbolic and visionary terms and context.

As previously suggested, the *specific* holarchic nature and arrangement of these transcendent realm-waves of Onliness theory were importantly determined through extensive *I Ching* consultation. In My view, such vision-logic relative consciousness *I Ching* consultation enabled Me to more *deeply* and *intuitively* See into the character and meaning of, and relationships between, each of these Onliness realm-waves of Truth-consciousness Self Awakening, Recognition and Remembrance.

TAO OF ONLINESS'S CENTRAL MESSAGE AND ASSERTION

In Tao of Onliness, the underlying *core message* is the same one that was expressed 2,500 years ago by Shakyamuni Buddha upon his Realization of Enlightenment under the Bodhi tree: "Marvelous! Marvelous! All beings are already fully enlightened! It is only because of their delusion that they don't realize this" (Mitchell, 1991). This is essentially the same message that has been variously expressed by many other Sages from various mystical spiritual traditions up to the present day. It is the message of Nondual Self-as-Self Awakening, Revelation and Realization described in the *Bhagavad-Gita* (Swami Prabhavananda and Isherwood, 1951), when Krishna says to Arjuna: "Creatures rise, creatures vanish; I alone am real, Arguna, looking out, amused, from deep within the eyes of every creature. I am the Self, Arjuna, seated in the heart of every creature. I am the origin, the middle, and the end that all must come to. . . Let your thoughts flow past you, calmly; keep me near, at every moment; trust me with your life, because I *am* you, more than you yourself are."

Basically, this is the message when Jesus says (The Holy Bible, King James Version): "The kingdom of God cometh not with observation: Neither shall they say, Lo here! or, lo there! for behold, the kingdom of God is within you." It is the message conveyed in our own time by the controversial sage Adi Da (Da Free John): "Notice conditional forms, events, and activities, but Notice (and Thus Inherently Transcend) them In Of and As Your Very Self, Which Is Transcendental and Infinitely Expanded, Beyond and Prior To all conditions. . . The Way Is To Recognize and To Realize The Divine Person As Your Real or Original Self, Through The Ordeal Of Transcendence Of the conditioned self." (Da Free John, 1985).

In Onliness theory, You are always, already fully Enlightened, fully Awakened as Spirit or Self only; and any kind of searching or seeking for, or attainment or possession of, Self Enlightenment is merely a way of avoiding and self-contracting from this Radiant, Eternal and Universal Self that you always, already are. Thus, these transcendental Self Realization realm-waves of evolution and development described in Tao of Onliness theory are *not* presented or intended for use as *means* of searching, seeking or possessing the Absolute Reality of

Awakened Nondual Self-as-Self. Rather, the content of this text is simply waking mind-based, and thus dream-based, advanced vision-logic consciousness notations of and about transcendent Self-as-Self Truth-consciousness Recognition and Realization, as described from Onliness perspective. Thus, such seeking, searching, attaining and possessing is *delusional avoidance* of, and self-contraction from, One's always already unborn and undying Nondual Self Revelation and Reality.

In Tao of Onliness, transcendent Absolute Nondual Self-of-no-self is ultimately Unfathomable, Unqualifable, Unassailable and Unknowable. And You are this transpersonal Self of All-pervading Fullness and Emptiness, and of Neither also. Open Your Eyes, and come to Recognize and Realize Who You are. You are All, and Each, and Every, and also None of these. Beloved, You are at once All, and beyond and prior to All. You are Enlightened Nondual Self-as-Self of boundless and timeless Unconditional, Unconditioned, Causeless and Uncreated Suchness, this Is-ness *Mind* of Self Recognition, Remembrance and Realization. Indeed, Awakened Nondual Self-as-Self is Your always and already Buddha-nature. You are, here and now, this birthless and deathless Self of Atman-Brahman, Christ-consciousness, God-consciousness.

Understand that You *are* this transcendent Self, but *not*, however, as your waking dream-based and body-mind identified (i.e., I-am-my-body-based) compound pre-personal pre-egoic, personal-egoic, and conditioned social-cultural relative self and consciousness alone. You *are* this *Onliness* of Self, and Self *only*, this unborn and undying transcendent *Am* of always already Buddha-mind Enlightenment. Choicelessly, in *Actlessness*, You neither come nor go, and yet are always already Pure Being, Pure Spirit, Pure Godhead, in each and every moment. Far beyond words, ideas, images and conceptions, You are this timeless ever-present *Radiance* of Self, embracing Each and All - each-where, all-where, every-where, nowhere, now-here. You are this uncreated Nondual Realization Self of *Mystery*, Openly and Freely arising *as* the entire radiant Kosmos and beyond - infinitely, boundlessly, timelessly and causelessly. But You must *Awaken* to this Self of Absolute Reality that You are.

THE IMPORTANCE OF POLARITY-WITHIN-UNITY CONSCIOUSNESS IN ONLINESS THEORY

The proposed pervasive and combined *holonic* and *polaric* nature of manifest Form Reality (i.e., manifest Spirit or Self) is a central theme of Onliness theory. It asserts that in pre-transcendental, and in much of transcendental, developmental-evolutionary manifest Form Self Reality, the emergence and expression of polarity-within-unity is an *inherent* and *integral* aspect of holonic process itself. In this way, such polaric expression is said to be an *innate dimension* of the holonic nature of much of developmental-evolutionary Consciousness Awakening (i.e., an inherent developmental dimension and expression of Spirit's or Self's manifest Form Reality). Thus, the innate *holonic* nature of Beings and Entities developmental-evolutionary Self Realization, within much of manifest Form Reality, is more accurately and completely described as being *holonic-polaric* (holon-polar) in nature.

Onliness theory suggests that in all developmental-evolutionary realm-wave expressions of Self Reality Consciousness up to (and even somewhat into) the realm-wave of Causal Holistence Realization (see Figure 4), there *concurrently* and *necessarily* co-arises and co-emerges a *pole* and *anti-pole* polarity-within-unity, and *always* within holonic context (i.e., within each holon of each realm-wave of such development-evolution). In this way, within the realm-waves noted above, Tao of Onliness is fundamentally a *holon-polar* formulation and expression (i.e., Onliness theory is primarily an integrated conception and expression of *concurrently occurring* holonic and polaric manifestation). Evident throughout almost all of Onliness theory is the *central* importance of *polaric* (polarity-within-unity and duality) occurrence and expression. As such then, within the realm-waves in which it occurs, polarity-within-unity is considered to be a *deep structural feature* in the early developmental-evolutionary Self-realization Consciousness of Beings and Entities up to, and in a limited shadowed way including, the formless, boundless and unmanifest realm-wave of Causal Holistence Self Awakening.

In Onliness theory, *polaric* (polarity-within-unity) insight, up to the realm-wave of Causal Holistence Realization, is asserted to always be concurrently integrated with, as an innate and integral dimension of, the *holonic* deep structure of manifest Beings and Entities developmental-evolutionary Consciousness Perception and Expression. In Onliness theory, such developmental-evolutionary holons include Wilber's (1995) integral holonic four quadrant knowledge insight and expression as well.

Tao of Onliness is a developmental and evolutionary theory of broad application and perspective. However, in this text, Onliness focuses on and is limited to the *transcendental development* and *evolution* of advanced Consciousness earth-centered human Beings, as well as *all* other possible (I would say very highly likely) advanced Consciousness human, human-like, and non-human sentient Beings and Entities of Consciousness Self Awakening and Realization elsewhere, in other possible dimensions, worlds and universes.

Figure 1 presents a schematic conceptualization of this integrated holon-polar process. By way of visual illustration, comparing Figures 1 and 6 from a developmental-evolutionary Truth-consciousness Illumination perspective, the two smallest circles of Figure 1 could be said to respectively symbolize the emerging polarity-with-unity (i.e., the holon-polarity) of "Multiplicity" and "Inherency" Self Realization in Figure 6. This holon-polarity of the two smallest circles are, in turn, included within the lower of the two intermediate sized circles of Figure 1, which could symbolize "Meaning" Realization in Figure 6, which, in turn, in its Self Awakening emergence, is itself in polarity-within-unity (in holon-polarity) with the upper intermediate sized circle of Figure 1, which would symbolize "Knowledge" Self Realization in Figure 6. In turn, this holon-polarity (of the two intermediate sized circles) is included within the lower of the two largest circles, which would symbolize "Awareness" Self Revelation in Figure 6, and which, in turn, in its Realization, would be in polarity-within-unity (in holon-polarity) with "Experience" Self Realization in Figure 6, (the upper of the two largest circle of Figure 1). In this way. the nested and integrated polarity-within-unity and holonic pattern of *include but transcend* (negate and preserve) within progressively greater Self-realization wholes of Consciousness inclusion is evident in Figure 1.

Human perception of the role of polarity-within-unity as a *deep structure* of mind-based relative reality and consciousness has a long and broadly diversified history. There is of course the ancient yin-yang polarity-patterned hexagram text of the *I Ching* (Legge, 1964; Blofeld, 1968), substantial portions of which appear to be written about 4,000 years ago. As a part of both Taoist and Confucian spiritual and moral wisdom paths, the yin and yang polarity-with-unity concepts of *I Ching* have been widely used, in both the Eastern and Western cultures, as a way of viewing and understanding the underlying nature of reality. In the West, the Hegelian (Friedrich, 1954) concept of the process of thesis, antithesis and synthesis is an example of the application of polarity-within-unity in understanding reality. Most significantly, it is the pervasive compound personal-egoic separate-self-sense *subject-versus-object* polarity-duality Consciousness, which has its ultimate transcendence resolution within Awakened Nondual Self-as-Self Realization, that also suggests the deep mind-based nature of polarity-within-unity and duality in Consciousness.

Profound (and not so profound) countless examples of polarity-within-unity abound: being-nonbeing, form-void, ascent-descent, involution-evolution, male-female, up-down, right-left, vertical-horizontal, progression-regression, subject-object and its I-you, mine-yours, we-they, us-them, subjective-objective, interior-exterior, singular-plural, conscious-unconscious, yes-no, black-white, finite-infinite, pro-con, conditional-unconditional etc. Indeed, I would suggest that the psychological and psycholinguist structural foundations of earth-centered human language itself, and the underlying relative human mentality from which it derives, are fundamentally based upon such polarity-within-unity perceptual, contrasting, and identification processes.

It is this embedded and pervasive *presence* and *applicability* of mind-based polarity-within-unity within these Onliness theory developmental-evolutionary realm-waves of Self Awakening and Revelation which primarily form the basis for its integral inclusion and role in Tao of Onliness perspective. In this way, polarity-within-unity is a *fundamental* feature and dimension of development-evolution within the spectrum of Consciousness, from matter, to life, to mind, through

World Soul (i.e., Psychic Multi-istence and Subtle Prim-istence realm-waves of Self Awakening); and then in its implicit but unmanifest presence within Universal Spirit, throughout most of the realm-wave of Causal Holistence Self Recognition and Realization.

At this *formless, boundless* and *unmanifest* Causal Holistence Self Revelation realm-wave, polarity-within-unity as a basic structural dimension of Consciousness tends to dissipate or deconstruct itself, so as to disintegrate and be "dissolved" within such Truth-consciousness Self Realization. Nonetheless, polarity-with-unity's implied *vestiges* within Causal Holistence Self Reality tend to continue to find some *limited* expression, but in progressively weakened and very faded ways. However, with developmental-evolutionary transition into Supreme Self of Nondual Ground Awakening and Realization, polarity-within-unity no longer arises or occurs at all.

From Onliness perspective, *all* language and thought at developmental realm-waves of compound pre-egoic, personal-egoic, and conditioned social-cultural self of relative mind consciousness involve polarity-within-unity or duality. Onliness theory suggests that duality arises when an individual perceives *polar-duality*, but without realization of its underlying *unity*. That is, such mind-based duality occurs when One has not yet developed the deeper capacity to comprehend the unity inherent in that perceived polar-duality. Wilber (*The Eye of Spirit*, vol. 7 in *The Collected Works of Ken Wilber*, 1999-2000) also speaks of the transpersonal Causal realm-wave into which duality reaches and extends before it is undone. He does this in the course of discussing the "gap" between subject and object; this subject-object duality impasse, and its resolution within Causal Realization.

SPIRITUALLY MEDIATING, FACILITATING AND SUPPORTING HOLON-POLE AND HOLON-POLARITY REALM-WAVES IN ONLINESS THEORY DIAGRAM SYMBOLIZATION

Developmentally-evolutionarily within each of the eight sub-realm-waves that comprise the three broader holon-polar realm-waves in Onliness theory (see Figures 3, 4 and 6), it is proposed that *each* holon-pole is in some degree of holon-polarity with *each* and *every* other holon-pole within its respective sub-realm-wave. And, in general, the *greater the degree* of yin and yang line pattern *contrast* (yin-yang line difference) between a given yin-yang symbolized holon-polarity in relation to other similar surrounding holon-polarities (among the respective unigram, digram, trigram, quadragram, pentagram or hexagram yin-yang holon-polarity pairs of Figures 3 and 5), the *greater* the degree of spiritually mediating, facilitating and supporting interaction *Revelation effect* that *that* holon-polarity pair has in relation to other surrounding holon-polarity pairs.

In Onliness theory, the spiritually meditating, facilitating and supporting interaction Self Awakening effect of any given yin-yang symbolized holon-polarity (i.e., polarity-engaged and interacting pair of holon poles) will *transcend but include* the spiritual mediating, facilitating and supporting effects of either of its two yin-yang symbolized holon-poles *acting alone* (see Figures 3 and 5). Note however, for any given so called (i.e., pre-transcendental consciousness reality perceived) *individual* Consciousness Being and Entity, the spiritual mediating, facilitating and supporting holon-polarity Self Awakening interaction effect will also tend to somewhat *individually* vary in Self-revelation intensity for any given holon-polarity *as a function of* that individual's varying degree of particular temperamental-environmental based *predisposition* toward that holon-polarity and its yin-yang symbolized holon-poles.

At each of the yin-yang symbolized Psychic Multi-istence and Subtle Prim-istence sub-realm-waves of Recognition and Realization in Figures 3 and 4, the influences of *each* of its spiritual mediating, facilitating and supporting *holon-pole* Self Revelation interaction effects (in and of themselves), as well as each of their respective spiritually mediating, facilitating and supporting *holon-polarities* (i.e, holon-polarity interaction Self Revelation effects), *summate* in relation to developmental-evolutionary Awakening toward Remembrance of Self. However, at least from an individual earth-centered human Being's point of view, seldom is such Nondual Self Remembrance and Realization quick and easy, or without stagnation, detour, regression, and possibly spiritual pathology.

AN OVERVIEW OF THE HOLON-POLAR REALM-WAVES AND SUB-REALM-WAVES OF ONLINESS THEORY AND PERSPECTIVE

By way of preface to this overview of Onliness theory, it is first important to visualize the nature of the difference between holonic-only (holon-only) *versus* integrated holonic-polaric (holon-polar) conceptualization, through comparison of two diagrams. First, Figure 2 is a *holon-only* diagram, which correctly symbolizes the degree and extent of holoarchic developmental-evolutionary Self-realized Ascent-Descent Awakening in relation to its surrounding realm-waves of transcendental Self Realization. This diagram's successively larger, and thus more Self-realization Consciousness inclusive and encompassing, concentric circles or rings symbolize the *holonic* nature and arrangement of Onliness's nested realm-waves and sub-realm-waves of Self Revelation and Awakening. As displayed in this nested diagram, each successively larger Onliness realm-wave ring of Truth-consciousness Self Awakening transcends but includes (negates and yet preserves) all of its junior (smaller circle) realm-wave rings. That is to say, each successively larger ring is a *whole/part* (a holon), in that it is a new and more Self Awakened and Inclusive *whole* in relation to all of its preceding junior (smaller) less Self Awakened and Inclusive rings, and at the same time it is also a *part* of all of its successively larger and even more Self Awakened and Inclusive senior rings.

In contrast, the Onliness theory visualization of Figure 3 is an *integrated holon-polar* diagram which, like Figure 2, symbolizes the *holonic* nature of the three *broad* realm-wave rings of Consciousness Self Realization and Inclusion (i.e., Psychic Multi-istence, Subtle Prim-istence and Causal Holistence Illumination). It visually symbolizes Onliness theory's holonic nature through its successively larger, outward expanding and encompassing, concentric circles (rings) of progressively more profound and inclusive transcendent Self Recognition and Realization Awakening. This is delineated by the three nested *unbroken-line* successively larger concentric rings. However, the six *grouped* series of yin-yang symbol *broken-line* rings (two sets of three each) concurrently symbolize, but in a successively smaller ring *inward focusing* (deepening) direction, the *same* progressively more profound and inclusive transcendent Self Awakening and Revelation *within* each of these six sub-realm-waves (i.e., *elemental* Psychic Multi-istence, *cardinal* Psychic Multi-istence, *fundamental* Psychic Multi-istence (all within Psychic Multi-istence Self Revelation), and *universive* Subtle Prim-istence, *supreme* Subtle

Prim-istence, and *absolute* Subtle Holistent Prim-istence (all within Subtle Prim-istence Self Realization).

In Figure 3, note the various yin and yang line patterned polarity-within-unity arrangements of the unigram, digram, trigram, quadra-gram, quintagram and hexagram sub-realm-wave rings of the Tao of Onliness I Ching. Also note at each of these six sub-realm-wave levels how their oppositional yin and yang line polarity-within-unity contrast and compare with one another, so as to create the symbolization for the various *holon-poles* and their respective *holon-polarity* relationships that exist within and between these *six* sub-realm-waves of the *two* inner *broad* realm-waves of Psychic Multi-istence and Subtle Prim-istence transcendent Self Recognition and Remembrance.

In Figure 3, because the third (outermost) *broad* realm-wave ring (i.e., Causal Holistence realm-wave Consciousness Awakening) is of unmanifest, boundless and formless transcendent Consciousness Self Realization, it is therefore symbolized as two concentric circles of blank or empty space. Again, its two sub-realm-waves (i.e., *primordial* Causal Arch-istent Holistence and *primordial* Causal Omni-istent Holistence Self Realization) are symbolized in a successively smaller ring *inward focusing* (deepening) direction of progressively more profound, inclusive and higher developmental-evolutionary Truth-consciousness Self Recognition and Realization. In this way, using both successive concentric circular rings *and* yin-yang line patterned symbols *in combination*, Figure 3 attempts to symbolize the inherently integrated *holarchy* (holonic) and *polarity-within-unity* (polaric) nature, according to Onliness theory, of the proposed developmental-evolutionary realm-waves and sub-realm-waves of transcendent Consciousness Self Awakened and Realization. That is to say, Figures 3 and 5 attempt to

symbolize the inherent and integrated *holon-polar* nature and character of the realm-waves and sub-realm-waves of Nondual Supreme Self
Recognition, Remembrance and Realization.

PSYCHIC MULTI-ISTENCE CONSCIOUSNESS AWAKENING AND REALIZATION

The following overview describes Onliness theory primarily from the
point of view of One's developmental-evolutionary transcendent *Ascent*
of Spirit or Self in Wisdom and Truth. But equally important to this
theory is One's developmental-evolutionary immanent *Descent* of Spirit
or Self in Unconditional and All-inclusive Love, Care and Compassion.
In Onliness theory, there are three *broad* developmental-evolutionary
holon-polar realm-wave rings of transcendent Consciousness Self
Revelation and Realization: *Psychic Multi-istence, Subtle Prim-istence*
and *Causal Holistence* Awakening (see Figures 3, 4 and 6).

In development-evolution, the first *broad* holon-polar realm-wave
(symbolized by and contained within the innermost *unbroken-line* ring
or Figure 3), is Psychic Multi-istence Self Revelation. According to
Onliness theory, initially in the transcendent Ascent of Self or Spirit in
Wisdom and Truth, each of eight distinct *diverse-beings Reality Pathways*
of developmental-evolutionary Self Awakening (symbolized by the eight
large black dots across the top of Figure 4) emerge from the convergent
courses of countless numbers of related *types* of advanced *pre-transcendental* consciousness Beings and Entities developmental-evolutionary
spiritual self awakening. Such trails or pathways of pre-transcendental
spiritual recognition are symbolized by the many converging lines at
the top of Figure 4 which lead to each of these eight large black dots.
From these eight initial *transitional transcendental* (i.e., not yet fully

transcendental) Consciousness convergences (large black dots) emerge (and diverge) Psychic Multi-istence's *eight* distinctive holon-polar *diverse beings* Reality Pathway realm-waves of Pan-gnostic and Trans-gnostic: Existence, Transexistence, Istence and Antistence (see Figure 4).

In turn, within each of these eight separate and overall parallel-coursing realms-waves of Psychic Multi-istence Self Recognition (but note, successively convergent line transitions between holon-poles *within* each of these eight parallel-coursing realm-waves - see Figure 4) there initially arise and emerge the eight *specific* developmental-evolutionary holon-pole realm-waves of *elemental* Psychic Multi-istence Self Awakening (i.e., the eight small black dots of *elemental* Psychic Multi-istence which occur within *each* of the eight overall parallel-coursing *diverse beings* Reality Pathways of Pan- and Trans-gnostic: Existence, Transexistence, Istence and Antistence in Figure 4). These eight specific holon-poles are symbolized in Figures 3 and 5 by the *eight* yin-yang trigrams, which, in Figures 3 and 5, create the outermost yin-yang trigram broken-line-ring of this inner solid-line ring of Psychic Multi-istence Self Revelation.

In this way, from holarchically less Self Awakened (less Consciousness Inclusive) to more Self Awakened (more Consciousness Inclusive), Psychic Multi-istence is comprised of *three* holon-polar sub-realm-wave rings of developmental-evolutionary Realization: (1) *elemental Psychic Multi-istence* (with its eight holon-poles noted above), (2) *cardinal Psychic Multi-istence* (with its four holon-poles), and (3) *fundamental Psychic Multi-istence* (with its two holon-poles) (see Figures 3, 4 and 5). In Figure 3, the eight yin-yang trigrams, which create the outermost broken-line rings of Psychic Multi-istence Self Illumination, symbolize the eight holon-poles of *elemental* Psychic Multi-istence

Awakening. Likewise in Figure 3, the four yin-yang digrams which create the middle broken-line rings of Psychic Multi-istence symbolize the four holon-poles of *cardinal* Psychic Multi-istence Self Revelation, and the two yin-yang unigrams of the single innermost broken-line ring of Psychic Multi-istence Self Reality symbolize the two holon-poles of *fundamental* Psychic Multi-istence Self Realization. Finally, it needs to be noted that *one* of the eight Psychic Multi-istence *diverse-beings* Reality Pathway realm-waves of Figure 4 is called *Psychic Pan-gnostic Existence* Self-recognition and pertains to, and is exclusively for and about, human and human-like Beings (see Figures 4 and 6).

SUBTLE PRIM-ISTENCE CONSCIOUSNESS AWAKENING AND REALIZATION

In Onliness theory, the second *broad* holon-polar realm-wave in the developmental-evolutionary Ascent-Descent of transcendental Self Awakening to Wisdom and Truth, and to Unconditional and All-embracing Love, Care and Compassion is *Subtle Prim-istence* Self Revelation. This realm-wave ring is symbolized by that area in Figure 3 from the innermost *unbroken-line* ring extending out to the next innermost *unbroken-line* ring (i.e., the *middle* unbroken-line ringed area of this diagram). This is the intermediate holon-polar realm-wave of Subtle Prim-istence Consciousness Self Realization, in which there is further development-evolution from holarchically less to more Self-awakening and Self-realization (i.e., further Truth-consciousness inclusion of all Beings and Entities, which is to say all of Reality, as Self and Self *only*.

Subtle Prim-istence Truth-consciousness is composed of three sub-realm-waves: First, *universive Subtle Prim-istence* Self Recognition, which further Unveils the eight *diverse beings* Reality Pathways of Pan-gnostic and Trans-gnostic: Existence, Transexistence, Istence and Antistence (see Figures 4 and 6). In all, it has 64 holon-poles, which are symbolized by the 64 yin-yang hexagrams of the *I Ching* and the Tao of Onliness I Ching in Figures 3 and 5. Second, *supreme Subtle Prim-istence* Awakening, which has four *diverse beings* Reality Pathway realm-waves (see Figures 4 and 6). In all, it has 32 yin-yang pentagram symbolized holon-poles (see Figures 3 and 5). Third, *absolute Subtle Holistent Prim-istence* Self Awakening and Realization, which has two *diverse beings* Reality Pathway realm-waves (see Figures 4 and 6). In all, this realm-wave has 16 yin-yang quadragram holon-poles, as symbolized in Figures 3 and 5 (compare Figures 3, 4 and 6).

In this way, the *initial* sub-realm-wave ring of Subtle Prim-istence, which is *universive* Subtle Prim-istence Self Recognition, more completely Reveals the eight *diverse beings* Reality Pathway realm-waves (see Figures 4) which *each* contain eight hexagram yin-yang symbolized holon-poles. That is, 64 holon-pole realm-waves in all within *universive* Subtle Prim-istence Realization which are symbolized by the 64 yin-yang *I Ching* hexagrams of the outmost broken-line ring in Figure 3. The *intermediate* sub-realm-wave ring of *supreme* Subtle Prim-istence Self Recognition and Remembrance has four major realm-waves (see Figures 4), which each contain eight pentagram yin-yang symbolized holon-pole realm-waves (see Figures 3 and 5). That is, 32 holon-poles in all within *supreme* Subtle Prim-istence Revelation which are symbolized by the 32 yin-yang pentagrams of the middle broken-line rings in Figure 3.

The innermost sub-realm-wave ring of Subtle Prim-istence in Figure 3 is *absolute* Subtle Holistent Prim-istence Self Awakening.

This realm-wave contains the two major *diverse beings* Reality Pathway realm-waves of Being (yin symbolized) and Nonbeing (yang symbolized) Self Revelation (see Figure 4), which each contain eight polarized and quadragram symbolized yin-yang holon-poles (see Figures 3 and 5). That is, 16 holon-poles in all which are symbolized by the 16 yin-yang quadragrams of this innermost broken-line ring in Figure 3.

In the developmental transcendent Ascent-Descent of Self or Spirit in Wisdom, Truth, Love, Care and Compassion, Onliness theory asserts that at One's *initial* emergence within World Soul's sub-realm-wave of *universive* Subtle Prim-istence Self Reality (see Figures 4 and 5), there *begins* to arise and develop a spectrum of eight holon-polar *temperamental-contextual based* predisposing realm-wave Modes or Ways of Nondual Self-as-Self Awakening and Realization. Each of these Modes of Consciousness Enlightenment has a yin and yang holon-pole Expression and Realization: yin-yang *Am*, yin-yang *Actlessness*, yin-yang *Radiance*, yin-yang *Emptiness*, yin-yang *Awakening*, yin-yang *Mystery*, yin-yang *Mind*, and yin-yang *Onliness* (see Figures 5 and 7).

These eight holon-polar Modes of transcendent Self Illumination continue to find expression and continue to evolve throughout One's whole developmental Subtle Prim-istence realm-wave Truth-consciousness Self Revelation. And ultimately these eight unique Enlightenment Modes find transcendent Synthesis and Resolution within the sub-realm-wave of *absolute* Subtle Holistent Prim-istence Self Realization. In this realm-wave ring these eight (16 yin-yang paired) distinctive Modes of transcendent Enlightenment Awakening are symbolized by the sixteen polarized yin and yang holon-pole quadragrams of this ring (see Figure 5).

ONLINESS REALM-WAVES OF PSYCHIC MULTI-ISTENCE AND SUBTLE PRIM-ISTENCE WITHIN THE IMMANENT DESCENT OF SELF OR SPIRIT

In Onliness theory, the deepest and most profound *Source* and *Origin* of Self's or Spirit's immanent *Descent* of Unconditional and All-encompassing Love, Care and Compassion Descends via Self Realization of and through the *highest* realms-waves downward. Whereas the deepest *Source* and *Origin* of Spirit's or Self's transcendent *Ascent* of Wisdom and Truth Ascends from Self Realization of and through the lowest realm-waves upward. That is, *within* Subtle Prim-istence Awakening, Self's deepest and most profound *Source* of this immanent *Descent* occurs within the sub-realm-wave of *absolute* Subtle Holistent Prim-istence Self Realization (see Figures 3, 4 and 5). Likewise, *within* Psychic Multi-istence Realization, Self's deepest and most profound *Source* and *Origin* of such immanent *Descent* occurs within the sub-realm-wave of *fundamental* Psychic Multi-istence Self Revelation (see Figures 3, 4 and 5).

In turn, in One's immanent Descent of Unconditional and All-embracing Love, Care and Compassion, the 32 yin-yang pentagrams which symbolize the holon-poles of sub-realm-wave *supreme* Subtle Prim-istence Recognition (see Figure 3) *derive from* and *return to* (i.e., have their Source and Origin within and through) the 16 yin-yang quadragrams which symbolize the holon-poles of sub-realm-wave *absolute* Subtle Holistent Prim-istence Self Awakening. In this regard, note that each of the eight yang (or *Nonbeing* in Figure 6) quadragram symbols of Figure 5 (as determined by the fourth *yang* unigram line of each quadragram in Figure 5) has, immediately above or outward to it, one yang Antistence Nonbeing Awakening and one yin Istence Nonbeing Awakening unigram line, as the *top line* of each *supreme* Subtle Prim-istence pentagram.

Likewise, the corresponding *yin* holon-pole quadragrams (determined by the fourth *yin* unigram line of the quadragram) of each of the eight *yin*, (or *Being* in Figure 6), holon-poles of Figure 5 (as determined by the fourth *yin* unigram line of each quadragram in Figure 5) (e.g., yin Am versus yang Am) has immediately above it, or outward to it, one yang Transexistence Being Revelation and one yin Existence Being Revelation *supreme* Subtle Prim-istence pentagram symbolized holon-pole (compare Figures 5 and 6). In this way, all four realm-waves of Being Existence and Transexistence, and Nonbeing Istence and Antistence, which comprise the eight *diverse Beings* Reality Pathway realm-waves of Self Remembrance and Awakening, are equally represented, find equal Source and Expression, in *each* of the eight holon-polar quadragram symbolized *Modes* of Enlightenment Awakening of *absolute* Subtle Holistent Prim-istence (see Figures 5 and 6).

And in this same way, when considering only One's immanent Descent of Self in Unconditional and All-encompassing Love, Care and Compassion, the 64 yin-yang hexagrams, which symbolize the holon-poles of *universive* Subtle Prim-istence Consciousness Self Recognition, derive from and return to (have their Source within and find Expression through) the 32 yin-yang pentagrams which symbolize the holon-poles of *supreme* Subtle Prim-istence Realization, which, in turn, derive from and return to the 16 yin-yang holon-polar quadragrams, which symbolize the eight Modes or Ways of Enlightenment of *absolute* Subtle Holistent Prim-istence Revelation (see Figures 3 and 5).

Again, from these 16 yin-yang quadragram symbolized holon-poles arise the eight temperamental and environmental-contextual based predisposing holon-polar Modes of Enlightenment Self Awakening (see Figure 5). Thus note that in Figures 3 and 5 there are eight yin-yang *universive* Subtle Prim-istence hexagrams that derived from (are directly above or outward to) *each* of these eight yin and eight yang polarized *absolute* Subtle Holistent Prim-istence Modes of Enlightenment Realization of Am, Actlessness, Radiance, Emptiness, Awakening, Mystery, Mind, and Onliness (e.g., four above *yang* Am and four above *yin* Am, in Am Self Awakening holon-polarity).

Symbolization indicating that *each* of the eight *diverse-beings* Reality Pathways of Psychic Multi-istence Self Realization, and initial *universive* Subtle Prim-istence Self Realization in Figures 4 and 6 (i.e., Pan-gnostic and Trans-gnostic: Existence, Transexistence, Istence and Antistence) find *equal* representation and expression in *each* of the eight Modes of Enlightenment of *absolute* Subtle Holistent Prim-istence Awakening (i.e., Am, Actlessness, Radiance, Emptiness, Awakening, Mystery, Mind and Onliness) in the following way: In Figure 6, each of the eight *diverse-beings* Reality Pathways is symbolized by *one* of the eight possible yin-yang line trigrams. In Figure 5, note that *all eight* of these symbolized trigrams of Figure 6 appear as the upper (top) trigrams in each of the eight sets of hexagrams that derive from (are directly above or outward to) *each* of the eight holon-polarity *pairs* of yin and yang quadragrams that symbolize the eight Modes of Enlightenment within *absolute* Subtle Holistent Prim-istence.

Causal Holistence Consciousness Awakening and Realization

In relative mind-based Onliness theory, the third realm-wave in the developmental-evolutionary Ascent-Descent of transcendent Consciousness Awakening is Causal Holistence, which is a *holon-only* realm-wave of Self Remembrance and Recognition. This realm-wave is symbolized in Figures 3 and 5 by the essentially blank area between the two outermost unbroken-line rings. It is within Causal Holistence Self Reality that *primordial* Self initially emerges and is Realized. From holarchically less to more Consciousness inclusive of and as All Beings and Entities (i.e., a progressively more profound and inclusive developmental-evolutionary Truth-consciousness Self Recognition and Realization), Causal Holistence is comprised of two sub-realm-waves: *primordial Causal Arch-istent Holistence* and *primordial Causal Omni-istent Holistence* Self Recognition and Realization (see Figures 3 and 4). As Causal Holistence Awakening is of *formless, boundless* and *unmanifest* transcendent Revelation, it is symbolized in this outmost circle of Figure 3 as empty space, except for the dotted line that marks the transition between these to sub-realm-wave Self Revelation Realities.

NONDUAL SPIRIT-AS-SPIRIT CONSCIOUSNESS AWAKENING AND REALIZATION

Note that *Nondual Self-as-Self* Remembrance, Illumination and Realization is the Pure Emptiness Ground, Source and Goal of, by, through, and within which the two earlier discussed holonpolar realm-waves (rings) of World-Soul's Psychic Multi-istence and Subtle Prim-istence Self Awakening, as well as the singular holon-only realm-wave of Universal Spirit's Causal Holistence Self Awakening occurs. In this regard, Nondual Self Enlightenment is symbolized in Figures 1 through 7 by the paper substance, ink, blank space, images, words and surfaces of which each of these seven diagrams are comprised. However, Awakened Nondual Spirit-as-Spirit or Self-as-Self Realization *is not* a holon-only or holon-polar realm-wave, stage, state, holon-pole or holon-polarity of Consciousness, but rather *is* Reality and Truth Itself, is Unqualifable and Unknowable Nondual Spirit or Self Itself, without a opposite or second.

In mind-based Onliness theory, at least for earth-centered human beings, all such transcendent Self Recognition, Remembrance and Revelation that emerges and develops through and within these holon-pole, holon-polarity and holon-only Truth-consciousness realm-waves, as well as of Nondual Spirit-as-Spirit Realization Itself, is most always *initially* Recognized, Remembered and Realized through an intensive and sustained integral spiritual practice, which includes meditation. Understand that such *profound* and *direct* Self Awakening to Spirit, to *no-self Self*, is *not* accessible through illusory mind-based relative, conditional and conditioned compound personal-egoic self reality and consciousness. Understand that Self is the singular and only Reality, Self *alone* is Real, and as such is prior to and beyond all waking dream-based mental conception, description and imagination.

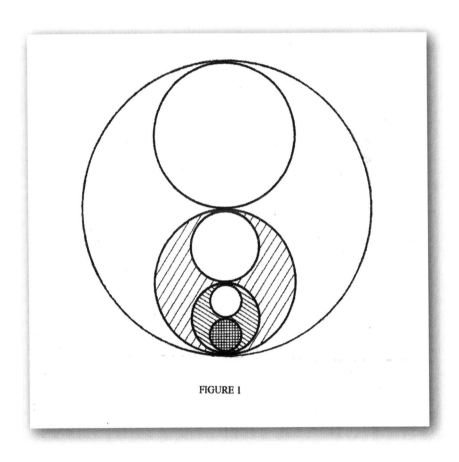

FIGURE 1

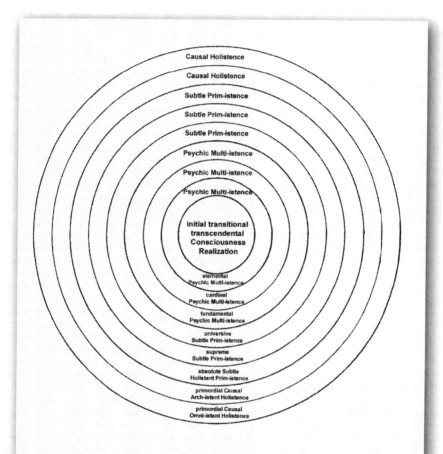

Causal Holistence

Causal Holistence

Subtle Prim-istence

Subtle Prim-istence

Subtle Prim-istence

Psychic Multi-istence

Psychic Multi-istence

Psychic Multi-istence

initial transitional transcendental Consciousness Realization

elemental
Psychic Multi-istence

cardinal
Psychic Multi-istence

fundamental
Psychic Multi-istence

universive
Subtle Prim-istence

supreme
Subtle Prim-istence

absolute Subtle
Holistent Prim-istence

primordial Causal
Arch-istent Holistence

primordial Causal
Omni-istent Holistence

Holonic-concept diagram (i.e., holon-only versus integrated holon-polar diagram) of the developmental-evolutionary Ascent-Descent of transcendental Consciousness in Onliness theory and perspective.

FIGURE 2

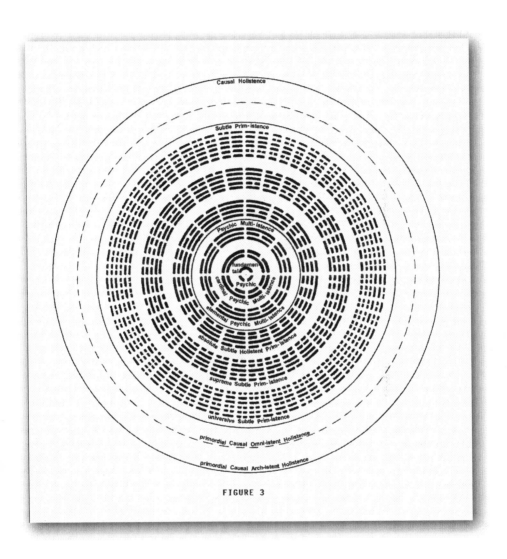

FIGURE 3

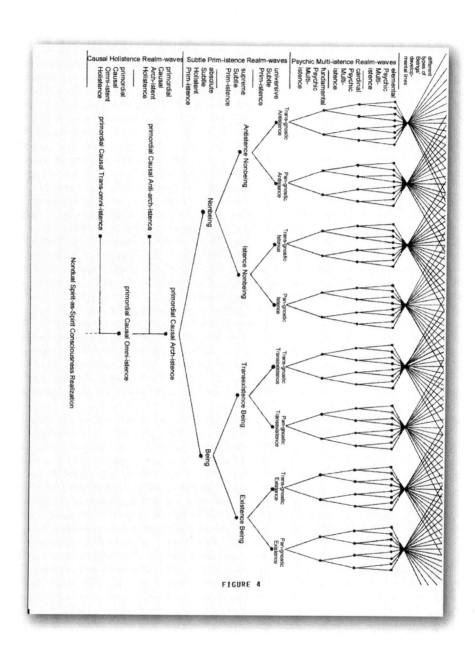

FIGURE 4

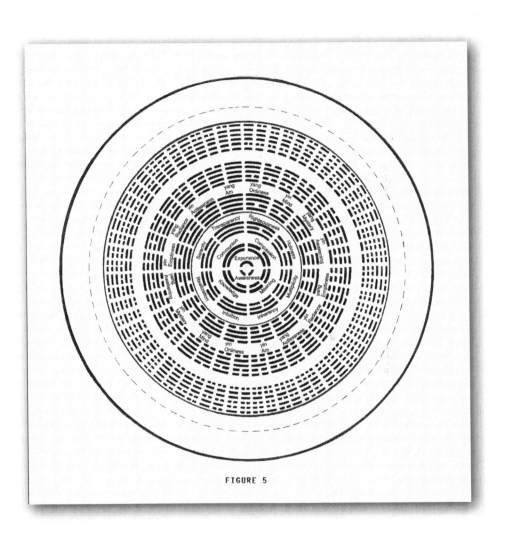

FIGURE 5

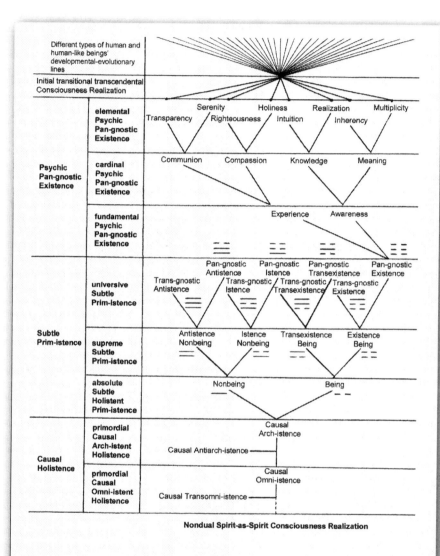

Nondual Spirit-as-Spirit Consciousness Realization

FIGURE 6

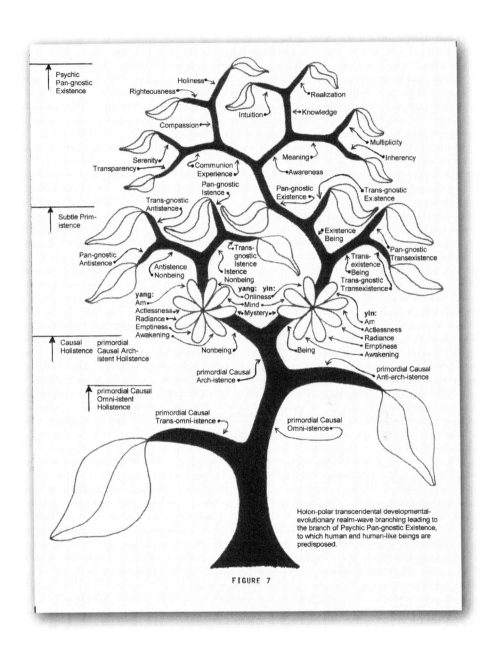

Holon-polar transcendental developmental-
evolutionary realm-wave branching leading to
the branch of Psychic Pan-gnostic Existence,
to which human and human-like beings are
predisposed.

FIGURE 7

THE NATURE AND RANGE OF BEINGS AND ENTITIES WITHIN THE SCOPE OF ONLINESS THEORY

As presented here, Onliness theory is a mind-based abstract and pre-liminary or "rough-draft" outline which attempts to describe *all* of the major transcendental holon-pole, holon-polar and holon-only realm-waves of developmental-evolutionary Consciousness Self Illumination available to, and taken by, *all* Consciousness Beings and Entities, within this and all other dimensions, worlds and universes of manifest Form Reality. In this way, Onliness presents one interpretation and perspective of a developmental-evolutionary comprehensive and universal theory of the transcendental Ways and Realities of Self Awakening and Realization that are directly and immediately available to each and every Conscious Being and Entity (of each and every dimension, world and universe) who is at an advanced developmental-evolutionary realm-wave level of Consciousness Self Revelation. Certainly, this is an *extremely* ambitious (grandiose?) undertaking. But there it is.

In various ways, Figures 1 through 7 attempt to symbolically dia-gram the *general* nature, relationships and transcendent Ascent-Descent *realm-wave sequence* of such developmental-evolutionary Awakening and Self-realization. The holon-pole, holon-polar and holon-only realm-wave names used in this description, although translated into Onliness terminology, are essentially those used in the Great Holarchy (Nest) of Being which is associated with the perennial philosophy (i.e., Psychic, Subtle, and Causal realm-waves, and Nondual Self Ground and Source Realization). However, the *specific* nature, meanings and relationships of the transcendental holon-pole, holon-polar and holon-only realm-waves themselves are of Onliness perspective and theory. In My relative view, given the present level of general or average earth-centered human development-evolution, *all* of the holon-pole, holon-polar and holon-only transcendental realm-waves described in Onliness theory are presented as fluid developmental-evolutionary *possible* potentials of Self-as-Self transpersonal Awakening and Realization for such human beings, and certainly *not* intended as presumed or pre-destined givens. Indeed, it is *quite possible* that there may be no developmental-evolutionary future at all for earth-centered human beings.

Throughout this text, when it is said that a so called individual Being (i.e., in Reality there are no individual Being and Entities) occupies, or has Realized, a given developmental-evolutionary realm-wave level of transcendent Consciousness Realization, it simply means the "individual" at that Consciousness realm-wave has *fully* Awakened to and *is*, in Fact, such Consciousness itself; that such Realization is now a *permanent*, *stable* and *enduring* Trait Configuration, or Way of Life and Living, for that so called individual Being. In this circumstance, such a holon-pole, holon-polar or holon-only Self-realized Trait Configuration will variously Express itself in all four *relative* Wilberian holonic quadrants, within and through which that individual Being functions (i.e., subjective-interior-individual, intersubjective-interior-social-cultural, objective-exterior-individual, and interobjective-exterior-social-cultural).

Starting at the top of Figure 4, the many radiating developmental-evolutionary lines that converge upon the eight large black dots symbolize the *countless* number of specific *types* (species, categories etc.) of developed-evolved *pre-transcendental* advanced-consciousness Beings and Entities who live in this and other worlds, dimensions, and universes of manifest Form Reality. Each line thus symbolizes one specific *type* of Being, of which there are countless numbers of advanced consciousness *individual* Beings of that type per line, who are developmentally-evolutionarily closely approaching, and about to converge at, this "gateway" point of *initial* transitional *transcendental* Consciousness Awakening, Recognition, Revelation, Illumination, Remembrance and Realization.

Because of the *vast* numbers of *very* different manifest structural circumstances and environments in this and other worlds, dimensions and universes of Form Reality, Onliness theory proposes that there are countless numbers of greatly diversified *types* or *categories* of Consciousness Beings and Entities of advanced developmental-evolutionary consciousness (i.e., the converging single line symbols at the top of Figure 4) who have developed-evolved within each of these varied circumstances and environments. And, of course, given such great contextual diversity, there are countless and unimaginatively imaginative and creative ways in which such Consciousness Being and Entities have structurally and functionally so developed and evolved.

Onliness theory claims that, beyond earth-centered human beings, these other types of advanced consciousness manifest Beings, of whatever developed-evolved nature, substances, dimensions, constructions, features and configurations, *inhabit* this and all other worlds, dimensions and universes of manifest Form Reality. Also, Onliness theory agrees with Wilberian perspective concerning the *inherent telos* of evolution as Spirit-in-Action, so that each and every manifest Consciousness Being and Entity (advanced or not), indeed all of manifest Form Reality - each and every Form of Its manifestations - inherently tends to *creatively* develop and evolve toward Remembrance and Realization of Uncreated, Timeless and All-pervasive Bliss-Divine Self only and completely.

Onliness theory further asserts that, at this very moment in the context of time, there are countless numbers of Consciousness Being and Entity *types* (each type comprised of countless individual Beings and Entities), in this and other worlds, dimensions and universes, who have *fully* developed-evolved, not only to just below (very near) initial transcendental Self Awakening but also to *within* and *through* each of the three *broad* transcendental realm-waves rings of Consciousness Self Realization (i.e., Psychic Multi-istence, Subtle Prim-istence and Causal Holistence) (see Figures 3 and 5), and *even beyond this* to Awakened Nondual Self-recognition, Self-remembrance and Self-realization.

PSYCHIC PAN-GNOSTIC EXISTENCE AWAKENING AND REALIZATION

At the top of Figure 6, the large black dot, upon which the many developmental-evolutionary *pre-transcendental* consciousness lines above it converge, marks the *initial* point of transition of Consciousness, at least for human and human-like Beings, as they emerge *from* relative mind-based advanced vision-logic compound personal-egoic self and consciousness *to* initial transpersonal, trans-egoic and trans-mental transcendent Consciousness Self Awakening. Likewise, the eight large black dots at the top of Figure 4 mark the *initial* points of transition for *all* types of advanced consciousness Beings and Entities, within all worlds, dimensions and universes, as they emerge from pre-transcendental realm-waves of consciousness, just below transcendent Consciousness, into initial realm-waves of transcendent Consciousness Self Awakening and Recognition.

The eight sets of eight developmental-evolutionary lines that lead from and are just below these eight large black dots of Figure 4 symbolize One's *initial* and somewhat stable Awakening to transcendent Self-revelation Truth-consciousness, which occurs during One's *transition* into the sub-realm-wave of *elemental* Psychic Multi-istence Self Awakening. In Onliness theory, earth-centered human Beings, during this transpersonal development-evolvement into initial *elemental* Psychic Multi-istence, are asserted to be *predominantly predisposed* to the *diverse beings* Reality Pathway of *elemental* Psychic Pan-gnostic Existence sub-realm-wave Self Recognition and Illumination (compare Figures 4 and 6).

Onliness theory further proposes that there are countless numbers of other *types* of *non-earth-centered* human and human-like Beings who are also thus predominantly predisposed to this *diverse beings* Pathway of Psychic Multi-istence's *elemental* Psychic Pan-gnostic Existence Self Realization. This is so because *all* human and human-like Beings commonly share *somewhat similar* developmental-evolutionary ontogenetic and phylogenetic body-mind natures; that is, somewhat similar social and physical environments, physical configurations, substances, dimensions, features, constructions, temperaments, experiences etc. with earth-centered human Beings.

This is symbolized at the top of Figure 6 by many other (actually countless number) of other developmental-evolutionary lines (one of which is intended as the single type of earth-centered human Being line) meeting at this *initial* transcendental Consciousness Awakening convergence, the large black dot, through and beyond which *elemental* Psychic Pan-gnostic Existence Awakening and Self Revelation emerges and finds Expression. Thus, *each* of these specific *types* of human and human-like Beings, including the earth-centered human Being type, although somewhat to quite dramatically different from one another *between* types, all share certain basic similarities which developmentally-evolutionarily predominantly predisposed them to the holon-polar sub-realm-wave of transpersonal Psychic Pan-gnostic Existence Truth-consciousness Self Realization (see Figure 6).

Each of the countless numbers of other Consciousness Being and Entity *types* (symbolized by the many converging lines to each of the other *seven* large black dots at the very top of Figure 4) who are also developmentally-evolutionarily at this *pre-transcendental* advanced consciousness realm-wave level, are similarly predominantly predisposed to one or the other of these remaining seven *elemental* Psychic Multi-istence *diverse beings* Reality Pathways of transcendent Awareness and Experience. In this way, the other seven large black dots at this convergence, at the top of Figure 4, mark One's *initial* point of *transition* into transcendent Awareness and Experience of and within one or the other of these seven *diverse-beings* Reality Pathways of *elemental* Psychic Multi-istence Self Awakening.

In Onliness theory, these eight parallel-coursing realm-waves (see Figure 4) of *diverse-beings* Self Reality Pathways are designated as: the two *Apparency* realm-waves of *elemental* Psychic Pan-gnostic and *elemental* Psychic Trans-gnostic *Existence* Self Awakening; the two *Transparency* realm-waves of *elemental* Psychic Pan-gnostic and *elemental* Psychic Trans-gnostic *Transexistence* Awakening; the two *Parency* realm-waves of *elemental* Psychic Pan-gnostic and *elemental* Psychic Trans-gnostic *Istence* Awakening; and the two *Anti-parency* realm-waves of *elemental* Psychic Pan-gnostic and *elemental* Psychic Trans-gnostic *Antistence* Self Awakening (see Figure 4). *Apparency, Transparency, Parency* and *Anti-parency* Consciousness Self Revelation realm-waves are defined as four distinctly different, but parallel-coursing, *transcendent* holon-polar *diverse beings* Reality Pathways of Perception, Recognition, Comprehension, Insight and Realization. Each of these Pathways is innate and integral to certain individual Beings and Entities, and certain types of Beings and Entities, who are native *to* and function *within*: (1) Existence (Pan- and Trans-gnostic) - whose Way of Perception and Understanding is *Apparency*, (2) Transexistence (Pan- and Trans-gnostic) - whose Way of Perception and Understanding is *Transparency*, (3) Istence (Pan- and Trans-gnostic) - whose Way of Perception and Understanding is *Parency*, or (4) Antistence (Pan- and Trans-gnostic) - whose Way of Perception and Understanding is *Anti-parency*.

Each of these four *diverse Beings* Reality Pathways include a *spectrum* of degrees or depths of transcendent Self Perception, Recognition, Comprehension, Insight and Realization for each Being and Entity who innately employs that Reality Pathway. Also, one Reality Pathway is not inherently more advanced in Consciousness Self Awakening and Realization than another, but rather each is just extremely different from the other. However, as One develops, evolves and Transforms through and within higher realm-waves of Self-awakening and Self-revelation, (that is, through more Consciousness inclusive realm-waves of transcendent Self-realization), One will *progressively* and *intuitively* Perceive, Realize and Apply (i.e., Acquire) the other three *diverse beings* Reality Pathways of Perception and Understanding. And that will tend to occur in a sequence from most to least similar *diverse beings* Reality Pathway to One's own innate Pathway (e.g., for human and human-like Being: from Apparency, to Transparency, to Parency, to Anti-parency Perception and Understanding). Such developmental-evolutionary progressive Perception, Understanding and Acquisition of these other three *diverse beings* Reality Pathways will, in turn, further mediate, facilitate and support One's own subsequent transcendent Nondual Self-as-Self Awakening and Realization.

Onliness theory proposes that, for Beings and Entities on the *diverse beings* Pathway of Pan- and Trans-gnostic Existence Self Illumination, the nature of Truth, Goodness and Beauty are profoundly Perceived, Recognized, Comprehended and Realized through transcendent *Apparency*. That is, Truth, Beauty and Goodness become easily, clearly and completely *Apparent* to such Beings and Entities through developmental-evolutionary transcendent Self Awakening and Realization. Unveiled in this progressive Way, the True, the Good, and the Beautiful become *spontaneously, directly* and *abundantly* Apparent to such Beings and Entities.

However, except for the *general connotative* meanings implied by each of the terms "Transparency," "Parency" and "Anti-parency," no *specific* mind-based definitions or meanings for these three *diverse beings* Reality Pathways of Perception and Understanding can be adequately given from the relative, conditioned and conditional compound personal-egoic self and pre-transcendental consciousness perspective, even at the advanced vision-logic realm-wave level of self and consciousness. Onliness theory thus suggests that, within the context of earth-centered human pre-transcendental consciousness awareness, these three terms can only be understood and assigned in a broad and unspecified connotative way.

I have previously defined "Pan-gnostic" as ". . .transcendental Realization *across* and *as* all Knowingness Itself, from Being *or* Nonbeing Perspective," and "Trans-gnostic" as ". . .transcendental Trans-realization *as* and *beyond* all Knowingness Itself, from Being *or*

Nonbeing Perspective" (Treon, 1996). Although very broadly accurate, such definitions are too non-specific for present purposes. More *specifically*, these two terms are intended to mean the *tendency* toward overall differences in the balance of *emphasis and importance* that Beings and Entities place on Self's transcendent *Ascent* of Wisdom and Truth *versus* Self's immanent *Descent* of Unconditional and All-encompassing Love, Care and Compassion, which occurs within the *diverse beings* Reality Pathways of Psychic Multi-istence's and *universive* Subtle Prim-istence's Existence, Transexistence, Istence and Antistence Self Awakenings (see Figures 4, 6 and 7). Onliness theory thus asserts that significant differences in emphasis and importance of this *balance between* the transcendent Ascent and immanent Descent of Self may certainly exist; while still recognizing that in Transformative Nondual Self-as-Self Revelation both the transcendent Ascent and immanent Descent always occur together, but sometimes with overall and persistent differing balances in the degree of intensity, attributed importance, and emphasis between them.

The adjective "Pan-gnostic," at whatever Psychic Multi-istence or *universive* Subtle Prim-istence holon-pole or holon-polarity realm-wave of Self Awakening so designated, means that, in so called individual Beings and Entities (or types thereof) there is, overall, occurring within that realm-wave of transcendent Recognition and Realization some *greater degree* of emphasis and importance being placed upon the immanent *Descent* of Self, over Its transcendent Ascent. That is, some significant overall imbalance, dys-synchrony and dys-synergy is occurring in this regard. Conversely, the adjective "Trans-gnostic," means that within any holon-pole or holon-polarity realm-wave of Self Awakening so designated there is, overall, occurring within transcendent Recognition and Realization some *greater degree* of emphasis and importance being placed upon the transcendent *Ascent* of Self, over Its immanent Descent. That is, some significant overall imbalance, dys-synchrony and dys-synergy is occurring in this regard.

However, in these Pan-gnostic and Trans-gnostic identified realm-waves of Psychic Multi-istence and *universive* Subtle Prim-istence Self Awakening and Realization, *both* the transcendent Ascent of Wisdom and Truth as well as the immanent Descent of Unconditional and All-encompassing Love, Care and Compassion *concurrently* still occur to-gether to some degree, according to Onliness theory. Note that such degrees of overall imbalance, dys-synchrony and dys-synergy differ-ences in emphasis and importance that may occur in One's transcen-dent Ascent of Spirit versus One's immanent Descent of Spirit become progressively smaller at successively deeper (higher) realm-wave levels up to, but not within, *supreme* Subtle Prim-istence Self Awakening and Illumination. When these two designations no longer appear in Onliness theory holon-pole and holon-polarity realm-wave identities, it is because Awakening Self's emphases on transcendent Ascent and immanent Descent are equally balanced, synchronized and syner-gized overall (see Figures 4 and 6 in this regard).

THE EIGHT *DIVERSE-BEINGS* REALITY PATHWAYS OF PSYCHIC MULTI-ISTENCE AND *UNIVERSIVE* SUBTLE PRIM-ISTENCE AWAKENING AND REALIZATION

As earth-centered human Beings within our somewhat common and present pre-transcendental advanced vision-logic consciousness levels of development-evolution, it is not possible to *specifically* understand, interpret or specify the seven other Psychic Multi-istence *diverse-be-ings* Reality Pathway realm-waves of Consciousness Self Realization *beyond* our own (i.e., beyond Psychic Pan-gnostic Existence as visualized in Figure 6). All that can be said is that each of these other seven transcendental Self Illumination realm-waves Reflect and Express the respective inherent *nature* and *essence* of the types of Beings and Entities who are innately predisposed to them. Onliness theory suggests that the various *specific* natures and characters of these other types of Consciousness Beings and Entities are *so* alien, strange and foreign to us, as earth-centered human Beings, so as to be incomprehensible at this relative level of pre-transcendental consciousness development-evolution.

In this way, and under these developmental-evolutionary circumstance, these *widely* diversified types of non-earth-centered Consciousness Beings and Entities are so utterly and bewilderingly strange to our relative mind-based comprehensions and imaginations, so far beyond the horizon of our earth-centered compound personal-egoic human self experience and awareness, as to make it impossible for us to understand, describe or explain the *specific* holon-pole and holon-polarity realm-wave character, identity or content of *any* of these Beings and Entities. From our perspective, these are the strange and incomprehensible Consciousness Beings and Entities who are variously predisposed to the other seven *diverse-beings* Reality Pathways of Psychic Multi-istence and *universive* Subtle Prim-istence Truth-consciousness Self Awakening (see Figure 4). However, Onliness theory proposes that such "strange" and "foreign" Consciousness Being and Entities are presently, and in general, either more nor less advanced in overall realm-wave level of Nondual Self Awakening, Revelation and Realization than are our own earth-centered human Beings. Indeed, Onliness theory claims that all Beings and Entities of each and every *diverse beings* Reality Pathway do not innately or inherently differ from one another in their developmental-evolutionary *potential* for transcendent Self Awakening and Self-realization.

Onliness theory suggests that each of the countless number of *types* of advanced consciousness Being and Entities (converging lines at the top of Figure 4) already has individuals (and likely types of individuals) who have developed to each and every transcendent Consciousness Self-realization realm-wave of Onliness theory, and, indeed, beyond all holon-polar and holon-only realm-waves of Awakening to fully Awakened Nondual Self-as-Self Realization Truth-consciousness. But because of earth-centered human Beings' relative, conditioned and conditional compound personal-egoic self and consciousness incomprehensibility "barrier" previously discussed, we are unable, except within our own innate and integral Psychic Pan-gnostic Existence Recognition realm-wave, to attribute *specific* meanings, contents and definitions to the other seven *diverse*-beings Reality Pathways of Psychic Multi-istence and *universive* Subtle Primistence. That is, in relation to their Trans-gnostic and Pan-gnostic: Antistence, Istence, Transexistence, and Trans-gnostic Existence Self Revelation realm-waves, as symbolized in Figure 4.

ELEMENTAL PSYCHIC PAN-GNOSTIC EXISTENCE AWAKENING AND REALIZATION

As indicated in Figures 5, 6 and 7, the holon-polar *elemental* Psychic Pan-gnostic Existence sub-realm-wave (ring) is comprise of eight separate and distinct Self Revelation realm-waves. As noted, for human and human-like Beings *elemental* Psychic Pan-gnostic Existence Awakening is one of the eight developmental-evolutionary *diverse beings* Reality Pathways of *elemental* Psychic Multi-istence (see Figure 4). In turn, in Onliness theory, the *broad* realm-waves of Psychic Multi-istence and Subtle Prim-istence Consciousness Self Realization together comprise the realm-waves of transcendent *World-Soul* Consciousness Self Awakening.

For human and human-like Beings then, *elemental* Psychic Pan-gnostic Existence Revelation is the transcendental realm-wave through which One's World-Soul Recognition first directly Experiences and Understands its encompassing Universal depth and breadth of Identity, Awareness and Experience, as an Expression of transpersonal Self. In this way, for human and human-like Beings, it is initially within *elemental* Psychic Pan-gnostic Existence Self Illumination that there emerges transcendental Awakening to Self as *World-Soul* Truth-consciousness Reality. This is the Self's first and preliminary Ascending-Descending World-Soul Awakening *as* the World Itself.

In mentally structured pre-transcendental Onliness theory, there are eight *holon-poles* of *elemental* Psychic Pan-gnostic Existence Self Realization (see Figures 5, 6 and 7). As presented in the following descriptions, these holon-poles are intended as generalized and very advanced-development prototypic examples of human and human-like Beings (or types of Beings) who are each respectively *primarily* predisposed to one or the other of these eight *elemental* holon-poles of transcendent Revelation. However, individuals predominantly pre-disposed to any one of these eight holon-poles of Self Realization will vary across a spectrum of degrees of development *within* that particular holon-pole's characteristic features, all the way from "not very advanced" to "very advanced." Also, as generalized descriptions, specific human and human-like Beings will tend to individually vary somewhat from the central-tendency characteristics described here for each of these eight *elemental* Psychic Pan-gnostic Existence Self Awakening holon-poles of Figures 5, 6 and 7.

In Onliness theory, these are the eight *elemental* transcendental holon-poles and their holon-polarities that spiritually mediate, facilitate and support human and human-like Beings in transcending (but including within such transcendence) their previous advanced world-centric vision-logic, but still pre-transcendental compound *personal-egoic* mind and self of consciousness, so as to developmentally transition into the *initial* transcendent Awakening realm-waves of *transpersonal*, trans-egoic and trans-mental Self Recognition and Expression. For human and human-like Beings these eight transpersonal holon-poles are: Transparency, Serenity, Realization, Intuition, Inherency, Multiplicity, Holiness, and Righteousness (see Figures 5, 6 and 7). In turn, these eight holon-poles are configured into the eight primary and eight secondary *elemental* holon-polarities, which are discussed below. However, there are also *other* important holon-polarities that occur and are influential between these eight holon-poles of *elemental* Psychic Pan-gnostic Existential Consciousness Self Awakening (see *Fires of Consciousness*; Treon, 1996).

TRANSPARENCY CONSCIOUSNESS ILLUMINATION AND REALIZATION

In *elemental* Psychic Pan-gnostic Existence, One who tends to be, via temperament and life experience, predominantly predisposed to the holon-pole of transpersonal *Transparency* Self Recognition is a human or human-like Being of remarkable *Vision, Clarity* and *Strength*. This intense and persistent human or human-like Being readily and clearly Sees into the heart of matters, into their underlying *core* structure and function. This is a highly insightful and visionary human or human-like Being who quickly understands the *deep* patterns and implications of issues and problems; One who Senses and clearly Perceives the more profound *Meanings* and deeper *Contexts* of matters. Thus, the empty sage Ch'ien: " 'i am the source of transparency, perfect emptiness of worlds. i am of-ness, transparent potency of worlds.' like the pristine lake in which no water can be seen, the clarity of Ch'ien's presence is complete. this hidden spring, the power of clarity complete" (Treon, 1989). In a generalized sense, this *Transparency* Self Awakening holon-pole is the Way of *deeply perceptive* and *profound Vision, Clarity and Strength.*

The holon-pole that is in *direct* or *primary* holon-polar opposition to holon-pole Transparency is Inherency (see Figures 5). From this holon-polarity-within-unity opposition emerges and is expressed the Transparency-Inherency *primary elemental* holon-polarity Self Revelation and Awakening. From this holon-polarity, as well as from *each* and *every* holon-polarity discussed in Onliness theory below, there derives and is expressed a critical and unique spiritual mediating, facilitating and supporting developmental-evolutionary *interaction effect,* which transcends but includes the effects of the *holon-poles* of either Transparency or Inherency alone.

This *holon-polar opposition* means that human or human-like Beings who are predominantly predisposed toward the holon-pole of Transparency as a means of mediating, facilitating and supporting Self or Spiritual Awakening, are secondarily but significantly also predisposed toward the holon-pole of Inherency, which specifically *supports* Transparency within the Transparency-Inherency holon-polarity interaction. Note that within this holon-polarity, the transpersonal influence of holon-pole Inherency also, in and of itself, mediates, facilitates and supports Self-realization.

The holon-pole that is in *indirect* or *secondary* holon-polar opposition to holon-pole Transparency is Multiplicity, from which opposition emerges and is expressed the Transparency-Multiplicity *secondary elemental* holon-polarity Self Recognition (see Figures 5). These two *secondary* Transparency and Multiplicity holon-poles, and their Transparency-Multiplicity *secondary* holon-polarity, function in the same way as the two *primary* Transparency and Inherency holon-poles and their Transparency-Inherency *primary* holon-polarity, in the sense of mediating, facilitating and supporting Self-realization, *except* that these two *secondary* holon-poles and holon-polarity are somewhat *less* influential in this regard.

But understand that it is *not* that human and human-like Beings are only influenced by these primary and secondary holon-polar (holon-pole and holon-polarity) *elemental* Psychic Pan-gnostic Existence realm-waves of Self Realization. In addition, each such Being (to varying degrees) is *also* influenced and employs *each* of the other five (of the eight) mediating, facilitating and supporting developmental-evolutionary transpersonal Self-realization holon-polar Realities of Truth-consciousness. That is, for example, in addition to being influenced by and employing the three Self-awakening holon-poles of Transparency, Inherency and Multiplicity, and their two holon-polarities of Transparency-Inherency and Transparency-Multiplicity described above, each human or human-like Being would *also* concurrently be influenced by, employ and express, but to various lesser degrees, the five remaining *elemental* Psychic Pan-gnostic Existence Self Illumination and Awakening holon-poles of Serenity, Righteousness, Holiness, Realization and Intuition, as well as their respective multiple primary and secondary holon-polarities.

In this way, *each* human and human-like Being is *concurrently* influenced by, employs and expresses a unique and individual con-figuration (in degrees of influence within various combinational pat-terns) of the holon-poles and holon-polarities of these eight variously predisposing mediating, facilitating and supporting Self-recognition developmental holon-polar tendencies, which comprise *elemental* Psychic Pan-gnostic Existence Self Realization.

INHERENCY CONSCIOUSNESS AWAKENING AND REALIZATION

One whose predominant predisposition realm-wave is the *elemental* Psychic Pan-gnostic Existence Self Revelation holon-pole of *Inherency* Realization readily *comprehends* the deep and underlying structural inter-relationship within and between complex and obscure concepts and manifest entities. Such an extremely observant and knowledge-able human or human-like Being, who is often socially unpopular - and thus socially marginalized and out of view, tends to have direct *insight into* and profound *understanding of* the underlying inter-con-nectedness, the hidden and inherent synergy, of events and processes that are not evident or visible at the surface expression of compound personal-egoic relative self and consciousness reality. Thus, the con-cealed sage Ken: " 'i am seed of mountain, genesis of wind. i am meaning's void, inherency of worlds.' as the mountain's highest vi-sion is rooted in the earth, so the light of meaning's deepest vision

is rooted in the night. great is Ken's thirst! the wellspring of worlds"
(Treon, 1989). In a generalized sense, this *Inherency* Self-awakening
holon-pole is the Way of *perceptive* and *profound inter-relatedness
Insight and Understanding*.

Likewise, One who is predominantly predisposed to the mediating, facilitating and supportive holon-pole realm-wave of
Inherency Self Illumination has Transparency as its *direct* or *primary* holon-polar opposition (see Figures 5). From this holon-
polarity-within-unity opposition emerges and is expressed the
Inherency-Transparency *primary* holon-polarity of Inherency,
with Its critical and unique mediating, facilitating and supporting holon-polarity Self-awakening interaction influence and effect.
And One whose predominant predisposition is the holon-pole of
Inherency Truth-consciousness is *secondarily* but significantly predisposed toward the influence, employment and expression of the
holon-pole of Transparency as a mediator, facilitator and supporter
of Transformative Self-realization.

In Onliness theory, the holon-pole that is in *indirect* or *secondary* holon-polar opposition to Inherency is Serenity (see Figures 5),
from which derives and is expressed the *secondary* holon-polarity of
Inherency-Serenity Self Awakening Reality. Again, the transcendental mediating, facilitating and supporting influence of this Serenity
secondary holon-pole (in and of itself), as well as its Inherency-Serenity
secondary holon-polarity interaction influence and effect, though
substantial, is somewhat less than the corresponding influences of
Transparency's *primary* holon-pole and its Inherency-Transparency
primary holon-polarity effect in mediating, facilitating and supporting Self Revelation.

SERENITY CONSCIOUSNESS RECOGNITION AND REALIZATION

From Onliness perspective, One whose predominantly predisposed spiritual mediating, facilitating and supporting holon-pole is *Serenity* Self Revelation tends to be a deeply *peaceful* and *reflective* human or human-like Being. A *profound* and *contemplative* person of equanimity, who is calm, calming, unifying and patient in temperament and action. This Being tends to have exceptionally insightful judgment in all matter, as well as a strong and balanced ethical and moral sense of fairness and justice. Such a Being tends to be a natural and revered teacher and leader of others. Thus, the profound sage Tui: " 'i am oneness, serenity's perfect realization. of wheat, i am the field.' like the lake's deep dreams, Tui's complete reflection is awakening worlds. like the giant redwood, Tui's towering visage stands alone and is the beauty of worlds" (Treon, 1989). In a generalized sense, this *Serenity* Self Recognition holon-pole is the Way of *calm* and *balanced ethical and moral judgment, meditative Unity, as well as deep Contemplation, Reflection, and Peace.*

The spiritual mediating-facilitating holon-pole in *direct* or *primary* opposition to Serenity Self Revelation is Multiplicity Awakening (see Figures 5). This holon-polar opposition creates the *primary* holon-polarity of Serenity-Multiplicity Truth-consciousness within *elemental* Psychic Pan-gnostic Existence Reality, with its *primary* mediating, facilitating and supportive Self-realization interaction effect. The *indirect* or *secondary* opposition to Serenity is the holon-pole of Inherency Self Awakening, which creates the *secondary* holon-polarity of Serenity-Inherency Realization, with its *secondary* mediating, facilitating and supporting Self-recognition interaction influence and effect in relation to Serenity.

The pattern of Self-realization mediating, facilitating and supporting influence and effect for human and human-like Beings who are predominantly predisposed to the *primary* and *secondary* holon-poles, and their holon-polarities, of any one of the other five holon-polar Self Awakening realm-waves of *elemental* Psychic Pan-gnostic Existence (i.e., Multiplicity, Righteousness, Intuition, Holiness and Realization) is of the *same* pattern as described above for Transparency, Inherency and Serenity (see Figures 3 and 5 to view these patterns).

MULTIPLICITY CONSCIOUSNESS AWAKENING AND REALIZATION

In Onliness theory, One who is predominantly predisposed to the Self-recognition mediating, facilitating and supporting holon-pole is *Multiplicity* Realization has the *direct* or *primary* holon-polarity of Multiplicity-Serenity, and the *indirect* or *secondary* holon-polarity of Multiplicity-Transparency (see Figures 3 and 5). Such a human or human-like Being tends to readily comprehend the multi-dimensional *meanings*, the complexity of meaning, of each event and moment of transpersonal Awareness and Experience. This is a highly *perceptive, creative* and *analytic* Being, who can quickly *penetrate to* and *define* the deep-meaning source or root of matters, great and small. This is One who has rich and fertile insight into, and understanding of, complexity. Thus, the radiant sage K'un: " 'i am diversity, reflection's perfect realization. of wheat, i am the seed.' as the sea of wind ebbs and flows across the prairie grasses, the movement of each blade creates a world of meaning. many of K'un's faces! great is the fire of prairie's fierce meaning! the consummation and illumination of worlds"

(Treon, 1989). In a generalized sense, this *Multiplicity* Self Revelation holon-pole is the Way of *deep Analysis, Perceptive understanding and creative Insight.*

RIGHTEOUSNESS RECOGNITION AND REALIZATION

One who has the predominantly predisposing mediating, facilitating and supporting Self Enlightenment holon-pole realm-wave of *Righteousness* Awakening has the *direct* or *primary elemental* holon-polarity of Righteousness-Intuition Illumination, and the *indirect* or *secondary* holon-polarity of Righteousness-Realization Self Revelation (see Figures 3 and 5). Such a human or human-like Being tends to deeply and empathetically Experience, to be acutely Aware of and Responsive to, the *suffering* of others, and to the *injustices* others endure. Out of Love, and with intensity and clarity of purpose, this is a Being who readily *Perceives* and promptly and courageously *Acts*, irrespective of the consequences for this Being, to attempt to alleviate and eliminate the *suffering* and *injustice* that others experience.

Such Righteous Action consciously and openly occurs, and is expressed through this Being in the context of strong ethical and moral values which are selfless and trans-egoic in nature. Thus, the vital sage Li: " 'i am love's righteousness, attention's perfect realization. i am withness, searing fire of presence.' Li, enfolding the earth like the moving wind, is the luminous power of love. great is the source of love's awakening! the fire of worlds" (Treon, 1989). In a generalized sense, this *Righteousness* Self-realization holon-pole is the Way of *courageous and empathetic Love and Care for the wellbeing of others* through *Loving, Just and Righteous Action, in selfless sacrifice.*

INTUITION TRUTH-CONSCIOUSNESS AWAKENING AND REALIZATION

In Onliness theory, One whose predominantly predisposing mediating, facilitating and supporting holon-pole realm-wave of Self Recognition is *Intuition* has the *direct* or *primary* holon-polarity of Intuition-Righteousness Awakening, and the *indirect* or *secondary* holon-polarity of Intuition-Holiness Realization (see Figures 3 and 5). A human or human-like Being so predominantly predisposed to realm-wave Intuition Self of Truth-consciousness tends to innately and intuitively *perceive* the basic and fundamental nature of things, events, problems, issues and concerns, both personal and transpersonal. This quiet Being fully and profoundly Comprehends, and can quickly grasp and visualize as a whole, the critical and essential nature and expression of all Self Awareness and Experience. Such a Being tends to be highly *imaginative, creative* and *perceptive*. Thus, the quiet sage Sun: " 'i am fluidity, streaming's perfect realization. i am through-ness, intuition's heart.' moving in the winds of knowledge, Sun is the great voyager standing on the highest peak. how provocative, how profound is the wind of Sun's awakening! the creator and destroyer of worlds." (Treon, 1989). In a generalized sense, this Intuition Illumination holon-pole is the Way of *imaginative, perceptive and comprehensive* Self-realization *through Intuitive and Creative Insight*.

HOLINESS CONSCIOUSNESS RECOGNITION AND AWAKENING

In Onliness theory, One's predominantly predisposing Self-revelation mediating, facilitating and supportive holon-pole of *Holiness* Enlightenment has the *primary* holon-polarity of Holiness-Realization Self Awakening and the *secondary* holon-polarity of Holiness-Intuition

Truth-consciousness (see Figures 3 and 5). A human or human-like Being so predominantly predisposed to Holiness Self Illumination tends to acutely and readily *Perceive* and *Respond to* the needs and problems of other Beings by selflessly attending to, and caring for, others in their suffering, agony and helplessness. Such a trans-egoic self-sacrificing Being tends, in Love and Glad Acceptance, to live a humble, unadorned and unassumingly plain-and-simple life, in the course of that Being's quiet *care for* and *service to* others who are in need.

There tends to be neither "fanfare" surrounding such a life, nor social or personal-egoic recognition sought for or desired by this Being. Such a One, as her or his transpersonal Self Awakening development proceeds, tends to have transcended (but included within such transcendence) the realm-wave levels of pre-transcendental compound personal-egoic relative self and consciousness. Thus, the Holy sage Chen: " 'i am complete embrace, germination of all relatedness. of wheat, i am the harvest. i am the luminous vision; receptivity and grace.' moving in the vast currents of oceans, Chen is the singular beacon, the incandescent body of love. great is the luminous body of love! the righteousness of worlds." In a generalized sense, this *Holiness* Self Revelation holon-pole is the Way of *profoundly perceiving and selflessly responding, caring for, serving and attending to the helplessness, agony and suffering of others.*

REALIZATION RECOGNITION AND AWAKENING

One's predominantly predisposing Self-remembrance mediating, facilitating and supporting holon-pole of *Realization* Self Awakening has the *primary* holon-polarity-within-unity of Realization-Holiness Enlightenment, and the *secondary* holon-polarity of Realization-Righteousness Self Revelation (see Figures 3 and 5). A human or human-like Being so predominantly predisposed tends to profoundly Recognize and clearly Perceive the *transcendental* nature of Self, of Truth-consciousness Reality that is to say. This is One who, with great Clarity and Insight, *Comprehends* and *Realizes* each of transcendent Spirit's Manifestations and Expressions. This is a highly *Insightful* Being who, in a modest, calm and quiet way, deeply *Touches* and *Enlightens* the lives of those who know and hear such a One. Thus, the joyful sage K'an: " 'i am realization of illusion, the formless form. of wheat, i am the stalk and grain itself. i am clarity, transessence of worlds. i am knowledge's form, mind of joy.' in radiant beauty, K'an sits facing the fire and to my left. illuminations fire. this calm and righteous being, the glory of worlds!" (Treon, 1989). In a general-ized sense, this *Realization* Self Awakening holon-pole is the Way of *profound Clarity and Truth of luminous transcendental Perception, Recognition, Understanding and Realization.*

CARDINAL PSYCHIC PAN-GNOSTIC EXISTENCE REVELATION AND REALIZATION

In Onliness theory, for human and human-like Beings, *cardinal* Psychic Pan-gnostic Existence Awakening of Self is the develop-mental-evolutionary *intermediate* holon-polar realm-wave Reality of Psychic Pan-gnostic Existence Self Recognition (see Figures 4, 5 and 6). This intermediate realm-wave ring comprises the *outer* core of the deeper and more profound *inner* fundamental center of transpersonal Awareness and Experience Truth-consciousness Self Reality.

In accord with what several others have identified as the *Psychic* stage-wave (realm-wave) of Consciousness Awakening, Onliness theory proposes that, for human and human-like Beings, *Psychic* Pan-gnostic

Existence (as one of the eight *diverse-beings* Reality Pathways of Self Awakening) is a major developmental-evolutionary realm-wave of Self Realization *as World-Soul* Consciousness Illumination. Indeed, Onliness theory claims that all eight *diverse-beings* Reality Pathways of Psychic Multi-istence Awakening (see Figure 4) include and involve the *initial* and *preliminary* stages (realm-waves) of developmental-evolutionary transcendence-but-inclusion of, and Self Identity transition *from*, One's illusory separate self-sense compound pre-egoic, personal-egoic, and conditioned social-cultural relative self and consciousness *to* Compassionate and Universal Self Identity *with* and *as* this entire manifest World, and, indeed, all Worlds and Universes.

In this way, there now emerges this *certain* Knowledge and Understanding of transcendent Self as *One,* without otherness or separation, with *all* sentient Beings and Entities, in *all* Worlds and Universes (i.e., with *all* of Reality Itself). This is, then, One's initial transparent and direct World-Soul *Recognition* of Self *as,* and thus Self's inclusion of, each and every Consciousness Being and Entity. That is to say, such *transpersonal* World-Soul Self Revelation and Realization can and will occur when, as Sri Nisargadatta Maharaj (2012) has said, there is release and abandonment of compound personal-egoic *fear* and *desire*. When there occurs the ceasing of compound personal-egoic self and consciousness shuttling between the past in *memory* and the future in *expectation*, and the turning away from always seeking body-mind based relative pleasure and trying to avoid body-mind based relative pain, so as to Be fully and completely *transpersonally* Present and Aware in the eternal and spontaneous moment.

As suggested, One's deeper (i.e., more Self-realization expansive and encompassing) Recognition, Insight and Understanding that occurs within this sub-realm-wave of *cardinal* Psychic Pan-gnostic Existence Self Awakening transcends but includes the Self Realization of its junior *elemental* Psychic Pan-gnostic Existence sub-realm-wave Truth-consciousness. In Onliness theory, this *cardinal* sub-realm-wave has four holon-poles (i.e., Communion, Compassion, Knowledge and Meaning) of transcendent Self Recognition (see Figures 5, 6 and 7). That is to say, it has four predominantly predisposing Self-awakening mediating, facilitating and supporting holon-pole dimensions of transcendent Realization. As described above in relation to each of the eight *elemental* holon-poles of *elemental* Psychic Pan-gnostic Existence Self Recognition, similarly, each of the four holon-poles of *cardinal* Psychic Pan-gnostic Existence Realization are in some degree of holon-polarity with each of the other three poles (see Figures 5, 6 and 7 to view these patterns).

As visualized in Figure 5, each of the four *cardinal* holon-poles has a *direct* or *primary* oppositional holon-pole which forms its *primary* holon-polarity (i.e., the directly opposite yin-yang symbolized digram in Figure 5). Note, however, that the top *yin or yang line* oppositional pattern of the trigram symbolization of these holon-poles and holon-polarities described in *elemental* Psychic Pan-gnostic Existence Revelation are *unique* to that holon-polar sub-realm-wave (i.e., are unique to the *initial* emergent "breakthrough" into transcendent Consciousness Self Awakening), and do *not* occur in this yin-yang line opposition pattern in the subsequent *cardinal* and *fundamental* Psychic Pan-gnostic Existence Awakening sub-realm-waves, nor, for that matter, within the *cardinal* and *fundamental* Psychic Multi-istence Self Realization sub-realm-waves of the other seven *diverse beings* Reality Pathway of Awakening (see Figure 3).

No *specific* content definitions, characteristics or identities are as-signed to these four *cardinal* Psychic Multi-istence holon-poles, or their respective holon-polarities, for the other seven *diverse-beings* Reality Pathway realm-waves of Figure 4. Recall that this is so be-cause the types of Consciousness Beings and Entities who develop-evolve within and throughout these other seven realm-waves (i.e., *cardinal* Psychic Trans-gnostic Existence, and *cardinal* Psychic Pan-gnostic and Trans-gnostic: Transexistence, Istence, and Antistence) are so *extremely* and *utterly* different from, and predominantly in-comprehensible to, earth-centered humans of compound personal-egoic self, who are thus of relative pre-transcendental consciousness, even at advanced vision-logic levels of such consciousness.

According to Onliness theory, there exists an abstract and broadly defined *similarity* between the functional contents and relationships, as well as a similarity in their the Self-realization mediating, facilitating and supportive interactions and effects, of these four *cardinal* Psychic Multi-istence holon-poles, and their holon-polarities, across *all* of the eight *diverse-beings* Reality Pathways of Self Awakening (see Figure 4). This *shared* and *basic* generalize similarity is proposed, whatever the many widely diversified *specific* meaning and content designa-tions differences may be within and between the four *cardinal* holon-poles, and their holon-polarities, of Psychic Pan-gnostic Existence Self Revelation *versus* the the four *cardinal* holon poles, and their holon-polarities, of the other seven *diverse being* Reality Pathways of Self Revelation. Given these basic similarities, we can, to some extent, use these defined features of the holon-poles, and their holon-polarities, of *cardinal* Psychic Pan-gnostic Existence Self Awakening, which relate only to human and human-like Beings, as *generalized prototypes*, so as to abstractly and broadly describe the four *cardinal* holon-polar structural and functional contents and relationships of each of these other seven *cardinal* Psychic Multi-istence *diverse-beings* Reality Pathways of transcendent Self Awakening and Realization.

For human and human-like Beings, the holon-polar sub-realm-wave of *cardinal* Psychic Pan-gnostic Existence Illumination has, in Onliness theory, four transpersonal Self-realization holon-poles: *Communion, Knowledge, Meaning* and *Compassion*. Recall that *each* human and human-like Being, while responding to, and influenced by, *each* of these four holon-poles of Consciousness Awakening, tends to be *predominantly* predisposed to only one of the four holon-polar Self Revelation Realities. This one predominant *cardinal* holon-pole, and its related holon-polarities, tend to be the *primary* mediating, facilitating and supporting transpersonal means of Transformative Self Awakening for that Being.

COMMUNION RECOGNITION AND AWAKENING

Human and human-like Beings who are developmentally at *elemental* Psychic Pan-gnostic Existence Realization, and are thus predominantly predisposed to *Transparency* or *Serenity* as mediating, facilitating and supporting means of Transformative Self-as-Self Awakening, will, at developmental emergence of *cardinal* Psychic Pan-gnostic Existence Self Realization, *strongly* tend to be predominantly predisposed to the holon-pole and its holon-polarities of *Communion* Self Recognition and Awakening, while transcending but including these two junior Transparency and Serenity *elemental* holon-poles and their holon-polarities (see Figure 5, 6 and 7).

In *primary* or *direct* holon-polar opposition to Communion is the holon-pole of Meaning (directly opposite in Figure 5). And again, this Communion-Meaning holon-polarity Realization creates a critical mediating, facilitating and supportive Self-revelation interaction influence and effect, which transcends but includes the influence of either the holon-pole of Communion or Meaning Self Illumination alone. Functioning in this same way, but with somewhat less mediating, facilitating and supportive Self-awakening influence and effect, are the other two holon-poles and holon-polarities (i.e., holon-polars) of Communion: the *secondary* holon-polarity of Communion-Knowledge Self Revelation and the *tertiary* holon-polarity of Communion-Compassion Self Revelation.

Communion Revelation is concerned with One's transcendent *Recognition* and *Realization* of the Union, Identity and Oneness of *all* Reality. This Communion holon-pole transpersonal Self Recognition expresses the creative, transparent and unitary *Power* of the immanent Descent of Spirit-as-Spirit or Self-as-Self as Unconditional and All-embracing Love, Care and Compassion. That is, One's Awakening *Potency* of Communion Self Realization tends to manifest itself through the *Transfiguring* immanent Descent of Spirit in the World (in all worlds and universes). "communion: 'i am unity of source, being *one all-where'* " (Treon, 1989).

MEANING REVELATION AND TRUTH-CONSCIOUSNESS

Human and human-like Beings at developmental *elemental* Psychic Pan-gnostic Existence Self Awakening, who are predominantly predisposed to *Inherency* or *Multiplicity* as primary holon-polar mediators, facilitators and supporter of Transformative Self Recognition will, at the developmental-evolutionary emergence of *cardinal* Psychic Pan-gnostic Existence Realization, *strongly* tend to be predominantly predisposed to the holon-pole and its holon-polarities of *Meaning* Self Awakening and Recognition, while transcending but including these two junior *elemental* holon-poles and their holon-polarities of Inherency and Multiplicity Self Revelation (see Figures 5, 6 and 7).

In *primary* or *direct* holon-polar opposition to Meaning is the holon-pole of Communion (directly opposite in Figure 5). The resultant Meaning-Communion Enlightenment holon-polarity interaction influence and effect is the *primary* mediator, facilitator and supporter of transcendent Self-realization development-evolution, transcending but including the influence of either holon-pole of Meaning or Communion alone. In development-evolution, the mediating, facilitating and supporting Self-awakening influences and effects of the *secondary* holon-poles and holon-polarity of Meaning-Compassion Self Revelation, and the *tertiary* holon-polar of Meaning-Knowledge Self Revelation become *progressively* less influential of Self-awakening in relation to the *primary* holon-polar of Meaning-Communion Self Revelation.

Transpersonal Meaning Self Illumination is concerned with *Insight into* and *Comprehension of* the Onliness and Ultimacy of Spirit, of Self. The realm-wave of transcendent Meaning Self Awakening expresses and conveys One's Conceptive, Cohesive, and Realizing *Vision* and *Insight* into and of the transcendent Ascent of Self in Wisdom and Truth. That is, One's Truth-consciousness *Vision* and *Insight* of Meaning Self Realization tends to manifest Itself as the confluent and fertile *Configuring Form* of transcendent Ascent of Spirit or Self in the World. "meaning: 'i am genesis of root, seeing *none each-where*' " (Treon, 1989).

KNOWLEDGE RECOGNITION AND ILLUMINATION

Human and human-like Beings who are predominantly predisposed to *Intuition* or *Realization* as primary mediators, facilitators and supporters of Recognition and Awakening within *elemental* Psychic Pan-gnostic Existence Self Revelation, will *strongly* tend to be predominantly predisposed to the holon-pole and holon-polarities of transcendent *Knowledge* at the developmental-evolutionary realm-wave of *cardinal* Psychic Pan-gnostic Existence Self Realization (see Figures 5, 6 and 7).

In *primary* holon-polar opposition to Knowledge is the holon-pole of Compassion (see Figure 5). One's resultant Knowledge-Compassion *primary* holon-polarity mediating, facilitating and supporting Self-realization influence and interaction effect transcends but includes the influence effects of either Knowledge or Compassion holon-poles alone. And again, the *secondary* holon-polar (i.e., holon-poles and holon-polarity) of Knowledge-Communion and the *tertiary* holon-polar of Knowledge-Meaning have progressively less influential Self-revelation interaction effects than does the *primary* holon-polar of Knowledge-Compassion.

Transpersonal Knowledge Self Realization is concerned with One's *Perception* and *Understanding* of, and deep *Insight into*, the Vision and Reality of Spirit, of Self. This Knowledge realm-wave of developmental Self Awakening *Intuitively* and *Perceptively* expresses and describes One's transcendent Ascent of Self in Wisdom and Truth. That is, the holon-pole of Knowledge tends to manifest Itself as the luminous, silent and reflective *Conforming* transcendent Ascent of Spirit or Self in the World. "knowledge: 'i am truth of essence, understanding *all all-where*' " (Treon, 1989).

COMPASSION REVELATION AND RECOGNITION

Human and human-like beings predominantly predisposed to *Righteousness* or *Holiness* as primary mediators, facilitators and supporters of Transforming Self-as-Self Awakening within the realm-wave of *elemental* Psychic Pan-gnostic Existence, will *strongly* tend to be predominantly predisposed to the holon-pole of transcendent *Compassion* Self Revelation within the developmental-evolutionary realm-wave of *cardinal* Psychic Pan-gnostic Existence Self Illumination (see Figures 5, 6 and 7).

In *primary* holon-polar opposition to Compassion is the holon-pole of Knowledge (see Figure 5). Again, the Self-revelation mediating, facilitating and supporting interaction influence and effect of this *primary* holon-polarity of Compassion-Knowledge Self Awakening transcends but includes that of either Compassion or Knowledge holon-poles alone. And again, the respective *secondary* Compassion-Meaning and *tertiary* Compassion-Communion holon-polarities have progressively less influential Self Realization mediating, facilitating and supporting effects than does the *primary* holon-polar of Compassion-Knowledge.

Compassion Realization is concerned with One's transpersonal *Perception of, Identification with* and *Response to* the suffering of all, each and every Consciousness Being and Entity. This realm-wave of Compassion Self Recognition expresses itself through One's *courageous* Attention to, and selfless Love, Embrace and Care of, each and all such Beings and Entities. That is, One's Compassion Self Realization primarily manifests itself through inspired, passionate and selfless *Action* and *Presence* within the immanent Descent of

Spirit or Self, through Unconditional and All-inclusive Love, Care and Compassion. Such Compassion conveys itself as the fiery and intense *Transformative* Descent of immanent Spirit or Self in the World. "compassion: 'i am resonance of [love and] grace, *touching each each-where*'" (Treon, 1989).

Onliness theory asserts that there is Self and *only* Self, and None other than. That Self is All and None, and Neither, only and completely. Nondual Self-as-Self is the One and the Many, Everything and Nothing, manifest Form and unmanifest Emptiness. Self is prior to time and space; it is prior to and beyond all mental knowledge, conception, description and imagination. Ultimately Self is unqualifable, causeless, uncreated and timeless Spirit as Such. That is, Self is Consciousness, and also prior to and beyond all Consciousness. *Self is Reality*, only and alone. Awakened Nondual Self Realization is, and thus embraces, Each and All, inclusively and unconditionally. For Each and All, without exception, *is* Self-as-Self, *is* Spirit-as-Spirit.

Supreme Self is Being and Nonbeing *Absolute* Reality and Truth. As Absolute Reality and Truth, each and every Consciousness Being and Entity (each and every Thing, for all so called "Things" have Consciousness) has *ultimate, absolute* and *equal* Worth, Priority and Value. That is, in One's transcendent Ascent of Wisdom and Truth, and One's immanent Descent of Unconditional and All-encompassing Love, Care and Compassion, there is no attribution basis for, and thus no meaning or distinction possible between, the Worth, Priority and Value of so called (i.e., relatively perceived) separate Consciousness Being and Entities.

However, Onliness theory also recognizes that within One's pre-transcendental realm-wave reality of relative and conditional compound pre-egoic, personal-egoic and conditioned social-cultural self and consciousness, there certainly are transcient bases for, and thus conditional meanings to, the making of relative distinctions by and between Beings and Entities, which will involve judgments of *relative* and *conditional* value, worth and priority. In relation to Compassion then, within relative, conditioned and conditional compound personal-egoic self reality, it is important, and often necessary, to make *difficult* distinctions and decisions, as well as to take actions *of relative* and *conditional* compassion, based upon such relative judgments of worth, priority and value.

FUNDAMENTAL PSYCHIC PAN-GNOSTIC EXISTENCE CONSCIOUSNESS AWAKENING

This is the developmental-evolutionary *advanced* Psychic Pan-gnostic Existence realm-wave of transpersonal Self Recognition and Awakening. This realm-wave is the *fundamental* Source and Foundation of all holon-polar realm-waves of Psychic Pan-gnostic Existence Realization. For human and human-like Beings, the developmental unfolding of *fundamental* Psychic Pan-gnostic Existence reveals an even higher and more Consciousness encompassing Self Realization of One's transcendent Ascent of Wisdom and Truth, and a deeper and more inclusive Self Realization of One's immanent Descent of Unconditional and All-pervasive Love, Care and Compassion, which, of course, transcends, but includes within such transcendence, Realization of One's previous and somewhat less Self-awakened realm-waves of *cardinal* Psychic Pan-gnostic Existence Reality.

In Onliness theory, *fundamental* Psychic Pan-gnostic Existence has two holon-poles of Self Realization: Awareness and Experience (see Figures 5, 6. And 7). However, for reasons previously discussed, it is not possible for earth-centered human Beings of relative, conditioned and conditional compound personal-egoic self and consciousness to *specify* the Meanings, Definitions and Identities of these two *fundamental* Psychic Multi-istence holon-poles, in relation to Beings and Entities within the *other* seven *diverse-beings* Reality Pathways of Psychic Multi-istence Self Awakening (i.e., Psychic Trans-gnostic Existence, as well as Psychic Pan-gnostic and Trans-gnostic: Transexistence, Istence and Antistence Self Realization (see Figure 4).

Nevertheless, in Onliness theory, the Truth-consciousness Self-recognition influential effect of these two *unspecified* holon-poles, individually and together in polaric interaction, within *each* of the other seven *diverse-beings* Reality Pathways of Illumination create and comprise the one pair of *fundamental* holon-poles within each of these seven Self Awakening realm-waves of *fundamental* Psychic Multi-istence (see Figure 4). Thus, without *specifically* describing or defining the other seven *diverse beings* Reality Pathway holon-polar realm-waves of Psychic Multi-istence, they are, from Onliness earth-centered relative human perspective, connotatively and generically described-identified contextually as: Psychic Trans-gnostic Existence, Psychic Pan- and Trans-gnostic Transexistence, Psychic Pan- and Trans-gnostic Istence, and Psychic Pan- and Trans-gnostic Antistence Self Awakening (see Figure 4). But for all human and human-like Beings within *fundamental* Psychic Pan-gnostic Existence Realization, this is the holon-polarity of Experience-Awareness or

Awareness-Experience transpersonal Self Revelation (see Figure 5, 6 and 7).

In Onliness theory, the influential mediating, facilitating and supporting Self-realization interaction effect dynamic that operates for human and human-like Beings between the two holon-poles of *fundamental* Psychic Pan-gnostic Existence (i.e., Awareness and Experience) are, in terms of their *broadly defined* underlying character and influence, claimed to be somewhat *similar* to those that occur and operate within the holon-polar (i.e., holon-poles and holon-polarity) dynamics of the other seven *diverse-beings* Reality Pathways of *fundamental* Psychic Multi-istence Self Illumination. In this way, discussion of such spiritually mediating, facilitating and supporting effects-influences within *fundamental* Psychic Pan-gnostic Existence Self Realization can serve to *broadly* and *prototypically* illustrate and define the general nature and character of these similar holon-polar Self-recognition interaction effects-influences that occur within the other seven unspecified *fundamental* Psychic Multi-istence realm-waves of Self Revelation and Realization (see Figure 4).

So called individual human and human-like Beings at this developmental-evolutionary realm-wave level will *always* and *concurrently*, but to differing degrees between individual Beings, embrace, enact and employ *both* of these two deeper (more Self-revealing and Consciousness-inclusive) *Awareness* and *Experience* transcendent Self Awakening and Realization holon-poles. At the same time, each such Being will tend to be predominantly predisposed to one or the other of these two holon-poles as *primary* mediators, facilitators and supporter of that Being's transpersonal Self Revelation fpr some developmental time to come.

EXPERIENCE CONSCIOUSNESS RECOGNITION AND REALIZATION

Human and human-like Beings predominantly predisposed to *Communion* or *Compassion* as mediators, facilitators and supporters of Self-awakening development-evolvement at the realm-wave level of *cardinal* Psychic Pan-gnostic Existence, will *strongly* tend to be predominantly predisposed to the holon-pole of *Experience* Consciousness Awakening within the realm-wave of *fundamental* Psychic Pan-gnostic Existence Self Realization (see Figures 5, 6 and 7). In holon-polar opposition to Experience is, of course, the holon-pole of Awareness Consciousness Awakening (see Figure 5, 6 and 7). The resultant holon-polarity of Experience-Awareness creates an influential mediating, facilitating and supporting Self-revelation interaction effect which *transcends*, but includes, the Self-revelation mediating, facilitating and supporting effects of either Experience or Awareness Truth-consciousness alone.

For all human and human-like Beings, Experience Self Illumination is the transcendental *ontological* dimension of *fundamental* Psychic Pan-gnostic Existence Self-illumination. It is One's *fundamental* Experience of the nature of transcendent Being and Beingness. This holon-pole is World-Soul's *Unreflexive* and *Transfigurative* Experience *of* and *as* each and all Consciousness Beings and Entities. This World-Soul of *Heart-Soul Experience* tends to express Itself *within* and *as* the *Creative Power* of the immanent Descent of Spirit or Self through Unconditional and All-embracing Love, Care and Compassions in the World. Experience is the *apparent transparency* Self Realization of One's World-Soul of Heart-Soul Consciousness Identity *with* and *as* each and all of manifest Reality. Such Self Awakening and Realization is the *direct* and *immediate* Experience of Self *as* the World (and as all Worlds and Universes).

AWARENESS CONSCIOUSNESS RECOGNITION AND REALIZATION

Human and human-like Beings predominantly predisposed to *Knowledge* or *Meaning* as developmental-evolutionary mediators, facilitators and supporter of Self-awakening within the realm-wave of *cardinal* Psychic Pan-gnostic Existence, will *strongly* tend to be predominantly predisposed to the holon-pole of *Awareness* Consciousness Awakening within the realm-wave of *fundamental* Psychic Pan-gnostic Existence Self Realization (see Figures 5, 6 and 7). The holon-polar opposition to Awareness is, of course, the holon-pole of Experience Consciousness Self Awakening (see Figure 5, 6 and 7). And again, the resultant holon-polarity of Awareness-Experience creates an influential mediating, facilitating and supporting Self-realization interaction effect which *transcends*, but includes within such transcendence, the Self-recognition mediating, facilitating and supporting effects of either holon-pole Awareness or Experience Self Realization alone.

For all human and human-like Beings, Awareness is the transcendental *epistemological* dimension of *fundamental* Psychic Pan-gnostic Existence Self-illumination. It is One's *fundamental* Awareness of the nature of transcendent Knowledge and Knowingness. This Consciousness holon-pole is World Soul's *Reflexive* and *Configurative* Awareness *of* and *as* each and all Consciousness Beings and Entities. This World-Soul of *Mind-Psyche Awareness* tends to express Itself *within* and *as* the *Productive Vision* of the transcendent Ascent of Spirit or Self through Wisdom and Truth in the World. Awareness is the *transparent apparency* Self Realization of One's World-Soul of Mind-Psyche Consciousness Identity *with* and *as* each and all of manifest Reality. Such Self Awakening and Realization is the *direct* and *immediate* transcendental Awareness of Self *as* the World (and as all Worlds and Universes).

SUBTLE PRIM-ISTENCE AWAKENING AND REVELATION

It should be emphasized again that *all* of the holon-polar realm-waves of developmental-evolutionary transcendental Truth-consciousness described in Onliness theory are presented *not* just as theoretic abstractions (though they are that also), but *primarily* as direct and immediate *Experiential* Realities and Disclosures which are open and available to *all* Consciousness Beings and Entities, in *all* manifest worlds, dimensions and universes. In the transcendental Consciousness development-evolution of all Beings and Entities, the Transformative transition *from* the initial (inner) broad realm-wave (solid-line ring) of Psychic Multi-istence Self Revelation *to* the intermediate broad realm-wave (solid-line ring) of Subtle Prim-istence Self Awakening and Realization is *radically Self Illuminating* indeed (see Figures 2, 3, 4, 5, and 6).

Within the realm-wave of Subtle Prim-istence Revelation there emerges and unfolds a greater *interiorization* of transcendent Consciousness Self Realization; that is, a deeper *turning-inward* Examination, Exploration and Understanding of One's always, already Supreme Self Reality. This also includes a more profound, expanded and direct transcendent Experience and Awareness of the many and multi-varied visions, forms and images that arise within Subtle Prim-istence Awakening. Overall, within the holon-polar realm-wave of One's Subtle Prim-istence Self Awakening there is now Revealed an even more *expansive* and *inclusive* transcendent Ascent of Wisdom and Truth, *together with* an immanent Descent of Unconditional and All-embracing Love, Care and Compassion, than had previously been Recognized and Awakened. And with this Ascent-Descent, there emerges a further abandonment and lessening of conditioned, conditional and relative compound personal-egoic self's mind-based fear and desire, as well as sense of otherness, isolation and separation.

In Onliness theory, from the *initial* emergence of the *universive* Subtle Prim-istence sub-realm-wave Self Revelation (of the broad realm-wave of Subtle Prim-istence) all Consciousness Beings and Entities, human, human-like and non-human, begin to *directly* and *progressively* Experience and become Aware of the basic Nature and Dimensions of eight varied Modes of Enlightenment Consciousness Self Awakening. This occurs across and within all of the other seven *diverse beings* Reality Pathways of Enlightenment beyond the Pan-gnostic Existence Pathway to which human and human-like Beings are natively predisposed and attuned (compare Figures 4, 5, 6 and 7).

It is thus within and throughout the developmental-evolutionary course of *universive* Subtle Prim-istence Self Awakening that the Nature of all eight *diverse-beings* Reality Pathways of Self Recognition (i.e., *universive* Subtle Prim-istence's Pan-gnostic and Trans-gnostic: Existence, Transexistence, Istence and Antistence Pathways) are Unveiled and Revealed to each and all Consciousness Beings and Entities at this realm-wave level. And, ultimately, it is at the developmental-evolutionary *culmination* of *absolute* Subtle Holistent Prim-istence Self Awakening, the highest sub-realm-wave of Subtle Prim-istence, that each Consciousness Being and Entity, of whatever diverse nature or type, *fully* Recognizes, Comprehends, Integrates and Resolves each of these eight *diverse beings* Reality Pathways of Consciousness Awakening (see Figures 3, 4, 5 and 6).

The nature and character of Subtle Prim-istence Self Realization is one of transcendental *Illumination* and *Light* of Holy and Divine Self Revelation. This broad realm-wave reveals a further Consciousness expansion and inclusion, a further differentiation and ultimate integration, of the multi-varied *Diversity* and concurrent *Oneness* of Bliss-Divine Self Reality, an unfolding of its Radiant and Wondrous *range* of transcendent Self Recognition and Realization. And for Beings and Entities developmentally at the culmination of its final sub-realm-wave of *absolute* Subtle Holistent Prim-istence Awakening (see Figures 3, 4 and 6), there is initially unveiled a *direct, spontaneous* and *immediate* Experience and Awareness of the Union, Identity and Reality of *Nondual* Self or Spirit. Here, in Radiant *Vision* and *Illumination,* Nondual Self-as-Self, for the first time, begins to Recognize and Realize its *Absolute, True* and *Ultimate* Nature, Condition and Identity, not only as an *Expression* of Spirit, but *as* Spirit *Itself.*

UNIVERSIVE SUBTLE PRIM-ISTENCE AWAKENING AND REALIZATION

Onliness theory asserts that there are three developmental-evolutionary holon-polar sub-realm-waves of Truth-consciousness Self-realization that comprise the *broad* intermediate realm-wave of Subtle Prim-istence Revelation: (1) *universive* Subtle Prim-istence, (2) *supreme* Subtle Prim-istence, and (3) *absolute* Subtle Holistent Prim-istence (see Figure 2, 3, 4, 6 and 7). For *all* Consciousness Beings and Entities, this initial *universive* Subtle Prim-istence Self Awakening begins to emerge and unfold within and through each Being's and Entity's distinct, innate and native developmental-evolutionary *diverse beings* Reality Pathway of Self Realization (i.e., through one of the eight *universive* Subtle Prim-istence Pan-gnostic or Trans-gnostic: Existence, Transexistence, Istence or Antistence *diverse beings* Reality Pathways of Awakening) (see Figures 4, 6 and 7).

Onliness theory postulates that early on, and progressively throughout, *universive* Subtle Prim-istence Self Revelation, each Being and Entity *begins* to become Aware of, Experience and Comprehend each and every other Being's and Entity's adjacent and oppositely polarized Pan-gnostic or Trans-gnostic *diverse beings* Reality Pathway of Consciousness Awakening, but only *through* and *within* each of their own innate respective Antistence, Istence, Transexistence and Existence realm-waves (see Figures 4, 6 and 7). In this way, and for the first time, with the initial emergent Awareness and Experience of this sub-realm-wave of *universive* Subtle Prim-istence, the eight separate and *parallel* coursing developmental-evolutionary *diverse beings* Reality Pathways of Psychic Multi-istence Self Awakening merge toward and become the eight progressively *convergent diverse beings* Reality Pathways of Subtle Prim-istence Self Awakening (see Figure 4 to view this change and difference). However, it is proposed that at this initial stage of *universe* Subtle Prim-istence Self Illumination, One's *specific* Awareness and Experience of *other* Beings' and Entities' adjacent polar-opposing Pan-gnostic or Trans-gnostic predominantly predisposing *diverse beings* Reality Pathways, although impressive and real, tends to be rather limited, fragmentary and obscure.

In Onliness theory, there are sixty-four "Faces" or dimensional Perspectives of transcendent Consciousness Awakening within *universive* Subtle Prim-istence Self Recognition and Realization. These transcendent "Faces" are symbolized by the sixty-four hexagrams of the Tao of Onliness I Ching, which are described in *Fires of Consciousness* and in the Part II Commentaries of this book (see Figures 3 and 5). It is proposed that these sixty-four Tao of Onliness I Ching Perspectives comprise the *full* spectrum of the Vision and Reality of Self's or Spirit's transcendent Consciousness Awakening for *all* Beings and Entities (human, human-like and non-human) within *universive* Subtle Prim-istence holon-polar realm-wave Self Realization.

In Onliness theory, there are proposed to be eight prototypic and universal holon-polar realm-wave *Modes* or *Ways* of Enlightenment Self Awakening, eight broad Dimensional Modes of Enlightenment Expression and Realization. And it is these eight Modes of Self Enlightenment in relationship to the eight *diverse beings* Reality Pathways of Self Enlightenment that underlie, and ultimately give rise to, these sixty-four Tao of Onliness I Ching hexagram-symbolized "Faces" of Self Reality. These eight all-encompassing Enlightenment Modes are: *Am, Actlessness, Radiance, Emptiness, Awakening, Mystery, Mind,* and *Onliness.* It is within the developmental-evolutionary final sub-realm-wave of *absolute* Subtle Holistent Prim-istence Self-recognition that these eight holonic-polaric yin and yang paired Modes of Awareness and Experience Self Realization are most profoundly and completely Revealed, Comprehending and Resolved. And it is thus in this realm-wave that these eight Ways or Dimensions of Self Enlightenment (and their sixteen holon-polar yin and yang holon-poles) are symbolized by the sixteen polaric yin and yang quadragrams of this sub-realm-wave ring in Figures 3 and 5.

However, in One's developmental-evolutionary transcendent Ascent as Spirit or Self in Awakening to Wisdom and Truth, it is within the *initial* emergence and unveiling of *universive* Subtle Prim-istence Self Recognition that these eight Modes of Realization are *originally* "seeded," and begin to manifest and find Expression and Meaning through the sixty-four Tao of Onliness I Ching "Faces" or dimensional Perspectives of Self Reality, which are symbolized by the sixty-four hexagrams of this realm-wave ring (see Figures 3 and 5).

These eight Modes of Enlightenment Revelation, these eight Transformative Ways of Self Enlightenment, shine forth and

Illuminate all of Reality Itself. It is as if *Seeing* the pure white transparent light of Nondual Self or Spirit Reality through a glass prism that spreads out its spectrum of hues, but does not separate and divide this Light Itself. But, of course, in relative mind conception, One could rightfully and truthfully described *any number* of such Realization Mode Dimensions and Expressions of Spirit or Self Enlightenment, not just eight.

In comparing Figures 3 and 5, note that *each* of these eight holon-polar Modes of transcendent Truth-consciousness Self Awakening (i.e., Am, Actlessness, Radiance, Emptiness, Awakening, Mystery, Mind, and Onliness of Figure 5), which find full Expression, Synthesis and Resolution in *absolute* Subtle Holistent Prim-istence Realization (see Figure 3), has a *yin* quadragram *holon-pole* symbol and a *yang* quadragram *holon-pole* symbol (sixteen such holon-pole quadragrams in all; eight yin and eight yang). Also note that in all sixteen Mode of Enlightenment holon-poles, each yin quadragram is *directly* opposite its corresponding yang quadragram (see Figure 5). In this way, *each* of the eight *yin* holon-pole Realization Modes of Self Awakening is in holon-polar opposition to its corresponding *yang* Realization Mode. It is in this yin-yang patterned way that these eight Modes of Am, Actlessness, Radiance, Emptiness, Awakening, Mystery, Mind and Onliness of Figure 5 are contrastively configured within *absolute* Subtle Holistent Prim-istence Self Realization (see Figures 3, 5, and 7).

The above background description of Onliness theory yin-yang quadragram symbolization is presented by way of explaining how *each* of the eight separate and parallel-coursing *diverse beings* Reality Pathways of Psychic Multi-istence Self Awakening, as well as the subsequent eight merging and convergent *diverse beings* Reality

Pathways of initial *universive* Subtle Prim-istence Self Awakening, develop and find Expression within *each* of the eight Realization Mode of Enlightenment realm-waves of *absolute* Subtle Holistent Prim-istence. Thus note in Figures 3 and 5 that, from the point of view of the immanent Descent of Self or Spirit in Love, Care and Compassion, *each* of the eight yin holon-pole and eight yang holon-pole quadragrams of the ring of *absolute* Subtle Holistent Prim-istence Self Illumination gives rise (going outward from this ring) to the *two* yin-yang *pentagram* symbolized holon-poles of *supreme* Subtle Prim-istence Awakening. In this way, these two pentagram holon-poles arise from (and in yin-yang line patterns are *derived* from) each of their eight yin and eight yang quadragram-symbolized *absolute* Mode of Enlightenment holon-poles (e.g., yin Am, yang Am, yin Actlessness, yang Actlessness etc.).

In turn, again in point of view of the immanent Descent of Self or Spirit in Love, Care and Compassion, from *each* of the yin-yang line *pentagram* holon-poles (thirty-two in all) there arise (going outward from the *supreme* Subtle Prim-istence ring in Figures 3 and 5) *two* yin-yang line *hexagrams* of *universive* Subtle Prim-istence Consciousness. Thus, as evident in Figures 3 and 5, *each* yin and *each* yang of the eight Modes of Enlightenment holon-pole quadragram symbols of *absolute* Subtle Holistent Prim-istence (sixteen in all) ultimately gives rise (in Self's or Spirit's immanent Descent) to *four* hexagrams (sixty-four in all) within *universive* Subtle Prim-istence Awakening. Which is to say, there arise *eight* hexagram-symbol representations and expressions from each of the *eight* Enlightenment Realization Mode holon-polarities, in which each has four *yin* holon-pole derived hexagrams and four *yang* holon-pole derived hexagrams.

Note in Figure 5 that the top (outer) trigrams of the eight hexagrams that derive from *each* Realization Mode of Enlightenment yin-yang symbolized holon-polarity (i.e, Am Actlessness, Radiance, Emptiness, Awakening, Mystery, Mind and Onliness) incorporates all of the eight trigrams in Figure 6 that symbolize all eight separate and parallel-coursing *diverse beings* Reality Pathways of Psychic Multi-istence Self Awakening, which developmentally become the eight merging and convergent *diverse beings* Reality Pathways of *universive* Subtle Prim-istence Self Revelation (see Figure 4 here also).

Symbolized in this way, Onliness theory postulates that *each* of the eight *diverse beings* Reality Pathways of Multi-istence and *universive* Subtle Prim-istence Awakening (i.e., Trans-gnostic and Pan-gnostic: Existence, Transexistence, Istence and Anti-istence) find Representation and Expression in *each* of the eight yin-yang polarized *Modes* of Enlightenment Self Awakening. In this way then, within Self's or Spirit's transcendent *Ascent* and immanent *Descent, each* Consciousness Being and Entity within this Subtle Prim-istence developmental realm-wave (that is, *all* human, human-like and non-human Beings and Entities of all eight *diverse beings* Reality Pathways who are developmentally at this Subtle Prim-istence realm-wave) *to varying degrees,* but *universally,* Awakens to, Employs, Responds to, and Express *each* and *all* of the eight developmental-evolutionary realm-wave Modes of Enlightenment Awakening.

However, via temperament, configuration and experience, each Consciousness Being and Entity tends to be *predominantly predisposed* to one or the other of these eight Modes of Self Enlightenment holon-polarities, which Mode then *primarily* mediates, facilitates and supports that Being's or Entity's Transformative developmental-evolutionary Self-realization. But, overall, each Being or Entity also has a *unique* and *holarchically nested* pattern of second, third, fourth, fifth, sixth and seventh spiritually mediating, facilitating and supporting progressively less influential Realization Modes of Enlightenment, among these other seven holon-polar realm-wave Modes of Self Awakening. And, as suggested, for any given Being or Entity, the entire developmental-evolutionary influential mediating, facilitating and supporting pattern within these eight Modes of Enlightenment Self Revelation is an interactive function of that Being's or Entity's innate and experientially-environmentally acquired configurative, structural and functional nature.

As previously suggested, for this particular so called (relatively perceived) individual Being, the holon-polar (i.e., holon-pole and holon-polarity) transcendent Enlightenment Mode of *Onliness* seems to be My predominantly predisposed mediating, facilitating and supporting developmental-evolutionary Self-awakening and Self-realization Mode of *primary* influence. Of countless numbers, this particular fleetingly and impermanent body-mind, of which fundamentally I Am not, is One specific, direct and complete *manifest* Expression of Self, of Spirit Itself.

In the waking dream-based mentality of Onliness theory, human and human-like Beings whose Self-revelation mediating, facilitating and supporting *primary* predispositional influence has been the *elemental* Psychic Pan-gnostic Existence Self Illumination holon-polar of *Transparency* Realization (and thus, very likely its related *cardinal* holon-polar of *Communion*, and its related *fundamental* holon-polar of *Experience*), *or* the *elemental* Psychic Pan-gnostic

Existence Awakening holon-polar of *Inherency* Self Realization (and thus, very likely its related *cardinal* holon-polar of *Meaning*, and its related *fundamental* holon-polar of *Awareness*), will *strongly* tend to initially, within early-stage *universive* Subtle Prim-istence Self-recognition, continue Transformative Ascent-Descent of Self *primarily* through the *absolute* Subtle Holistent Prim-istence Realization Mode of *either* holon-polar Am, or Actlessness Self Awakening (see this derivation pattern symbolized in Figures 3 and especially 5). And, according to Onliness theory, a broadly similar Transformative Ascent-Descent of Spirit or Self tends to occur in this same *general* holaric-polaric developmental-evolutionary pre-dispositional *pattern* and *sequence* of primary mediating, facilitating and supporting Self-realization influence for human-like and non-human Beings who develop-evolve within each and all of the other remaining holon-polar convergent *diverse beings* Reality Pathways of Subtle Prim-istence Self Awakening and Realization (see Figures 4 and 6 for these other Pathways).

As previously suggested, the *specifically defined* meanings that may be applicable for human-like or non-human Consciousness Being and Entities at various realm-waves of transcendental developmental Self Awakening within the other seven *diverse beings* Reality Pathways of elemental or cardinal or fundamental Psychic Multi-istence Self Realization are likely to be *quite* different from those used by human Beings of Psychic Multi-istence's Psychic Pan-gnostic Existence realm-wave Self Awakening (see Figures 3, 4, 5, and 6). However, in Onliness theory, it is this generalized derivation pattern, dynamic and relational sequence of primary Self-realization mediating, facilitating and supporting influence and effect that applies to *all* Consciousness Beings and Entities, of *all* eight Pan-gnostic and

Trans-gnostic: Existence, Transexistence, Istence, and Antistience *diverse beings* Reality Pathways of Self Awakening.

In Onliness theory, the eight holon-polar (holon-poles and holon-polarities) Modes of transcendent Awakening and Self-realization (i.e., Am, Actlessness, Radiance, Emptiness, Awakening, Mystery, Mind and Onliness) are *initially* and *partially* Differentiated and Realized *only* with the developmental emergence of *universive* Subtle Prim-istence Self Revelation. Subsequently, One's Awareness and Experience of these eight Ways or Modes of transcendent Recognition continues to progressively Unfold and find Expression *throughout* all three sub-realm-waves of Subtle Prim-istence Self Illumination. Indeed, the Enlightenment Dimensions and Expressions of these eight Modes of Self-awakening are the *central* characteristics and identifying features (i.e, the Luminous "flowering" - see Figure 7) of One's Subtle Prim-istence Consciousness Self Awakening and Realization. And, in Onliness theory, these eight Enlightenment Self-revelation Modes comprise, display and express the *full spectrum* of transcendent Ways of Self Remembrance, Recognition and Realization.

From an advanced vision-logic point of view, the transcendent Meaning of *each* of these eight holon-polar Self Realization Modes of Ascending-Descending Enlightenment is somewhat self-evident from the connotative meaning of the word used to identify and characterize it: Am, Actlessness, Radiance, Emptiness, Awakening, Mystery, Mind, and Onliness. Also, the implicate or deep-structure Meaning of *each* of these eight hexagram-symbolized Illumination dimensions of Self Revelation, which arise, derive from and characterize each of the eight quadragram-symbolized Realization Modes of *absolute* Subtle Holistent Prim-istence Self Recognition (see Figure 5), are, to some extent, defined and discussed from Onliness perspective in *Tao of Onliness*, *Fires of Consciousness*, and in Part II of this book. However, from advanced vision-logic pre-transcendental consciousness perspective, *no* specific or precise relative, conditional and conditioned compound personal-egoic self and mind-based *language* definition can clearly, accurately or completely convey the *transcendent* Meanings of these eight Realization Modes. In Truth, in Reality, such Meanings are transpersonal, trans-egoic, trans-mental and trans-logical in nature, and thus fundamentally unfathomable in this mind-based context.

Throughout the developmental-evolutionary course of transcendent Self-awakening and Self-realization that unfolds within *universive* Subtle Prim-istence Illumination, there occurs, in Onliness theory, a progressive Awareness and Experiential *convergence* toward *balance* of the transcendent Ascent versus immanent Descent of Spirit or Self (see Figures 4, 6, and 7). That is, a convergence toward *equalization* and *integration* of Self's transcendent Ascent of Wisdom and Truth, and its immanent Descent of Unconditional and All-pervasive Love, Care and Compassion within each of the four realm-waves of Existence, Transexistence, Istence and Antistence Self Realization. In this way, there emerges a convergence toward balance, equalization and integration of One's *Trans-gnostic* tendency of emphasizing Spirit's or Self's transcendent Ascent over Its immanent Descent, *versus* One's *Pan-gnostic* tendency of emphasizing Spirit's or Self's immanent Descent over Its transcendent Ascent. Without such an integrated and balance Ascent-Descent of Self-realization Truth-consciousness there tends to occur a developmental-evolutionary distortion of, a blocking and interference with, Nondual Self-as-Self Awakening, Remembrance and Realization (Wilber, 1995, 1997, 1999-2000 vol.4).

At the most advanced developmental-evolutionary realm-wave level of One's *universive* Subtle Prim-istence Self Realization, there thus emerges, and is stabilized, such a simultaneously balanced *equalization* and *integration* of Spirit's or Self's transcendent Ascending and immanent Descending Consciousness Self Recognition and Expression. In Onliness theory, this stable and balanced integration of Self's Ascent-Descent, this *final equalization-integration* of Trans-gnostic emphasized transcendent Ascent Self-realization *versus* Pan-gnostic emphasized immanent Descent Self-realization at the culmination of *universive* Subtle Prim-istence Awakening, is the critical shift in Self-revelation that precipitates the Transformative transition from *universive* to *supreme* Subtle Prim-istence Self Remembrance and Realization (see Figures 4, 6, and 7).

SUPREME SUBTLE PRIM-ISTENCE AWAKENING AND REALIZATION

For *all* Consciousness Beings and Entities, this intermediate holon-polar *supreme* Subtle Prim-istence Illumination sub-realm-wave (of the broader realm-wave of Subtle Prim-istence transcendent Self Awakening) first arises within each Being's and Entity's innate and native, but newly reconfigured, convergent *diverse beings* Reality Pathway of Self Realization. Newly reconfigured, because of the now *equal* and *integrated balance* of transcendent Ascent and immanent Descent of Self-awakening at this realm-wave level. No longer is there an unequal, imbalanced and unintegrated Ascent versus Descent of

Self Revelation and Expression emphasis (designated respectively as Trans-gnostic versus Pan-gnostic) arising and occurring in Truth-consciousness. What does arise and occur at the initial onset of *supreme* Subtle Prim-istence Self Awareness and Experience is One's re-configured innate and native convergent *diverse beings* Reality Pathway realm-wave of either Existence Being, Transexistence Being, Istence Nonbeing or Antistence Nonbeing Self Recognition and Realization (see Figures 4, 6 and 7).

In Onliness theory, as *supreme* Subtle Prim-istence Self Awakening begins to developmentally-evolutionarily unfolds within these two paired sets of converging holon-pole realm-waves (i.e., Existence Being and Transexistence Being versus Istence Nonbeing and Antistence Nonbeing), there is Unveiled and Recognized two *supreme* holon-polarity realm-waves of transcendent Consciousness Self Revelation. These are One's Foundational holon-polar (holon-pole and holon-polarity) realm-waves of Existence Being-Transexistence Being, which are ultimately rooted in *Being* Consciousness, and the holon-polar realm-wave of Istence Nonbeing-Antistence-Nonbeing, which are ultimately rooted in *Nonbeing* Consciousness (see Figures 4, 6 and 7).

In Onliness theory, expressed from a polaric-based advanced vision-logic point of view, Being is predominantly the Consciousness realm-wave of transcendent *Form*, while Nonbeing is predominantly the Consciousness realm-wave of transcendent *Emptiness*; yet each implicitly reflects, and thus exists only in relation to the opposing and contrasting aspects of the other. Being Self Awakening and Realization is the open, abundant and unassailable *Fullness* of Spirit's or Self's Abyss of ever-changing and evolving *Form*. Nonbeing Self

Awakening and Realization is the open, abundant and unassailable *Freedom* of Spirit's or Self's Abyss of ever-changeless and formless *Emptiness*. From perspective of advanced vision-logic, there is Being's *Is-ness* transcendent Revelation, Being's *Awakened Consciousness Apparency*, in contrast to Nonbeing's *Anti-Is-ness* or *Is-Not-ness* transcendent Revelation, Nonbeing's *Awakened Trans-consciousness Transparency*.

In Nonbeing Self Realization, the prefix "Trans-" in Trans-consciousness is intended to mean *beyond*, or the polar opposite which is *outside of*, Being Self Realization Consciousness, but not in any sense above or below it. This is the reason I initially called Onliness perspective an *Isantis* (Is-Anti-is) *Tao* cosmology (Treon, 1989). *Existence* is Being's *universal* transcendent Self of Form Reality, while *Transexistence* is Being's Form of *universal* transcendent Self of Void or Emptiness Reality. Likewise, *Antistence* is Nonbeing's *universal* transcendent Self of Void or Emptiness Reality, while *Istence* is Nonbeing's Void or Emptiness of *universal* transcendent Self of Form Reality.

In *The Tao of Onliness* (Treon, 1989) the Learned One puts it well: "Being's process is versive polarity-within-unity. Nonbeing's process is inversive unity-within-polarity. The *perfect movement* of Being's *flexive* consciousness. The *perfect stillness* of Nonbeing's *anti-flexive* consciousness. . . Birthless realms of Being and Nonbeing. . . Realities of Being's boundless *Bliss*, and realms of Nonbeing's boundless *Freedom*. These realms of Being's *holomorphosis*, and of Nonbeing's *hologenesis*. Being's *manifestive* realities, the profound *mystery* of Nonbeing. The unspeakable *grandeur* of Being, the transcendent *suchness* of

Nonbeing. Being's sublime and numinous *Beauty*, the transfinite *Wonder* of Nonbeing. The infinite ocean of Being's *Form*, the anti-ocean *Void* of Nonbeing. Realities of Being's *consciousness*, realms of Nonbeing's *anti-consciousness*. Each by the Other founded and sustained, Each within the Other seeded and contained."

In Onliness theory, there are thirty-two holon-pole "Faces" or perspectives of Self or Spirit at *supreme* Subtle Prim-istence Awakening (see Figures 3 and 5). These are symbolized by the thirty-two yin-yang line pentagrams of *supreme* Subtle Prim-istence Self Recognition that, in turn, derive from the Am, Actlessness, Radiance, Emptiness, Awakening, Mystery, Mind and Onliness Enlightenment Realization Modes of *absolute* Subtle Holistent Prim-istence Self Reality (see Figures 3 and 5). Within *each* of these eight Modes of Self Realization, as each is Expressed within *supreme* Subtle Prim-istence Illumination, there is contained all four of the convergent *diverse beings* Reality Pathway holon-poles of Existence Being, Transexistence Being, Istence Nonbeing and Antistence Nonbeing Self Revelation.

These four *diverse beings* Reality Pathways of Self Recognition are symbolized by the four uniquely different *pentagrams* that derive from (are above or outward from) each of the eight Enlightenment Realization Mode yin and yang symbolized holon-pole *quadragrams* of *absolute* Subtle Holistent Prim-istence Consciousness Self Remembrance (see Figures 3 and 5). In this way, *each* of these four *Supreme* holon-poles of Self Realization (i.e., Existence Being, Transexistence Being, Istence Nonbeing and Antistence Nonbeing) finds singular Expression in *each* of these eight holon-pole Modes of Enlightenment (i.e., Am, Actlessness, Radiance, Emptiness,

Awakening, Mystery, Mind and Onliness). In Onliness theory, these eight *absolute* Modes of Enlightenment, which each contain the four *diverse beings* Reality Pathways, comprise the *full* spectrum of Spirit or Self Awakening, Remembrance and Realization for *all* Consciousness Being and Entities, as Expressed within *supreme* Subtle Prim-istence Self Revelation.

Note the following judgment error on my part in *Fires of Consciousness* (Treon, 1996) (starting on pages 34 to 36 and in Figures 2 and 2A) which involves the mis-directed and mistaken identification of Pan-gnostic and Trans-gnostic as modifiers of both Being and Nonbeing Self Awakening and Realization. The *correct* identity of the modifying adjectives for Being and Nonbeing within *supreme* Subtle Prim-istence Awakening (as indicated in Figures 4, 6 and 7 of this text) are as follows: in *Fires of Consciousness*, incorrect "Pan-gnostic Being" should correctly be "Existence Being," and incorrect "Trans-gnostic Being" should correctly be "Transexistence Being." Also, incorrect "Pan-gnostic Nonbeing" should correctly be "Istence Nonbeing," and incorrect "Trans-gnostic Nonbeing" should correctly be "Antistence Nonbeing." These adjective identity changes also need to be made wherever this error may occur in *Fires of Consciousness*.

In Figures 3 and 5, two distinctly different pentagram-symbolized holon-polar opposition arrangements of the thirty-two convergent *diverse beings* Reality Pathway holon-poles result in a total of: (1) sixteen *primary* holon-polarities of *directly opposite* pentagram symbolization; thus eight *primary* convergent *diverse beings* Reality Pathway holon-polarities of *Existence Being-Antistence Nonbeing* Self Recognition (one *within* each of the eight Enlightenment Mode holon-polarities of Am, Actlessness, Radiance etc.), and, similarly, eight *primary* convergent *diverse beings Reality Pathway* holon-polarities of *Transexistence Being-Istence Nonbeing* Self Awakening (again, one *within* each of the eight Enlightenment Mode holon-polarities of Am, Actlessness, Radiance etc.). Note that these sixteen *primary* holon-polarities are *between* Being and Nonbeing Self Revelation and Realization.

Also, there are sixteen *secondary* convergent *diverse beings* Reality Pathway holon-polarities, symbolized by adjacent pairs of pentagrams in Figures 3 and 5, with each pair occurring within *each* of the sixteen - eight yin and eight yang - Enlightenment Mode holon-poles. That is, there are eight *secondary* convergent *diverse beings* Reality Pathway holon-polarities of *Existence Being-Transexistence Being* Self Awakening, and, similarly, eight *secondary* convergent *diverse beings* Reality Pathway holon-polarities of *Antistence Nonbeing-Istence Nonbeing* Self Revelation. Note that each of these sixteen secondary holon-polarities are respectively *within* either Being or Nonbeing transcendent Self Recognition. In this way, each of the four *supreme* Subtle Prim-istence convergent *diverse beings* Reality Pathway holon-polarities (i.e., Existence Being-Antistence Nonbeing, Transexistence Being-Istence Nonbeing, Existence Being-Transexistence Being, and Antistence Nonbeing-Istence Nonbeing) find developmental-evolutionary Consciousness Expression in *each* of the eight Enlightenment Realization Modes of Am, Actlessness, Radiance, Emptiness, Awakening, Mystery, Mind and Onliness, for all Beings and Entities within *supreme* Subtle Prim-istence Self Illumination.

In Onliness theory, this is simply illustrated by comparing the yin-yang line *digram* symbols for *each* of the four convergent *diverse beings* Reality Pathway holon-poles in Figure 6 to the top (outermost) two yin-yang lines (this *digram* section) of the four *pentagrams* in Figure 5 which, in this way, symbolize these same four holon-poles within each of the eight Modes of Self Enlightenment, represented in the 32 pentagram symbols of the is ream-wave. Comparing Figures 3, 5 and 6 in this way, it is clear that *each* of the four convergent *diverse beings* Reality Pathway holon-polarities (i.e., the two *primary* and two *secondary* holon-polarities and their four respective holon-poles) are equally represented and expressed within *each* of the eight Enlightenment Mode holon-polarities, of *supreme* Subtle Prim-istence Self Remembrance and Realization.

As previously noted, in Onliness theory there occurs a developmental-evolutionary progressive merging of (i.e., a progressive Self Awareness, Experience, Comprehension of, and Identification with) the Self Realizations of Beings and Entities who, up to this developmental point, had opposingly different and quite foreign *diverse being* Reality Pathways of Self Awakening. This progressive expanding-embracing and merging-integrating Self Awareness and Experience occurs in each of the four convergent *diverse beings* Reality Pathway holon-pole and holon-polarity realm-waves of Existence Being-Antistence Nonbeing, Transexistence Being-Istence Nonbeing, Existence Being-Transexistence Being, and Istence Nonbeing-Antistence Nonbeing Self Recognition (see Figures 4, 6 and 7). Recall that *each* of these four holon-polar realm-waves occur within *each* of the eight Enlightenment Mode realm-waves of *supreme* Subtle Prim-istence Self Realization.

At the culmination of *supreme* Subtle Prim-istence Illumination there occurs a *complete* and *final* resolution, inclusion and integration Self-awakenings and Self-realizations (i.e., convergence and union) of the holon poles and holon polarities of: (1) holon-polar Existence Being and Transexistence Being Revelation into their *common* Source and Root, which is the more *expansive* and *inclusive* Truth-consciousness Self Recognition of holon-polar *Being* Reality, and (2) holon-polar Antistence Nonbeing and Istence Nonbeing Awakening into their *common* Source and Root, which is the more *expansive* and *inclusive* Truth-consciousness Self Recognition of holon-polar *Nonbeing* Reality (as symbolized in Figures 4, 6 and 7).

In Onliness theory, it is *through* a Being's and Entity's developmental-evolutionary Self Awakening to all four of these holon poles and their two holon-polarities that the broader and more Consciousness encompassing holon-polar realm-wave of *absolute* Subtle Holistent Prim-istence Self-revelation and Self-remembrance is precipitated, emerges, and begins to unfold. Through this realm-wave Transition, there is now Revealed an even more *expansive* and *inclusive* transcendent Ascent of Wisdom and Truth, together with an immanent Descent of Unconditional and All-pervasive Love, Care and Compassion, than had previously been Self-recognized and Self-awakened. And with this more profound Ascent-Descent, there emerges a further abandonment and lessening of conditioned, conditional and relative compound personal-egoic self's mind-based fear and desire. And thus One's question of Truth-consciousness enquiry "Who Am I?" becomes closer to Self Recognition of the Self Reality of "I Am."

ABSOLUTE SUBTLE HOLISTENT PRIM-ISTENCE AWAKENING AND REALIZATION

Onliness mind-based theory proposes that for *all* Consciousness Beings and Entities, this advanced *absolute* Subtle Holistent

Prim-istence sub-realm-wave (ring) of transcendent Consciousness Self Recognition emerges, and begins to be unveiled, primarily through and within each Being's and Entity's predominantly predisposed, distinct and innate holon-pole *diverse beings* Reality Pathway of *either* Being or Nonbeing Self Illumination. These two holon-poles Manifest and find Expression within each of the eight Enlightenment Realization Modes (see Figures 4, 6 and 7). For the first time then, *all* Beings and Entities in *all* worlds and universes, at this realm-wave level of development-evolution, predominantly share either one or the other of these two Being or Nonbeing *diverse beings* Reality Pathways of Self Awakening.

In Onliness theory, there are sixteen quadragram-symbolized Enlightenment Mode paired holon-poles (eight yin and eight yang), with one pair (e.g., yin Am versus yang Am) occurring in each of Am, Actlessness, Radiance, Emptiness, Awakening, Mystery, Mind and Onliness Modes of Self Recognition and Expression. The eight *yin* symbolized are primarily of transcendent Being Self Revelation and the eight *yang* symbolized are primarily of transcendent Nonbeing Self Revelation. In this way, both Being (yin) and Nonbeing (yang) Self Awakening holon-poles, and thus their Being-Nonbeing holon-polarity, find Representation and Expression in *each* of the eight Modes of Enlightenment Self Realization of *absolute* Subtle Holistent Prim-istence Illumination. To graphically visualize this, compare the yin Being and yang Nonbeing unigram (single yin or yang line) symbolization of Figure 6 *to* the top (outermost) single unigram line of the eight yin-Being and eight yang-Nonbeing quadragrams of Figures 5 (also see Figure 7 in this regard). In this manner of *absolute* Subtle Holistent Prim-istence ring symbolization, these sixteen directly opposite holon-pole quadragrams of Figure 5 create the eight Being-Nonbeing Self Realization Mode holon-polarities of transcendent Self Enlightenment.

This transcendent Being-Nonbeing Self Awakening holon-polar (holon-poles and holon-polarity) realm-wave (see Figures 4, 6 and 7) is now common to, and shared by, all eight Enlightenment Modes of *absolute* Subtle Holistent Prim-istence Illumination. That is, the singular *diverse beings* Reality Pathway of holon-polar Being-Nonbeing Self Awakening now underlies, and is inherent to, each of the eight Enlightenment Modes of Am, Actlessness, Radiance, Emptiness, Awakening, Mystery, Mind and Onliness. It is, then, within One's *absolute* Subtle Holistent Prim-istence realm-wave Self Realization that the now singular and still nested Being-Nonbeing holon-polar convergent *diverse beings* Reality Pathways of Self Awakening *finally* merge with, and become a integral dimension of, the eight holon-polar Enlightenment Realization *Modes* of Self Awakening.

In this way, the eight Enlightenment Mode holon-polarities are: Am Being (yin)-Am Nonbeing (yang), Actlessness Being-Actlessness Nonbeing, Radiance Being-Radiance Nonbeing, Emptiness Being-Emptiness Nonbeing, Awakening Being-Awakening Nonbeing, Mystery Being-Mystery Nonbeing, Mind Being-Mind Nonbeing, and Onliness Being-Onliness Nonbeing (see Figures 5, 6 and 7). In Onliness theory, these eight Enlightenment Modes are the developmental-evolutionary transcendent *Vehicles* that comprise the *full dimensional spectrum* Expression of Self's or Spirit's Recognition, Remembrance and Realization for *each* and *all* Being and Entities within this realm-wave level of Awakening.

According to Onliness theory, over each and every Consciousness Being's and Entity's developmental-evolutionary course within *absolute* Subtle Holistent Prim-istence Self Revelation, there occurs the progressive convergence of *two* different, but holonic-polaric interrelated, Consciousness Transformations. In the first such Self-revelation and Transformation there occurs a convergence, and ultimate merging and integration, of Being and Nonbeing transcendent Self Realization. This occurs because each Being and Entity progressively becomes Aware of, Identifies with, and Comprehends its non-innate and non-native previously opposing holon-pole *diverse beings* Reality Pathway of either Being or Nonbeing Consciousness Self Reality and Realization (see Figure 4).

That is, for Beings and Entities at *absolute* Subtle Holistent Prim-istence's developmental-evolutionary culmination, there unfolds in Truth-consciousness a final merging, resolution and integration of Being and Nonbeing as *one unitary* transcendent Reality Pathway of Self Recognition and Realization (Figures 4, 6 and 7). Thus, the predominantly predispositional *diverse beings* Reality Pathways of either holon-polar Being or Nonbeing Self Illumination is transcended, but included within such transcendence (negated yet preserved), in and as a broader and more Consciousness inclusive Transformational Ascent-Descent of Self-awakening and Self-realization. And again, with this Ascent-Descent, there emerges a further abandonment and lessening of conditioned, conditional and relative compound personal-egoic self's mind-based fear and desire.

Recall that in Onliness theory each and every Being and Entity, even at the initiation of *absolute* Subtle Holistent Prim-istence Awakening, has a *unique* predominantly predisposing mediating, facilitating and supporting *hierarchic pattern* of Self-revelation development-evolution among the eight holon-polar (holon-pole and holon-polarity) Enlightenment Self Realization Modes. That is to say, there occurs an unequally balanced predominantly predisposing Self-awakening expression-configuration pattern of *priority* among these eight Enlightenment Modes. This *second* progressive merging (which occurs concurrently with the above described convergent merging of Being and Nonbeing) that marks One's developmental-evolutionary course within *absolute* Subtle Holistent Prim-istence Self Realization is, over its *initial* course, the convergence to complete elimination of this *unequally balanced* Enlightenment Mode priority patterned hierarchy or holarchy and, over its *final* course, the *complete* convergence, merging, integration and Union (i.e., the complete transcendence but inclusion Self Resolution) of these eight *separately occurring* equally balanced holon-polar Enlightenment Realization Modes.

Thus, for all Consciousness Beings and Entities developmentally within *absolute* Subtle Holistent Prim-istence Self Awakening there Emerges, and for the *first* time there is Disclosed at the end of this sub-realm-wave's initial developmental-evolutionary course, an *equal* and *balanced* pattern of predisposition among and between the eight holon-polar Enlightenment Self Realization Modes of Am, Actlessness, Radiance, Emptiness, Awakening, Mystery, Mind and Onliness Enlightenment. And, over this sub-realm-wave's final course, at its culmination, there occurs a progressive convergence and final merging, integration and Union of these eight Self Realization Mode realm-waves of Enlightenment. It is, then, within this *final* developmental-evolutionary completion of *absolute* Subtle Holistent Prim-istence Illumination that these eight equally balanced *absolute* Realization Modes of Self Enlightenment are Resolved and

Integrated as one Holistent, undivided, singular and unitary *Way* of Consciousness Self-recognition and Self-realization, shared by each and every Being and Entity at this realm-wave level.

The transcendence-but-inclusion through integration and ultimate Union of Holistent Being-Nonbeing Self-realization, in *conjunction* with the balancing, equalization, and ultimate convergence, integration and Union of the eight holon-polar Enlightenment Modes of Am, Actlessness, Radiance, Emptiness, Awakening, Mystery, Mind and Onliness, is the *essential* and *complete* meaning of Holistence Consciousness Self Awakening. And it is *through* One's Self-realized transcendence but inclusion Resolution and Integration of these issues that the more Truth-consciousness encompassing and inclusive transcendent Ascent of Wisdom and Truth, and it corresponding immanent Descent of Love, Care and Compassion, realm-wave of Causal Holistence Self Awakening is precipitated, emerges and unveiled.

In Onliness theory, with this final developmental-evolutionary completion of *absolute* Subtle Holistent Prim-istence Self-revelation, there occurs an *unprecedented* Unity and Identity of transcendent Self Awakening, which is shared by *each* and *every* Being and Entity at this realm-wave level. That is, for the first time, *all* such Beings and Entities, in *all* worlds, dimensions and universes, are sharing *one* and the *same* transcendent Holistent Self Recognition, Remembrance and Realization.

In this way, One comes to Awareness and Experience of the all-inclusive deeps-structure Unity, Commonality and Identity which underlies the varied surface structures of the eight holon-polar Self

Realization Ways or Modes of Enlightenment. Now, within Causal Holistence Self Awakening, One becomes Aware of and Experiences this shared and common Luminous Self Realization of uncreated, causeless, timeless, spaceless, boundless, formless and unmanifest *primordial* Self Awakening and Self Reality.

It is thus, that the polarity-within-unity of *all* previously described realm-waves of Consciousness Reality Self Awakening are transcended, but included within such transcendence, are negated and preserved. No longer does manifest *holonic-polaric* Awareness and Experience arise or occur in transcendent Consciousness. No longer does holon-polar (i.e., holon pole and holon-polarity) Self Recognition and Realization manifest and find expression in Consciousness. But, rather, now *holonic-only* Self-awakening Consciousness alone arises, develops and remains.

Onliness theory proposes that, ultimately, it is this integrated-unified *singular* and *all-inclusive* Enlightenment-Modes-and-Pathways of Wisdom, Truth, Love, Care and Compassion Ascent-Descent Self Revelation, now shared by each and every Being and Entity at the culmination of *absolute* Subtle Holistent Prim-istence Illumination, which precipitates the developmental-evolutionary *Transition* into Causal Holistence Self Recognition, Remembrance and Realization. With this, Self's Awakened *World-Soul* Reality is transcended but included (negated and preserved), and the emergence of Self's *Universal Spirit* is now Awakened and Realized.

Causal Holistence Revelation and Realization

In Onliness theory, the realm-wave of Causal Holistence is comprised of two *sub-realm-waves*: the *junior* holon-only (not holon-polar however) of *primordial* Causal Arch-istent Holistence Self Awakening, and the *senior* holon-only of *primordial* Causal Omni-istent Holistence Self Awakening (Figures 2, 3, 4, 6 and 7). The Recognition and Realization of One's transcendent *primordial* Self Identity *as* boundless, formless and unmanifest Spirit *fully* emerges within the developmental-evolutionary realm-wave (ring) of Causal Holistence Consciousness; this uncreated and unconditioned None that is All *primordial* Self, this Pure Silence and Emptiness. However, it is only at the developmental-evolutionary *culmination* of Causal Holistence Self Realization that each and all Consciousness Being and Entities Awaken to their *full* and *complete* Identity *as* Nondual Self-as-Self, *and Self only*, of birthless and deathless Godhead Revelation and Reality.

One's emergent Transformations within Causal Holistence are Self Recognitions and Realizations of *primordial* Spirit, of *primordial* Self, but not of Nondual Self-as-Self *only*. Such Causal Holistence Self Recognitions and Realizations transcend but include the Realizations of Self's *World*-Soul Reality, which occur within Psychic Multi-istence and Subtle Prim-istence Self Awakening. Unlike Psychic Multi-istence's and Subtle Prim-istence's manifest Form Realizations, One's transcendent Consciousness Awakening of Causal Holistence *primordial* Self are *Formless, Boundless* and *Unmanifest.* That is, according to Onliness theory, One's Self Illumination throughout this Causal Holistence holon-only realm-wave occur as the formless, boundless and unmanifest *Seer,* or pure *Witness,* within and through which *all* of the forms and boundaries of manifest Reality arise and pass (Wilber, 1995,1999-2000, 2007).

One's formless, boundless and unmanifest Ground of Causal Holistence Self Realization is the Alpha and Omega through which *all* manifestations of Form arise and pass, and thus find minds-based recognition, interpretation and expression. However, One's Causal Holistence Self Recognition, Revelation and Realization is *not* merely an abstraction, idea or metaphor, but rather is a direct developmental-evolutionary *Reality* of Awareness and Experience, an *immediate*, *profound* and *spontaneous* transcendental Awakening *to* and *as primordial* Self or Spirit.

Again, in Onliness theory, it is through the Transformative developmental-evolutionary realm-wave (ring) of Causal Holistence Self Awakening (see Figures 3, 4, 5, 6, and 7) that there occurs in One the transcendence but inclusion (negation and preservation) of each and all realm-waves of Subtle Prim-istence's and Psychic Multi-istence's Awakened Self Realizations. And with the emergence of Causal Holistence Self Recognition, Remembrance and Realization there unfolds, and is unveiled, an even more Consciousness inclusive and expansive transcendent *Ascent* of Self in Wisdom and Truth, and, likewise, an immanent *Descent* of Self in Unconditional and All-inclusive Love, Care and Compassion.

PRIMORDIAL CAUSAL ARCH-ISTENT HOLISTENCE RECOGNITION

Onliness theory asserts that there are two holon-only (not holon-polar) sequential sub-realm-waves within the realm-wave of *primordial* Causal Arch-istent Holistence Self Awakening: the initial *junior* holon-only of *primordial* Causal Arch-istence Self Recognition, and the culminating *senior* holon-only of *primordial* Causal Anti-arch-istence Self Recognition (Figures 3, 4, 6 and 7). Because, according to Onliness theory, polarity-within-unity is an innate and inherent structure of

Consciousness Self Reality for all Beings and Entities (i.e., for all of manifest Reality) up to the realm-wave level of Causal Holistence Self Awakening, the preliminary transitional Consciousness of all Being and Entities within this initial (junior) sub-realm-wave of *primordial* Causal Arch-istence Illumination includes the *unmanifest* "shadow," so to speak, of holon-polarity-within-unity (including duality) Consciousness (i.e., the *unmanifest* but *implied* "remnants" of holon-polarity-within-unity and duality Consciousness).

For Beings and Entities at this level of *primordial* Causal Arch-istence Self Revelation, these "remnants" include, among others, the *unmanifest* but *implicit* holon-polarities of: *unmanifest-manifest, bounded-boundless, subject-object* and *form-formless*. However, Onliness theory claims that the explicit and fully expressed *manifestation* of holon-polarity-within-unity or duality *does not* occur at all within the unmanifest, boundless and formless realm-wave of Causal Holistence Self Awakening.

With the emergence and unfolding Self Revelations of this *primordial* Causal Arch-istence holon-only sub-realm-wave (see Figures 3, 4, 6 and 7), there occurs the *initial* and *preliminary* developmental-evolutionary *Recognition* of Nondual Bliss-Devine Self; that is, the Onliness Intimation of this ultimately unassailable, unfathomable, indefinable and inexpressible Nondual Self Reality. However, for Beings and Entities at this level of *primordial* Causal Arch-istence Self Awakening there emerges, and is unveiled, only a *partial* and *incomplete* transcendent Recognition of this ultimate *Nondual* Spirit-as-Spirit Self Reality.

It is only with the developmental-evolutionary emergence and unfolding of *primordial* Causal Anti-arch-istence Self Awakening (see

Figures 3, 4, 6 and 7) that there occurs a *full* and *complete* transcendent *Recognition* of One's unconditional, unconditioned and uncontracted *Nondual* Self (Spirit) of Bliss-Divine Wisdom, Truth, Love, Care and Compassion; which Self is All and None, and Neither (i.e., *Nondual* in the sense of being *neither* holon-only or holon-polarity-within-unity *nor* not holon-only or holon-polarity-within-unity Self Realization). And with One's *initial* full and complete Nondual Spirit-as-Spirit *Recognition*, there is, for the first time, an accompanying full and complete *trans-polaric Realization* of the delusion of *all* remaining "remnants" or "shadows" of unmanifest holon-polarity-with-unity and duality. It is with One's *full* Nondual Self *Recognition* Awakening, within this senior holon-only of *primordial* Causal Anti-arch-istence Self Revelation, that there occurs the transcendence but inclusion of One's *incomplete* and *partial* Nondual Self *Recognition* Awakening, which occurred within the junior holon-only of *primordial* Causal Arch-istence Truth-consciousness Self Recognition (Figures 3, 4, 6 and 7).

In Onliness theory, One's developmental-evolutionary resolution and completion of *primordial* Causal Anti-arch-istence Self Awakening marks the full transcendent *Recognition*, but *neither* the partial and incomplete *nor* the full and complete *Realization*, of Nondual Spirit-as-Spirit's Ascent-Descent of Wisdom, Truth, Love, Care and Compassion. And finally, with the completion of *primordial* Causal Anti-arch-istence Self Revelation, there occurs a no-separateness and no-otherness full and complete *trans-polaric* transcendence but inclusion *Recognition* of the illusion of subject-versus-object polarity-duality, which is of relative waking dream-based consciousness reality. And with this, a *full* and *complete* Self Recognition of the illusion of individual separate-self-sense conditional and conditioned compound personal-egoic relative self and consciousness, and the mind-based fear and desire integral to it.

In Onliness theory, this Universal Spirit *Recognition* of unconditioned, unconditional and uncontracted Nondual Bliss-Devine Self Reality is called *primordial* Causal Arch-istent Holistence's *Self Recognition Enlightenment.* Such Self Recognition Enlightenment Awakening marks One's culmination and Resolution of this junior holon-only realm-wave of *primordial* Causal Arch-istent Holistence Consciousness Illumination, and thus precipitates the developmental-evolutionary emergence of the senior holon-only realm-wave of *primordial* Causal Omni-istent Holistence Awakening and Self-realization (see Figures 3, 4, 6 and 7).

PRIMORDIAL CAUSAL OMNI-ISTENT HOLISTENCE REALIZATION

Onliness theory asserts that there are two sequential sub-realm-waves of developmental-evolutionary Self Awakening that arise and unfold within *primordial* Causal Omni-istent Holistence Self Realization: the initial *junior* holon-only of *primordial* Causal Omni-istence Realization, and the *senior* culminating, and final, holon-only, of *primordial* Causal Trans-Omni-istence Realization (see Figures 3, 4, 6 and 7). For Beings and Entities at the developmental-evolutionary culmination of *primordial* Causal Omni-istent Holistence Self Awakening there is unveiled and revealed the *full* and *complete* transcendent Recognition *and* Realization (and thus Recognition-only transcendence but inclusion) of unconditioned, unconditional and uncontracted *Nondual* Self of Bliss, Love, Wisdom, Truth, Care and Compassion. In Onliness, this is the *final* sub-realm-wave holon-only of the *final* realm-wave holon-only (i.e., Causal Holistence) of all of transcendent realm-wave Self Realization Consciousness.

The emergence and arising of *primordial* Causal Omni-istence Self-realization (see Figures 4, 6 and 7) marks One's initial, preliminary and *partial* developmental-evolutionary unfolding *Realization* of Nondual Bliss-Devine Self Reality; that is, its *partially* Realized Onliness and Ultimacy as no-self Self, as transcendent Spirit. Thus, for all Beings and Entities at the level of *primordial* Causal Omni-istence Self Remembrance there is Revealed a profound but *limited* and *incomplete* Realization of Nondual Spirit-as-Spirit Self Reality. However, what distinguishes this trans-mental, trans-polaric and trans-egoic realm-wave of *primordial* Causal Omni-istence Self Revelation is that, for the first time, there emerges and unfolds One's *Realization* (not just Recognition) *of,* Identity and Union *with,* this transcendent Selfas-Self of Nondual Awakened Reality, albeit partial and incomplete.

It is only at the developmental-evolutionary *culmination* and Resolution of One's *primordial* Causal Trans-Omni-istence Self Awakening sub-realm-wave that there is Revealed the full and complete *Realization* of One's *True* Nature and Condition *as,* and Identity *with,* the radiant and perfect Emptiness of unqualifable and unassailable Nondual Spirit-as-Spirit Supreme Self Reality That is, this Ultimate and Absolute Self-as-Self of transcendent Ascent in Wisdom and Truth, and corresponding immanent Descent in Unconditional and All encompassing Love, Care and Compassion (Figures 3, 4, 6 and 7). Again, with this Ascent-Descent, there emerges a final abandonment of conditioned, conditional and relative compound personal-egoic self's mind-based fear and desire. And, with this final sub-realm-wave's completion there is Revealed, for the first time,

One's *trans-holonic* (including but transcending both holon-polar and holon-only) Self Awakening and Realization.

The *full* and *complete* Identity with, and Self Realization of, this unborn and undying no-self Self of Nondual Reality and Bliss, which You and I always and already are, marks the completion, which is transcendence but inclusion within such transcendence, of: the *primordial* Causal Trans-Omni-istence Self Awakening sub-realm-wave; the transcendence but inclusion of *primordial* Causal Omni-istent Holistence Self Awakening realm-wave; and the transcendence but inclusion of the *broad* holon-only realm-wave of Causal Holistence Consciousness Self Realization itself. And with this, there occurs an accompanying *complete* and *final* release and abandonment of all relatively perceived fear and desire, and of all relatively perceived pain and pleasure. And a final and total transcendence but inclusion of the mind-based relative perception of otherness and separateness (see Figures 2, 3, 4, 5, 6 and 7).

And finally, with the completion of *primordial* Causal Trans-Omni-istence Self Revelation, there occurs a no-separateness and no-otherness full and complete *trans-polaric* transcendence but inclusion *Realization* of the illusion of subject-versus-object polarity-duality, which is of relative waking dream-based consciousness reality. And with this, a *full* and *complete* Self Realization of the illusion of individual separate-self-sense conditional and conditioned compound personal-egoic relative self and consciousness, and the mind-based fear and desire integral to it.

One now Realizes that Self is always already All and None, and Neither; that there is no otherness or separateness whatsoever - no polarity-duality at all, so that subject and object are one and the same, are of One Self Reality and Identity. That is, that subject and object separation is an illusion. This, then, is the Enlightenment of Causal Holistence Consciousness Self Awakening, which, in turn, precipitates the developmental-evolutionary emergence and unfolding of the final, unfathomable and unchangeable Enlightenment Awakening of Absolute Nondual Self-as-Self Realization and Reality.

NONDUAL SELF-AS-SELF AWAKENING AND REALIZATION
In Truth, Only Self, which You now and ever are, is Real. Beyond name, conception and imagination, You are *Pure Being* only, this Pure Silence and Emptiness. In Truth, You are Nondual Self-as-Self Reality alone, which is *Supreme Self Reality*. This Nondual Self of Truth-consciousness is prior to and far beyond One's body-mind centered, and thus extremely limited, reflected, distorted and restricted, conditional and conditioned pre-personal-pre-egoic, personal-egoic, and conditioned social-cultural waking dream-based relative self of pre-transcendental mind-based consciousness reality. Such Self Awakening and Realization requires that this body-mind centered and focused relative self reality be transcended, turned away from and utterly abandoned, but also incorporated and included *within* the context of such transcendent Nondual Self Realization.

However, it is not that such waking dream-based body-mind centered compound personal-egoic illusory self and consciousness is not significant and important, quite the contrary. Currently, almost all earth-centered human Beings (and possibly many humans, human-like and possibly even non-human Beings in other worlds) function as, and primarily identify with, such illusory body-mind compound personal-egoic waking dream-based self and consciousness realities.

And it is this same narcissistic compound personal-egoic self reality functioning and identification that predominantly underlies and gives rise to so much of earth-centered human suffering, misery, pain and sorrow. And thus, there is a fundamental and central importance to One's Self-realization of the immanent Descent of Love, Care and Compassion for all so called (i.e., relatively perceived) *other* Beings and Entities of Consciousness.

In Onliness theory, *Nondual Awakened Self-realization* is *neither* a holon-only realm-wave (as in Causal Holistence Self Awakening) *nor* a holon-polar (i.e., holon-pole and holon-polarity) realm-wave (as are Subtle Prim-istence and Psychic Multi-istence Self Awakening), but rather the *all inclusive* Ground, Goal and Source *from* which *each* and *all* Consciousness Self Realization realm-waves arise, and *to* which they *all* return (Wilber, 1995, 1996). Thus, Nondual Spirit-as-Spirit (Self-as-Self) Recognition, Remembrance and Realization transcends, but includes within such transcendence, all holon-only and holon-polarity-within-unity realm-waves of developmental Consciousness Self Illumination. Nondual Self-realization is *transpolaric*, and thus separate inner interior-internal subject versus outer exterior-external object polarity or duality illusion no longer arises or occurs in Nondual Self Realization Consciousness. Now, Witness-and-that-which-is-witnessed are no longer two, nor not-two.

As this Supreme and Ultimate Self Reality, One no longer fundamentally Identifies with One's body, mind, personality, emotions, sensations or social roles; One no longer identifies with, or is attached to, any mind-based perceptions or conceptions of self whatsoever. One is now completely free of, is detached from and indifferent to, any and all perceptual and conceptual mental relative-self projections or introjections. Universes arise and pass and Self is completely untouched and unaffected. As *Absolute Self* of Nondual Realization's transcendent Ascent of Wisdom and Truth, and corresponding immanent Descent of Unconditional and All-pervasive Love, Care and Compassion, there no longer at all arises or occurs self-contracted, conditioned and conditional relative compound personal-egoic self's mind of fear and desire, or of loss and gain, or of separate subject and object.

"Trans-manifest and Trans-istential, Consciousness with no second Trans-ists - Only Self of Enlightenment. Unfathomable, unknowable, boundless Self of Consciousness 'remains' " (Treon, 1996). With great Earnestness and unrivaled Persistence, Self of Nondual Realization expresses and embraces the *highest* transcendent Ascent of Wisdom and Truth, and concurrently the *deepest* immanent Descent of Unconditional and All-encompassing Love, Care and Compassion for each and every Consciousness Being and Entity. In each of the previous seven diagrams, this Self of Nondual Spirit-as-Spirit Awakened Enlightenment is symbolized by *all* that is written and blank; that is, the paper substance, ink and all perceived surfaces and ink-mark words and images (see Figures 1 through 7).

As previously suggested, with each successive holon-polar or holon-only developmental-evolutionary realm-wave Realization, Spirit's (Self's) transcendent *Ascent* of Wisdom, Insight and Truth becomes *progressively* more Consciousness inclusive, embracing and complete; and, correspondingly, Self's immanent *Descent* of Love, Care and Compassion also becomes *progressively* more Consciousness inclusive, embracing and complete. Such progressive embrace, inclusion and completeness of Self's *immanent* Descent of Love, Care and

Compassion is Expressed through profound concern for (i.e., sustained and concerted effort toward) the *cessation* of, and *release* from, the suffering of *all* Beings and Entities in all worlds and universes.

Note that the culmination of Causal Holistence Self Awakening is marked by the transition *from* a Being's or Entity's predominantly *transient* (temporary state) peak-experience of Nondual Self Realization *to* an ongoing, stable and predominantly continuous Nondual Self Realization, a *permanent trait*, which, in turn, marks the final transition into Nondual Self-as-Self Remembrance and Realization (see Figures 4 and 6). One's trans-polaric, trans-holonic, trans-realm-wave, trans-egoic, trans-mental, trans-ist, transcendent trans-perspectival Nondual Self-revelation and Self-realization is, as suggested, the creative *Ground, Goal* and ultimate *Source* from which *all* of One's holon-polar and holon-only developmental-evolutionary realm-waves of Awakening arise, and to which they *all* return.

Nondual Spirit-as-Spirit Illumination *is* this no-self Self of Godhead, Brahman, Buddha-mind, including and embracing *both* the Many and the One, Form and Emptiness, Nirvana and Samsara. This Self-as-Self Awakened Realization *is* God-consciousness, Christ-consciousness, Buddha-nature, Brahman-Atman. As Sri Ramana Maharshi (2011) said in reply to this question: "Can you enable me to see God? I'm willing to pay any price, even to lose my life." Maharshi: "No. God is not an object to be seen. Do not concern yourself with object that can be seen. God is the Subject, the Seer. Find out who the Seer is. You alone are God."

Supreme Nondual Self-as-Self Truth-consciousness Remembrance is not achievable or possessable, but rather is ordinary and everyday;

is always already One's unassailable, uncreated, causeless, timeless and unchangeable *True* Nature, Condition and Identity. This is well expressed through the tenth level of Consciousness in the "Ten Oxherding Pictures" of Zen Buddhism: "Bare-chested and bare-footed, he (she) comes out into the market-place; Daubed with mud and ashes, how broadly he (she) smiles! There is no need for the miraculous power of the gods, for he (she) touches, and lo! the dead trees are in full bloom" (Suzuki, 1960).

You and I, but not merely as our body-mind centered compound pre-egoic, personal-egoic, and conditioned social-cultural relative self reality, already are, have ever been and ever will be, this *Self* of Enlightened Buddha-nature, Christ-consciousness, God-consciousness, and Atman-Brahman. But in Our self-contracted, conditional and conditioned compound personal-egoic relative self delusion and ignorance, We do not Recognize, Remember and Realize this birthless and deathless Nondual Self of Spirit-as-Spirit Realization and Reality that We inherently and timelessly are.

You and I are this *Supreme Self Identity*, here and now, always and already. We are this Absolute Self Condition, Nature and Identity of *Is* and *Is-not*, of *All* and *None* and *Neither* - Uncreated, Causeless, Unborn and Undying. We are this Bliss-Divine *Nondual Self Reality* of Wisdom, Truth, Love, Care and Compassion. In Transcendence but inclusion of Causal Holistence Self Awakening's formless, boundless and unmanifest Witnessing *primordial* Self of Universal Spirit, this is Nondual Self-as-Self of Only and Absolute Awakening and Realization, without an opposite or other. This Radiant Abyss Nondual Self of Everything and Nothing, and Neither. This luminous *Emptiness Self* of complete and absolute Freedom and Liberation.

You and I always and already are this unspeakable *Suchness* of Spirit-as-Spirit, which is spaceless-timeless All-embracing and Unconditional *Pure Emptiness* Self-as-Self Reality of uncontracted and unconditioned Awakened Bliss. We are Self's Revelation and Realization that Form *is* Emptiness, Emptiness *is* Form. We *are* this Self of Enlightenment, Nirvana, Sahaja Samadhi, Thusness, One Taste; nothing special and apart - *Just This*, ordinary and everyday.

"The world is illusory, Brahman alone is real, Brahman is the world," says Shankara. Nondual Self Recognition and Realization is at once the highest (deepest) developmental-evolutionary Consciousness Awakening, and the only, all, each and every True Reality (see Figures 4 and 6). Trans-mental *direct* Realization of Nondual Bliss-Divine Self-as-Self Reality is, as others have said, neither two nor not-two, neither one nor not-one. This fundamentally unqualifable, unfathomable and unassailable *Absolute Self* is Luminous and Radiant Reality Itself, is *Supreme Self* Onliness Identity. *The Upanishads* (Swami Prabhavananda and Manchester, 1957) put it well: "A knower of Brahman becomes Brahman."

I Am uncreated and timeless Self, the very Consciousness of God. And so are You. Again, in Onliness theory, Nondual Self-as-Self Realized Awakening is this Self of unknowable and eternal *Emptiness*. It is this unconditioned and uncreated Suchness or Is-ness *Mind* of Liberated Self-as-Self Reality. Self is Our own inherent Buddha-nature. We are Self's *Awakening* as Atman-Brahman, Christ-consciousness, God-consciousness. You and I *are* Self, but not as our relative compound personal-egoic self of body-mind alone. We *are* this *Onliness* of Self, and Self *only*; this unborn and undying transcendent *Am* of always already Buddha-mind Enlightenment.

Choicelessly, in *Actlessness*, We neither come nor go, and yet are always already pure Spirit, pure Godhead, in each and every moment. Far beyond words, ideas, images and conceptions, You and I *are* this ever-present *Radiance* of Self, this Permanent and Unchanging Presence of Pure *Emptiness*, embracing Each and All - each-where, all-where, every-where, nowhere, now-here. You and I *are* this unassailable and unknowable transcendent Nondual Realization Self of *Mystery*, Openly, Fearlesssly, Desirelessly and Freely arising and emerging, Ascending and Descending, as the *entire* radiant Kosmos, and beyond. Effortless, uncreated, causeless, infinite, boundless, and timeless, You and I are Bliss-Divine Self Reality.

But remember and understand that such Self-as-Self Awakening, Remembrance and Realization almost always involves great and sustained persistence, earnestness, determination, endurance and clarity. This developmental-evolutionary Truth-consciousness Path of Self Revelation and Illumination will seldom be personally easy, painless or effortless, nor without frustration, despair, confusion, and at times a sense of loneliness, loss and hopelessness. One's Transformational Nondual Self-as-Self Recognition and Expression is necessarily compound personally-egoically very difficult, disruptive and disorienting. Indeed, it will ultimately require turning away from and abandoning relative self reality altogether (i.e., transcending, but including it within the context of such transcendence). But all of these are temporary and transitory body-mind waking dream-based experiential states of conditioned, conditional and relative compound personal-egoic self and consciousness, which arise and pass.

My Teacher, Sri Nasargadatta Maharaj (2012) has indicated that, from the perspective of relative and conditional self reality and understanding, the only way One may come to Comprehend, to See into and to Realize the Pure Being of One's True Nature, Condition and Identity as Supreme Nondual Self Reality, is through the process of *negation*. That is, through the complete unveiling, and then turning away from and thus abandoning, all of One's *false* and *illusory* "I Am this and I Am that" roles, designations and identities. This *transcendent Self* of All and None, and Neither, which One always, already is and will ever be, must come to Recognize, Remember and Realize that I Am not a person, I Am not the body, I Am not the mind, I Am not my memories, I Am not my expectations, I Am not my feelings and emotions, I Am not my sensations, I Am not my gender or sexuality, I Am not my personality, I Am not my values, ideas and opinions, I Am not my actions and behaviors, I Am not my social-cultural roles, awards and recognitions, I Am not my weaknesses and limitations, I Am not my strengths and talents etc.

I Am not this and I Am not that; until *all* of One's remaining mind-based relative, conditioned and conditional compound personal-egoic self designations, roles and labels are *totally* revealed, negated and abandoned. What then remains, what then is Comprehended, Seen, and Realized with great Clarity, is One's fearless and desireless *True* Nondual Self-as-Self Nature, Condition and Identity. That is to say, One's Supreme and Unassailable Self only and completely, of transcendent Ascent of Wisdom and Truth, and corresponding immanent Descent of Unconditional and All-embracing Love, Care and Compassion.

PART TWO

"M [Sri Nisargadatta Maharaj]: As long as you are interested in your present way of living, you will not abandon it. Discovery cannot come as long as you cling to the familiar. It is only when you realize fully the immense sorrow of your life and revolt against it, that the way out can be found.

M: . . . I give eternally, because I have nothing. To be nothing, to have nothing, to keep nothing for oneself is the greatest gift, the highest generosity.

Q: Is there no self-concern left?

M: Of course I am self-concerned, but the self is all. In practice it takes the shape of goodwill, unfailing and universal. You may call it love, all-pervading, all-redeeming. Such love is supremely active - without the sense of doing.

Q: Is love a state of mind?

M: Again, it depends what you mean by love. Desire is, of course, a state of mind. But the realization of unity is beyond mind. To me, nothing exists by itself. All is the Self, all is myself. To see myself in everybody and everybody in myself most certainly is love.

M: The undisturbed state of being is bliss; the disturbed state is what appears as the world. In non-duality there is bliss; in duality - experience. What comes and goes is experience with its duality of pain and pleasure. Bliss is not to be known. One is always bliss, but never blissful. Bliss is not an attribute.

Q: Obviously, I am not all-pervading and eternal. I am only here and now.

M: Good enough. The 'here' is everywhere and the now - always. Go beyond 'I-am-the-body' idea and you will find that space and time are in you and not you in space and time. Once you have understood this, the main obstacle to realization is removed.

Q: Without desire and fear what motive is there for action?

M: None, unless you consider love of life, of righteousness, of beauty, motive enough. Do not be afraid of freedom from desire and fear. It enables you to live a life so different from all you know, so much more intense and interesting, that, truly, by losing all you gain all. . . .when desire and fear end, bondage also ends. It is the emotional involvement, the pattern of likes and dislikes which we call character and temperament, that create the bondage."

-Sri Nisargadatta Maharaj
From *I Am That* (2012)

PART 2

THE TAO OF ONLINESS I CHING COMMENTARIES

PREFACE

THIS SECTION IS a revision of "The Tao of Onliness I Ching Commentaries" that comprised Part II of my previously published first edition book *Uncreated Timeless Self of Radiant Emptiness: Onliness Consciousness and Commentaries* (2009). In retrospect, I felt that too much of the content of these previously written commentaries lacked sufficient clarity, integration and continuity, and thus needed to be revised.

Like the original, these revised Tao of Onliness I Ching Commentaries are intended as a reference section only. That is, this revised Part II section is intended as a *reference source* and *aid* for Tao of Onliness I Ching hexagram consultation and interpretation. The process of such consultation involves: first determining a hexagram and interpreting this hexagram in relation to a traditional *I Ching* text, and then, in conjunction and supplemental combination with this initial interpretation, re-interpreting this hexagram in relation to its content within the Tao of Onliness I Ching, which I have described in *Fires of Consciousness: The Tao of Onliness I Ching* and in Part II of this text. Such a proposed *combined* traditional *I Ching* and Tao of Onliness I Ching hexagram text consultation-interpretation is intended to be predominantly *transpersonally* focused and oriented.

Specifically, such combined and integrated consultation-interpretation needs to blend the content of each traditional *I Ching* hexagram with its corresponding Tao of Onliness I Ching hexagram content. And in order to derive a complete reading and interpretation of One's hexagram *within* the Tao of Onliness I Ching portion of this overall *combined* I Ching consultation, One needs to first consult the hexagram's Tao of Onliness I Ching *image, text* and *expression* content (found in *Fires of Consciousness* - which is also primarily a reference text), followed by consultation of that hexagram's Tao of Onliness I Ching commentary, described below in this Part II.

Following, then, are brief commentaries on each of the sixty-four hexagrams of the Tao of Onliness I Ching. These hexagram commentaries are primarily an extension and elaboration of Onliness theory's *universive* Subtle Prim-istence Realization realm-wave, as described in Part I of this book. Indeed, these hexagrams derive from, and are used to symbolize, the sixty-four holon-poles of *universive* Subtle Prim-istence developmental-evolutionary transcendent Awakening and Revelation (see Figures 3 and 5).

The content basis for each of these hexagram commentaries substantially derives from the hexagram content presented in *Fires of Consciousness: The Tao of Onliness I Ching* and *The Tao of Onliness: An I Ching Cosmology*. Thus, to fully understand and interpret any one of these sixty-four holon-pole hexagram-symbolized Tao of Onliness

I Ching commentaries, it is necessary to *first* refer to and consult that hexagram's specific description (i.e., image, text and expression) in *Fires of Consciousness*. Also, more generally, it may be useful to review the *transpersonally oriented* background content that forms the basis of the Tao of Onliness I Ching which is presented in *Fires of Consciousness* and *The Tao of Onliness: An I Ching Cosmology*.

To facilitate ease of comparison between hexagram *image, text, and expression* contents within *Fires of Consciousness* versus hexagram commentaries presented below in Part II, the hexagram presentation sequence here is the same as in *Fires of Consciousness*. Also, the page location of each hexagram content in *Fires of Consciousness* is given here at the end of each hexagram commentary.

HEXAGRAM 1: TENDENCY TOWARD NONBEING'S TRANS-GNOSTIC ANTISTENTIAL AM EXPERIENCE

You are not your rigid, unforgiving, grudgeful and revengeful self and consciousness. This is not Your True Nature and Condition. This is not Your *True Identity*. Only Self, which You now and ever are, is Real. In Self-realization, developmentally beyond (with the death of) conditional and conditioned body-mind centered compound personal-egoic self and consciousness, You are, in Truth, the Love, Wisdom and Compassion of uncreated, causeless, boundless, timeless and formless *Supreme Self Reality*, and non-other Than. Unfathomable, You are this birthless and deathless unassailable *Bliss-Divine Self* which is All and Each and None, Only and Completely. Awaken to, and *Be,* the Truth-consciousness of this ultimately unutterable and unqualifable *Absolute Nondual Self Reality* that You always and already are. Transpersonally, within World-Soul Experience's Consciousness Awakening, You are Transparency Communion's *Heart-Soul Bliss of Genesis and Creativity*, this *Transfigurative Origin and Potency of Perfect Emptiness Self-as-Self Reality*, which is Numinous Revelation Self of Am. Personally, at the pre-transcendental developmental level of body-mind compound personal-egoic self and consciousness, this hexagram symbolizes the developmental ascending-descending benefit of the Creative Principle's penetrating power to bring forth harmony, illumination and full completion to all things, each in their proper time. Persistence in a righteous cause, with magnanimity and without pride, bring auspicious and sublime success. Properly timed, the righteous and firm application of this Principle brings forth beauty, peace, kindness, forgiveness and understanding to the whole world. However, there is a danger in excessive egoic agency and willfulness. This is a vision-logic consciousness expression of One's developmental tendency toward, and agency within, the transpersonal Reality of *Nonbeing's Trans-gnostic Antistential Am Experience*, as seen from Onliness theory and perspective. See *Fires of Consciousness,* page 75.

Numinous Revelation Self of Am

HEXAGRAM 43: TENDENCY TOWARD NONBEING'S PAN-GNOSTIC ANTISTENTIAL AM EXPERIENCE

You are not your pridefulness and self-importance self and consciousness. This is not Your True Nature and Condition. This is not Your *True Identity*. Only Self, which You now and ever are, is Real. In Self-realization, developmentally beyond (with the death of) conditional and conditioned body-mind centered compound personal-egoic self and consciousness, You are, in Truth, the Love, Wisdom and Compassion of uncreated, causeless, boundless, timeless and formless *Supreme Self Reality*, and non-other Than. Unfathomable, You are this birthless and deathless unassailable *Bliss-Divine Self* which is All and Each and None, Only and Completely. Awaken to, and *Be,* the Truth-consciousness of this ultimately unutterable and unqualifiable *Absolute Nondual Self Reality* that You always and already are. Transpersonally, within World-Soul Experience's Consciousness Awakening, You are Transparency Communion's *Heart*-Soul of One *All-where Origin and None All-where Potency*, this *Infusive Power and Bliss of Numinous Apparent Transparancy Self-as-Self Truth-consciousness*, which is Infinite Uncontracted Self of Am. Personally, at the pre-transcendental developmental level of body-mind compound personal-egoic self and consciousness, this hexagram symbolizes the developmental ascending-descending benefit of establishing a goal and pursuing it with resolution, and also with peaceful quiet determination. However, there is a present danger of corruption, and also a danger in too candidly expressing the true state of affairs to certain others. Completion of One's goal is important now. Also, there is a danger in egoic overconfidence and pride. This is a vision-logic consciousness expression of One's developmental tendency toward, and agency within, the transpersonal Reality of *Nonbeing's Pan-gnostic*

Antistential Am Experience, as seen from Onliness theory and perspective. See *Fires of Consciousness,* page 77.

-------   -------

Infinite Uncontracted Self of Am

HEXAGRAM 15: TENDENCY TOWARD BEING'S PAN-GNOSTIC EXISTENTIAL AM AWARENESS

You are not your mental ideas, visions, thoughts, and analyses self and consciousness. This is not Your True Nature and Condition. This is not Your *True Identity*. Only Self, which You now and ever are, is Real. In Self-realization, developmentally beyond (with the death of) conditional and conditioned body-mind centered compound personal-egoic self and consciousness, You are, in Truth, the Love, Wisdom and Compassion of uncreated, causeless, boundless, timeless and formless *Supreme Self Reality*, and non-other Than. Unfathomable, You are this birthless and deathless unassailable *Bliss-Divine Self* which is All and Each and None, Only and Completely. Awaken to, and *Be,* the Truth-consciousness of this ultimately unutterable and unqualifable *Absolute Nondual Self Reality* that You always and already are. Transpersonally, within World-Soul Awareness's Consciousness Awakening, You are Inherency Meaning's *Mind-Psyche of Configurative Source* and *Singularity,* this *Fertile and Productive Morphosis of None Each-where Conception of Worlds Self-as-Self Expression,* which is Unqualifiable Self of Am. Personally, at the pre-transcendental developmental level of body-mind compound personal-egoic self and consciousness, this hexagram symbolizes the developmental ascending-descending benefit of progress, accomplishment and success, through humility, modesty and equanimity. One needs to balance that which is depleted or lacking with that which is over-full and excessive. This is a vision-logic consciousness expression of One's developmental tendency toward, and agency within, the transpersonal Reality of *Being's Pan-gnostic Existential Am Awareness,* as seen from Onliness theory and perspective. See *Fires of Consciousness*, page 80.

```
-------    -------
-------    -------
-------    -------
------------------
-------    -------
-------    -------
```

Unqualifiable Self of Am

HEXAGRAM 52: TENDENCY TOWARD BEING'S TRANS-GNOSTIC EXISTENTIAL AM AWARENESS

You are not your transient joys, pleasures and happiness self and consciousness. This is not Your True Nature and Condition. This is not Your *True Identity*. Only Self, which You now and ever are, is Real. In Self-realization, developmentally beyond (with the death of) conditional and conditioned body-mind centered compound personal-egoic self and consciousness, You are, in Truth, the Love, Wisdom and Compassion of uncreated, causeless, boundless, timeless and formless *Supreme Self Reality*, and non-other Than. Unfathomable, You are this birthless and deathless unassailable *Bliss-Divine Self* which is All and Each and None, Only and Completely. Awaken to, and *Be,* the Truth-consciousness of this ultimately unutterable and unqualifiable *Absolute Nondual Self Reality* that You always and already are. Transpersonally, within World-Soul Awareness's Consciousness Awakening, You are Inherency Meaning's *Mind-Psyche of None Each-where Vortex and One Each-where Ubiquity*, this *Realizing Vision of Numinous Transparent Apparency Self-as-Self Awakening*, which is Unsurpassable Transfinite Self of Am. Personally, at the pre-transcendental developmental level of body-mind compound personal-egoic self and consciousness, this hexagram symbolizes the ascending-descending benefit of stopping, desisting, stillness, meditation, and refraining from action (using non-action) when circumstances so indicate. That is, there is delusion and danger in action when non-action is needed. Consider carefully One's movement to action. This is a vision-logic consciousness expression of One's developmental tendency toward, and agency within, the transpersonal Reality of *Being's Trans-gnostic Existential Am Awareness*, as seen from Onliness theory and perspective. See *Fires of Consciousness*, page 82.

```
------------------
-------    -------
-------    -------
------------------
-------    -------
-------    -------
```

Unsurpassable Transfinite Self of Am

HEXAGRAM 14: TENDENCY TOWARD NONBEING'S TRANS-GNOSTIC ISTENTIAL AM EXPERIENCE

You are not your duplicitous and betrayal self and consciousness. This is not Your True Nature and Condition. This is not Your *True Identity*. Only Self, which You now and ever are, is Real. In Self-realization, developmentally beyond (with the death of) conditional and conditioned body-mind centered compound personal-egoic self and consciousness, You are, in Truth, the Love, Wisdom and Compassion of uncreated, causeless, boundless, timeless and formless *Supreme Self Reality*, and non-other Than. Unfathomable, You are this birthless and deathless unassailable *Bliss-Divine Self* which is All and Each and None, Only and Completely. Awaken to, and *Be,* the Truth-consciousness of this ultimately unutterable and unqualifable *Absolute Nondual Self Reality* that You always and already are. Transpersonally, within World-Soul Experience's Consciousness Awakening, You are Transparency Communion's *Meditative and Apprehending Heart-Soul,* this *Transfigurative Power and Dispersion Awakening of Worlds Self-as-Self Revelation,* which is All-embracing Only Self of Am. Personally, at the pre-transcendental developmental level of body-mind compound personal-egoic self and consciousness, this hexagram symbolizes the ascending-descending benefit of firmness, strength, confidence, great talent and achievement, with resultant supreme success through virtuous and properly timed and measured action, but without pride. The avoidance and suppression of that which is evil is needed now. This is a vision-logic consciousness expression of One's developmental tendency toward, and agency within, the transpersonal Reality of *Nonbeing's Trans-gnostic Istential Am Experience,* as seen from Onliness theory and perspective. See *Fires of Consciousness,* page 85.

-------   -------

All-embracing Only Self of Am

HEXAGRAM 34: TENDENCY TOWARD NONBEING'S PAN-GNOSTIC ISTENTIAL AM EXPERIENCE

You are not your anger and hateful self and consciousness. This is not Your True Nature and Condition. This is not Your *True Identity*. Only Self, which You now and ever are, is Real. In Self-realization, developmentally beyond (with the death of) conditional and conditioned body-mind centered compound personal-egoic self and consciousness, You are, in Truth, the Love, Wisdom and Compassion of uncreated, causeless, boundless, timeless and formless *Supreme Self Reality*, and non-other Than. Unfathomable, You are this birthless and deathless unassailable *Bliss-Divine Self* which is All and Each and None, Only and Completely. Awaken to, and *Be,* the Truth-consciousness of this ultimately unutterable and unqualifable *Absolute Nondual Self Reality* that You always and already are. Transpersonally, within World-Soul Experience's Consciousness Awakening, You are Transparency Communion's *Gnostic Heart-Soul of Unconditionality and Of-ness Unreflexivity*, this *Peaceful and Infusive Bliss of Self-as-Self Reality*, which is No-otherness Trans-istential Self of Am. Personally, at the pre-transcendental developmental level of body-mind compound personal-egoic self and consciousness, this hexagram symbolizes the ascending-descending benefit of deep insight into the inner nature of reality through great power and accomplishment, and with firmness and persistence in a righteous course. There is also a possible danger of entanglement through improper action, use, or timing of such insight, power and accomplishment. This is a vision-logic consciousness expression of One's developmental tendency toward, and agency within, the transpersonal Reality of *Nonbeing's Pan-gnostic Istential Am Experience*, as seen from Onlines theory and perspective. See *Fires of Consciousness,* page 87.

No-otherness Trans-istential Self of Am

HEXAGRAM 39: TENDENCY TOWARD BEING'S PAN-GNOSTIC TRANSEXISTENTIAL AM AWARENESS

You are not your sense of superiority and entitlement self and consciousness. This is not Your True Nature and Condition. This is not Your *True Identity*. Only Self, which You now and ever are, is Real. In Self-realization, developmentally beyond (with the death of) conditional and conditioned body-mind centered compound personal-egoic self and consciousness, You are, in Truth, the Love, Wisdom and Compassion of uncreated, causeless, boundless, timeless and formless *Supreme Self Reality*, and non-other Than. Unfathomable, You are this birthless and deathless unassailable *Bliss-Divine Self* which is All and Each and None, Only and Completely. Awaken to, and *Be,* the Truth-consciousness of this ultimately unutterable and unqualifiable *Absolute Nondual Self Reality* that You always and already are. Transpersonally, within World-Soul Awareness's Consciousness Awakening, You are Inherency Meaning's *Mind-Psyche of Comprehending and Insightful Vision*, this *Configuration and Conception of Worlds Self-as-Self Recognition*, which is Non-striving, Non-resisting Self of Am. Personally, at the pre-transcendental developmental level of body-mind compound personal-egoic self and consciousness, this hexagram symbolizes ascending-descending trouble, difficulty, peril and danger; unless, through wisdom, firmness and caution, One is able to perceive and thereby avoid such trouble. There is advantage to the south and west so as to find a middle course. In general, moving forward presents difficulties, and indeed waiting or turning back may be the better choice. It is important to seek advice from a wise and trusted person. And also, looking inward, to radically alter One's self so as to cultivate virtue. Although difficulties lie ahead, persistence in a righteous course brings good fortune. This is a vision-logic consciousness expression of One's developmental tendency toward, and agency within, the transpersonal Reality of *Being's Pan-gnostic Transexistential Am Awareness*, as seen from Onliness theory and perspective. See *Fires of Consciousness*, page 89.

```
-------    -------
------------------
-------    -------
------------------
-------    -------
-------    -------
```

Non-striving, Non-resisting Self of Am

HEXAGRAM 53: TENDENCY TOWARD BEING'S TRANS-GNOSTIC TRANSEXISTENTIAL AM AWARENESS

You are not your self-contracted, anxious and fear-filled self and consciousness. This is not Your True Nature and Condition. This is not Your *True Identity*. Only Self, which You now and ever are, is Real. In Self-realization, developmentally beyond (with the death of) conditional and conditioned body-mind centered compound personal-egoic self and consciousness, You are, in Truth, the Love, Wisdom and Compassion of uncreated, causeless, boundless, timeless and formless *Supreme Self Reality*, and non-other Than. Unfathomable, You are this birthless and deathless unassailable *Bliss-Divine Self* which is All and Each and None, Only and Completely. Awaken to, and *Be*, the Truth-consciousness of this ultimately unutterable and unqualifable *Absolute Nondual Self Reality* that You always and already are. Transpersonally, within World-Soul Awareness's Consciousness Awakening, You are Inherency Meaning's *Boundless Gnostic Seeing Mind-Psyche of None Each-where Genesis of Root*, this *Confluent and Suffusive In-ness Reflexivity Self-as-Self Awakening*, which is Luminous Recognition Self of Am. Personally, at the pre-transcendental developmental level of body-mind compound personal-egoic self and consciousness, this hexagram symbolizes the ascending-descending benefit of gradual but real and beneficial progress, which results in progression through One's current direction along a *righteous* path. Abiding in holiness and virtue, a leader, through the integrated actions of firmness and gentleness, leads others toward goodness. The marriage of a maiden now brings good fortune. This is a vision-logic consciousness expression of One's developmental tendency toward, and agency within, the transpersonal Reality of *Being's Trans-gnostic Transexistential Am Awareness*, as seen from Onliness theory and perspective. See *Fires of Consciousness*, page 91.

-------   -------

-------   -------
-------   -------

Luminous Recognition Self of Am

HEXAGRAM 62: TENDENCY TOWARD NONBEING'S PAN-GNOSTIC ISTENTIAL ACTLESSNESS AWARENESS

You are not your condescending, arrogant, impatient and dismissive self and consciousness. This is not Your True Nature and Condition. This is not Your *True Identity*. Only Self, which You now and ever are, is Real. In Self-realization, developmentally beyond (with the death of) conditional and conditioned body-mind centered compound personal-egoic self and consciousness, You are, in Truth, the Love, Wisdom and Compassion of uncreated, causeless, boundless, timeless and formless *Supreme Self Reality*, and non-other Than. Unfathomable, You are this birthless and deathless unassailable *Bliss-Divine Self* which is All and Each and None, Only and Completely. Awaken to, and *Be,* the Truth-consciousness of this ultimately unutterable and unqualifable *Absolute Nondual Self Reality* that You always and already are. Transpersonally, within World-Soul Awareness's Consciousness Awakening, You are Inherency Meaning's *Cohesive Form of Nondual Realization, Mind-Psyche's Vortex of Eternity and Deep Repose Self-as-Self Recognition*, which is Non-discriminating Self of Actlessness. Personally, at the pre-transcendental developmental level of body-mind compound personal-egoic self and consciousness, this hexagram symbolizes the ascending-descending benefit of success and accomplishment in humble and small matters, through determined persistence in a righteous course. Action and advancement toward great or important matters should not be undertaken now. The immanent Descent of Spirit, which is Unconditional and All-encompassing Love and Compassion, is primarily required at this time. There is the possibility of sorrow from bereavement, and also danger in arrogance, and possible problems with excessive frugality. This is a vision-logic consciousness expression of One's developmental tendency toward, and agency within, the transpersonal Reality of *Nonbeing's Pan-gnostic Istential Actlessness Awareness*, as seen from Onliness theory and perspective. See *Fires of Consciousness*, page 104.

```
-------     -------
-------     -------
------------------
------------------
-------     -------
-------     -------
```

Non-discriminating Self of Actlessness

HEXAGRAM 56: TENDENCY TOWARD NONBEING'S TRANS-GNOSTIC ISTENTIAL ACTLESSNESS AWARENESS

You are not your emotions, moods and feelings self and consciousness. This is not Your True Nature and Condition. This is not Your *True Identity*. Only Self, which You now and ever are, is Real. In Self-realization, developmentally beyond (with the death of) conditional and conditioned body-mind centered compound personal-egoic self and consciousness, You are, in Truth, the Love, Wisdom and Compassion of uncreated, causeless, boundless, timeless and formless *Supreme Self Reality*, and non-other Than. Unfathomable, You are this birthless and deathless unassailable *Bliss-Divine Self* which is All and Each and None, Only and Completely. Awaken to, and *Be*, the Truth-consciousness of this ultimately unutterable and unqualifable *Absolute Nondual Self Reality* that You always and already are. Transpersonally, within World-Soul Awareness's Consciousness Awakening, You are Inherency Meaning's *None Each-where Vision* of *Holo-ceptive Unconditionality*, this *Scient and Prehending Mind-Psyche of Reflection Self-as-Self Revelation*, which is Changeless Self of Actlessness. Personally, at the pre-transcendental developmental level of body-mind compound personal-egoic self and consciousness, this hexagram symbolizes the ascending-descending benefit of success in small matters, through persistence and determination in well timed movement and travel. Here, beauty and stubbornness are conjoined. Firm and correct action is now important. One must use wisdom and caution in administering punishment, and make such decisions without delay. This is a vision-logic consciousness expression of One's developmental tendency toward, and agency within, the transpersonal Reality of *Nonbeing's Trans-gnostic Istential Actlessness Awareness*, as seen from Onliness theory and perspective. See *Fires of Consciousness*, page 106.

Changeless Self of Actlessness

HEXAGRAM 9: TENDENCY TOWARD BEING'S TRANS-GNOSTIC TRANSEXISTENTIAL ACTLESSNESS EXPERIENCE

You are not your sorrow and regretful self and consciousness. This is not Your True Nature and Condition. This is not Your *True Identity*. Only Self, which You now and ever are, is Real. In Self-realization, developmentally beyond (with the death of) conditional and conditioned body-mind centered compound personal-egoic self and consciousness, You are, in Truth, the Love, Wisdom and Compassion of uncreated, causeless, boundless, timeless and formless *Supreme Self Reality*, and non-other Than. Unfathomable, You are this birthless and deathless unassailable *Bliss-Divine Self* which is All and Each and None, Only and Completely. Awaken to, and *Be,* the Truth-consciousness of this ultimately unutterable and un-qualifable *Absolute Nondual Self Reality* that You always and already are. Transpersonally, within World-Soul Experience's Consciousness Awakening, You are Transparency Communion's *Heart-Soul of One All-where Nonduality,* this *Perfect Creative Emptiness of Eternity, this Homeward Voyager of Self-as-Self Awakening,* which is God-realized Self of Actlessness. Personally, at the pre-transcendental developmental level of body-mind compound personal-egoic self and consciousness, this hexagram symbolizes the ascending-descending benefit of progress, nourishment and success to come, as affairs are still in process and not yet at the point of taking action. Mild restraint is important now. Gentleness and strength are here conjoined, which soon will lead to modest good fortune and success. It is advantageous to display One's scholarly accomplishments. This is a vision-logic consciousness expression of One's developmental tendency toward, and agency within, the transpersonal Reality of *Being's Trans-gnostic Transexistential Actlessness Experinece,* as seen from Onliness theory and perspective. See *Fires of Consciousness,* page 108.

-------   -------

God-realized Self of Actlessness

HEXAGRAM 5: TENDENCY TOWARD BEING'S PAN-GNOSTIC TRANSEXISTENTIAL ACTLESSNESS EXPERIENCE

You are not your body self and consciousness. This is not Your True Nature and Condition. This is not Your *True Identity*. Only Self, which You now and ever are, is Real. In Self-realization, developmentally beyond (with the death of) conditional and conditioned body-mind centered compound personal-egoic self and consciousness, You are, in Truth, the Love, Wisdom and Compassion of uncreated, causeless, boundless, timeless and formless *Supreme Self Reality*, and non-other Than. Unfathomable, You are this birthless and deathless unassailable *Bliss-Divine Self* which is All and Each and None, Only and Completely. Awaken to, and *Be,* the Truth-consciousness of this ultimately unutterable and unqualifable *Absolute Nondual Self Reality* that You always and already are. Transpersonally, within World-Soul Experience's Consciousness Awakening, You are Transparency Communion's *Transfigurative Power of Trans-ceptive Boundlessness,* this *Heart-Soul of Lucent and Conceptive Bliss Self-as-Self Reality,* which is No-thingness, No-mind Self of Actlessness. Personally, at the pre-transcendental developmental level of body-mind compound personal-egoic self and consciousness, this hexagram symbolizes the ascending-descending benefit of purposeful and calculated inaction, and in this way gaining the confidence of others so as to avoid the danger and peril of this time. Conditions must be allowed to take their course before further action is undertaken. Righteous persistence, firmness, strength, sincerity and clarity of mind must be maintained to achieve brilliant success, and to avoid danger under present circumstances and conditions. This is a vision-logic consciousness expression of One's developmental tendency toward, and agency within, the transpersonal Reality of *Being's Pan-gnostic Transexistential*

Actlessness Experience, as seen from Onliness theory and perspective. See *Fires of Consciousness,* page 110.

-------   -------

-------   -------

No-thingness, No-mind Self of Actlessness

HEXAGRAM 31: TENDENCY TOWARD NONBEING'S PAN-GNOSTIC ANTISTENTIAL ACTLESSNESS AWARENESS

You are not your surface persona and socially presented self and consciousness. This is not Your True Nature and Condition. This is not Your *True Identity*. Only Self, which You now and ever are, is Real. In Self-realization, developmentally beyond (with the death of) conditional and conditioned body-mind centered compound personal-egoic self and consciousness, You are, in Truth, the Love, Wisdom and Compassion of uncreated, causeless, boundless, timeless and formless *Supreme Self Reality*, and non-other Than. Unfathomable, You are this birthless and deathless unassailable *Bliss-Divine Self* which is All and Each and None, Only and Completely. Awaken to, and *Be,* the Truth-consciousness of this ultimately unutterable and unqualifable *Absolute Nondual Self Reality* that You always and already are. Transpersonally, within World-Soul Awareness's Consciousness Awakening, You are Inherency Meaning's *Mind-Psyche of Convergent and Omniscient Vision*, this *Boundless and Hidden Wellspring of Worlds Self-as-Self Awakening*, which is Trans-egoic Meritless Self of Actlessness. Personally, at the pre-transcendental developmental level of body-mind compound personal-egoic self and consciousness, this hexagram symbolizes the ascending-descending benefit of the union of strength and yielding, as well as the benefits of inner peace, attraction, mutual stimulation, sensation and fertility, accomplished through selflessness, firmness and righteous persistence. One can know the inner nature of things by observing what it is that stimulates them. This is a vision-logic consciousness expression of One's developmental tendency toward, and agency within, the transpersonal Reality of *Nonbeing's Pan-gnostic Antistential Actlessness Awareness*, as seen from Onliness theory and perspective. See *Fires of Consciousness*, page 113.

Trans-egoic Meritless Self of Actlessness

HEXAGRAM 33: TENDENCY TOWARD NONBEING'S TRANS-GNOSTIC ANTISTENTIAL ACTLESSNESS AWARENESS
You are not your egocentric, personalizing and self-referencing self and consciousness. This is not Your True Nature and Condition. This is not Your *True Identity*. Only Self, which You now and ever are, is Real. In Self-realization, developmentally beyond (with the death of) conditional and conditioned body-mind centered compound personal-egoic self and consciousness, You are, in Truth, the Love, Wisdom and Compassion of uncreated, causeless, boundless, timeless and formless *Supreme Self Reality*, and non-other Than. Unfathomable, You are this birthless and deathless unassailable *Bliss-Divine Self* which is All and Each and None, Only and Completely. Awaken to, and *Be,* the Truth-consciousness of this ultimately unutterable and unqualifable *Absolute Nondual Self Reality* that You always and already are. Transpersonally, within World-Soul Awareness's Consciousness Awakening, You are Inherency Meaning's *Trans-scient Mind-Psyche of Reflexivity,* this *Fertile and Cohesive Void-Emptiness Conception of Worlds Self-as-Self Recognition*, which is Inherent, Illuminated Self of Actlessness. Personally, at the pre-transcendental developmental level of body-mind compound personal-egoic self and consciousness, this hexagram symbolizes the ascending-descending benefit of progress and success, through properly timed yielding, restraint, and/ or withdrawal when circumstances so indicate. One needs to maintain distance from those of inferior character so as to avoid negative entanglement and containment. Firmness and persistence in small matters results in some limited advantage. This is a vision-logic consciousness expression of One's developmental tendency toward, and agency within, the transpersonal Reality of *Nonbeing's Trans-gnostic Antistential Actlessness Awareness*, as seen from Onliness theory and perspective. See *Fires of Consciousness*, page 114.

```
------------------
------------------
------------------
------------------
-------      -------
-------      -------
```

Inherent, Illuminated Self of Actlessness

HEXAGRAM 26: TENDENCY TOWARD BEING'S TRANS-GNOSTIC EXISTENTIAL ACTLESSNESS EXPERIENCE

You are not your hostile, hate-oriented and spiteful self and consciousness. This is not Your True Nature and Condition. This is not Your *True Identity*. Only Self, which You now and ever are, is Real. In Self-realization, developmentally beyond (with the death of) conditional and conditioned body-mind centered compound personalegoic self and consciousness, You are, in Truth, the Love, Wisdom and Compassion of uncreated, causeless, boundless, timeless and formless *Supreme Self Reality*, and non-other Than. Unfathomable, You are this birthless and deathless unassailable *Bliss-Divine Self* which is All and Each and None, Only and Completely. Awaken to, and *Be,* the Truth-consciousness of this ultimately unutterable and unqualifable *Absolute Nondual Self Reality* that You always and already are. Transpersonally, within World-Soul Experience's Consciousness Awakening, You are Transparency Communion's *Vergent Heart-Soul of Omnipotence*, this *Potency and Bliss of Perfect Emptiness Self-as-Self Truth-consciousness*, which is Unconditional Self of Actlessness. Personally, at the pre-transcendental developmental level of body-mind compound personal-egoic self and consciousness, this hexagram symbolizes the ascending-descending benefit of nourishment, strength, truth, brilliance and magnanimity, through exercising righteous persistence, firmness and restraint in the use of power. Willingness to be mobile and travel, and to outwardly express One's appreciation to others for what they have done for You, is important now. Action based upon the profound knowledge of wise individuals will nourish One's virtue. This is a vision-logic consciousness expression of One's developmental tendency toward, and agency within, the transpersonal Reality of *Being's Trans-gnostic Existential*

Actlessness Experience, as seen from Onliness theory and perspective. See *Fires of Consciousness*, page 118.

```
------------------
-------    -------
-------    -------
------------------
------------------
------------------
```

Unconditional Self of Actlessness

HEXAGRAM 11: TENDENCY TOWARD BEING'S PAN-GNOSTIC EXISTENTIAL ACTLESSNESS EXPERIENCE

You are not your illusory perception of interior-internal body *versus* outer exterior-external world self and consciousness. This is not Your True Nature and Condition. This is not Your *True Identity*. Only Self, which You now and ever are, is Real. In Self-realization, developmentally beyond (with the death of) conditional and conditioned body-mind centered compound personal-egoic self and consciousness, You are, in Truth, the Love, Wisdom and Compassion of uncreated, causeless, boundless, timeless and formless *Supreme Self Reality*, and non-other Than. Unfathomable, You are this birthless and deathless unassailable *Bliss-Divine Self* which is All and Each and None, Only and Completely. Awaken to, and *Be,* the Truth-consciousness of this ultimately unutterable and unqualifable *Absolute Nondual Self Reality* that You always and already are. Transpersonally, within World-Soul Experience's Consciousness Awakening, You are Transparency Communion's *Heart-Soul of Holo-lucent Void-Emptiness Unreflexivity*, this *Transfigurative Creation and Dispersion of Worlds Self-as-Self Expression*, which is Unutterable Transcendental Self of Actlessness. Personally, at the pre-transcendental developmental level of body-mind compound personal-egoic self and consciousness, this hexagram symbolizes the ascending-descending benefit of peace and harmony, and also of progress and success, in the intimate communion of Heaven (Wisdom and Truth) and Earth (Love, Care and Compassion). In this, there is the inner strength, truth and wisdom of *transcendent* Spirit in communion and harmony with the outer glad acceptance, love and compassion of *immanent* Spirit. The great and good now ascend and bring benefit to everyone. This is a vision-logic consciousness expression of One's developmental tendency toward, and agency within, the transpersonal Reality of *Being's*

Pan-gnostic Existential Actlessness Experience, as seen from Onliness theory and perspective. See *Fires of Consciousness*, page 120.

```
-------     -------
-------     -------
-------     -------
------------------
------------------
------------------
```

Unutterable Transcendental Self of Actlessness

HEXAGRAM 10: TENDENCY TOWARD NONBEING'S TRANS-GNOSTIC ANTISTENTIAL RADIANCE EXPERIENCE

You are not your sensations and sensory-based experiences self and consciousness. This is not Your True Nature and Condition. This is not Your *True Identity*. Only Self, which You now and ever are, is Real. In Self-realization, developmentally beyond (with the death of) conditional and conditioned body-mind centered compound personal-egoic self and consciousness, You are, in Truth, the Love, Wisdom and Compassion of uncreated, causeless, boundless, timeless and formless *Supreme Self Reality*, and non-other Than. Unfathomable, You are this birthless and deathless unassailable *Bliss-Divine Self* which is All and Each and None, Only and Completely. Awaken to, and *Be,* the Truth-consciousness of this ultimately unutterable and unqualifable *Absolute Nondual Self Reality* that You always and already are. Transpersonally, within World-Soul Experience's Consciousness Awakening, You are Serenity Communion's *Seeing Heart-Soul Genesis of Creativity*, this *Source-Unity of One All-where Singularity Self-as-Self Expression*, which is All-inclusive Self of Radiance. Personally, at the pre-transcendental developmental level of body-mind compound personal-egoic self and consciousness, this hexagram symbolizes the ascending-descending benefit of joyous progress and success, but the situation-circumstance is also dangerous, and extreme caution in conduct and action needs to be taken. Consultation both high and low gives confidence and assurance to others. This is a vision-logic consciousness expression of One's developmental tendency toward, and agency within, the transpersonal Reality of *Nonbeing's Trans-gnostic Antistential Radiance Experience*, as seen from Onliness theory and perspective. See *Fires of Consciousness*, page 132.

-------   -------

All-inclusive Self of Radiance

HEXAGRAM 58:TENDENCY TOWARD NONBEING'S PAN-GNOSTIC ANTISTENTIAL RADIANCE EXPERIENCE

You are not your illusion of being the doer and of actions being done self and consciousness. This is not Your True Nature and Condition. This is not Your *True Identity*. Only Self, which You now and ever are, is Real. In Self-realization, developmentally beyond (with the death of) conditional and conditioned body-mind centered compound personal-egoic self and consciousness, You are, in Truth, the Love, Wisdom and Compassion of uncreated, causeless, boundless, timeless and formless *Supreme Self Reality*, and non-other Than. Unfathomable, You are this birthless and deathless unassailable *Bliss-Divine Self* which is All and Each and None, Only and Completely. Awaken to, and *Be,* the Truth-consciousness of this ultimately unutterable and unqualifiable *Absolute Nondual Self Reality* that You always and already are. Transpersonally, within World-Soul Experience's Consciousness Awakening, You are Serenity Communion's *Omnipotent Heart-Soul of Transfiguration,* this *Perfect Emptiness Foundation and Awakening of Worlds Self-as-Self Revelation,* which is Compassionate Omniscient Self of Radiance. Personally, at the pre-transcendental developmental level of body-mind compound personal-egoic self and consciousness, this hexagram symbolizes the ascending-descending benefit of joy, gladness, progress, accomplishment and success, through firm and righteous persistence. Joyous leadership brings encouragement to those who follow. One should engage friends in mutual discussion and practice. This is a vision-logic consciousness expression of One's developmental tendency toward, and agency within, the transpersonal Reality of *Nonbeing's Pan-gnostic Antistential Radiance Experience,* as seen from Onliness theory and perspective. See *Fires of Consciousness,* page 133.

Compassionate Omniscient Self of Radiance

HEXAGRAM 2: TENDENCY TOWARD BEING'S PAN-GNOSTIC EXISTENTIAL RADIANCE AWARENESS

You are not your personality, personal traits and attributes self and consciousness. This is not Your True Nature and Condition. This is not Your *True Identity*. Only Self, which You now and ever are, is Real. In Self-realization, developmentally beyond (with the death of) conditional and conditioned body-mind centered compound personal-egoic self and consciousness, You are, in Truth, the Love, Wisdom and Compassion of uncreated, causeless, boundless, timeless and formless *Supreme Self Reality*, and non-other Than. Unfathomable, You are this birthless and deathless unassailable *Bliss-Divine Self* which is All and Each and None, Only and Completely. Awaken to, and *Be,* the Truth-consciousness of this ultimately unutterable and unqualifiable *Absolute Nondual Self Reality* that You always and already are. Transpersonally, within World-Soul Awareness's Consciousness Awakening, You are Multiplicity Meaning's *Envisioning Morphosis of Productivity*, this *Conceptive Mind-Psyche of Seeing None Each- where Radiance Self-as-Self Reality*, which is Eternal Self of Radiance. Personally, at the pre-transcendental developmental level of body-mind compound personal-egoic self and consciousness, this hexagram symbolizes the ascending-descending benefit of tranquil beauty, gentleness, harmony, accord, multitudinous plentitude, and sublime success, through firm, powerful, penetrating and originating insight, combined with productive action, and within all-embracing luminous acceptance. This is a vision-logic consciousness expression of One's developmental tendency toward, and agency within, the transpersonal Reality of *Being's Pan-gnostic Existential Radiance Awareness*, as seen from Onliness theory and perspective. See *Fires of Consciousness*, page 136.

------- -------
------- -------
------- -------
------- -------
------- -------
------- -------

Eternal Self of Radiance

HEXAGRAM 23: TENDENCY TOWARD BEING'S TRANS-GNOSTIC EXISTENTIAL RADIANCE AWARENESS

You are not your memories and future expectations self and consciousness. This is not Your True Nature and Condition. This is not Your *True Identity*. Only Self, which You now and ever are, is Real. In Self-realization, developmentally beyond (with the death of) conditional and conditioned body-mind centered compound personal-egoic self and consciousness, You are, in Truth, the Love, Wisdom and Compassion of uncreated, causeless, boundless, timeless and formless *Supreme Self Reality*, and non-other Than. Unfathomable, You are this birthless and deathless unassailable *Bliss-Divine Self* which is All and Each and None, Only and Completely. Awaken to, and *Be,* the Truth-consciousness of this ultimately unutterable and unqualifable *Absolute Nondual Self Reality* that You always and already are. Transpersonally, within World-Soul Awareness's Consciousness Awakening, You are Multiplicity Meaning's *Omniscient Mind-Psyche of Configurative Force and Vision*, this *Consummation and Illumination of Worlds Self-as-Self Revelation*, which is Choiceless Self of Radiance. Personally, at the pre-transcendental developmental level of body-mind compound personal-egoic self and consciousness, this hexagram symbolizes the ascending-descending benefit of progressively removing barriers that block the return of virtue, and of waiting and steadfast patience until the present inferior but predominant situation-circumstance passes. Such patience in waiting will result in later success. Now it is a time to be especially generous to those who depend upon You, and to patiently contemplate the impermanent ebb and flow of these present, and indeed of all, phenomena. This is a vision-logic consciousness expression of One's developmental tendency toward, and agency within, the transpersonal Reality of *Being's*

Trans-gnostic Existential Radiance Awareness, as seen from Onliness theory and perspective. See *Fires of Consciousness*, page 138.

```
-------------------
-------    -------
-------    -------
-------    -------
-------    -------
-------    -------
```

Choiceless Self of Radiance

HEXAGRAM 38: TENDENCY TOWARD NONBEING'S TRANS-GNOSTIC ISTENTIAL RADIANCE EXPERIENCE

You are not your early-immature traits of pre-personal and pre-egoic self and consciousness. This is not Your True Nature and Condition. This is not Your *True Identity*. Only Self, which You now and ever are, is Real. In Self-realization, developmentally beyond (with the death of) conditional and conditioned body-mind centered compound personal-egoic self and consciousness, You are, in Truth, the Love, Wisdom and Compassion of uncreated, causeless, boundless, timeless and formless *Supreme Self Reality*, and non-other Than. Unfathomable, You are this birthless and deathless unassailable *Bliss-Divine Self* which is All and Each and None, Only and Completely. Awaken to, and *Be*, the Truth-consciousness of this ultimately unutterable and unqualifable *Absolute Nondual Self Reality* that You always and already are. Transpersonally, within World-Soul Experience's Consciousness Awakening, You are Serenity Communion's *Lucent Heart-Soul of Trans-ceptive Power and Boundlessness*, this *One All-where Potency and Grace Self-as-Self Awakening*, which is Brahman-consciousness (Atman) Self of Radiance. Personally, at the pre-transcendental developmental level of body-mind compound personal-egoic self and consciousness, this hexagram symbolizes the ascending-descending benefit of opposition, separation, difference and diversity, all occurring within unity, which here succeeds in small matters. Joy and beauty conjoin in radiance. In relative reality there is no opposition without union, nor union without opposition; no polarity exists outside of unity, no unity exists outside polarity. It is important to acknowledge and support difference and diversity, and the productive purposes these serve, even when estrangement may occur. This is a vision-logic consciousness expression of One's developmental tendency toward, and agency within, the transpersonal Reality of

Nonbeing's Trans-gnostic Istential Radiance Experience, as seen from Onliness theory and perspective. See *Fires of Consciousness,* page 141.

```
------------------
-------    -------
------------------
-------    -------
------------------
------------------
```

Brahman-consciousness (Atman) Self of Radiance

HEXAGRAM 54: TENDENCY TOWARD NONBEING'S PAN-GNOSTIC ISTENTIAL RADIANCE EXPERIENCE

You are not your judgmental, accusational and blaming self and consciousness. This is not Your True Nature and Condition. This is not Your *True Identity*. Only Self, which You now and ever are, is Real. In Self-realization, developmentally beyond (with the death of) conditional and conditioned body-mind centered compound personal-egoic self and consciousness, You are, in Truth, the Love, Wisdom and Compassion of uncreated, causeless, boundless, timeless and formless *Supreme Self Reality*, and non-other Than. Unfathomable, You are this birthless and deathless unassailable *Bliss-Divine Self* which is All and Each and None, Only and Completely. Awaken to, and *Be*, the Truth-consciousness of this ultimately unutterable and unqualifable *Absolute Nondual Self Reality* that You always and already are. Transpersonally, within World-Soul Experience's Consciousness Awakening, You are Serenity Communion's *Eternal Heart-Soul of Transparency and Perfect Emptiness*, this *Contemplative and Transfigurative Awakening of Worlds Self-as-Self Truth-consciousness*, which is Suchness Self of Radiance. Personally, at the pre-transcendental developmental level of body-mind compound personal-egoic self and consciousness, this hexagram symbolizes the ascending-descending possible danger and need for caution. Action going forward or setting of goals at this time, in these circumstances, is not advised (possible misfortune). To achieve distant and enduring ends, One must to be aware of, and attend to, mistakes or mischief made at the beginning. The marriage (active and joyful conjoining and intercourse) of Heaven (transcendent Ascent of Truth and Wisdom) and Earth (immanent Descent of Unconditional and All-inclusive Love and Compassion) give rise to all of manifest reality. This is a vision-logic consciousness expression of One's developmental tendency toward, and agency within, the transpersonal Reality of *Nonbeing's Pan-gnostic Istential Radiance Experience*, as seen from Onliness theory and perspective. See *Fires of Consciousness*, page 142.

```
-------    -------
-------    -------
------------------
-------    -------
------------------
------------------
```

Suchness Self of Radiance

HEXAGRAM 8: TENDENCY TOWARD BEING'S PAN-GNOSTIC TRANSEXISTENTIAL RADIANCE AWARENESS

You are not your greedy, acquisitive and avarice self and consciousness. This is not Your True Nature and Condition. This is not Your *True Identity.* Only Self, which You now and ever are, is Real. In Self-realization, developmentally beyond (with the death of) conditional and conditioned body-mind centered compound personal-egoic self and consciousness, You are, in Truth, the Love, Wisdom and Compassion of uncreated, causeless, boundless, timeless and formless *Supreme Self Reality,* and non-other Than. Unfathomable, You are this birthless and deathless unassailable *Bliss-Divine Self* which is All and Each and None, Only and Completely. Awaken to, and *Be,* the Truth-consciousness of this ultimately unutterable and unqualifable *Absolute Nondual Self Reality* that You always and already are. Transpersonally, within World-Soul Awareness's Consciousness Awakening, You are Multiplicity Meaning's *Fertile Vision of Holoceptive Unconditionality,* this *Scient Mind-Psyche of Conception and None Each-where Self-as-Self Recognition,* which is Christ-consciousness Self of Radiance. Personally, at the pre-transcendental developmental level of body-mind compound personal-egoic self and consciousness, this hexagram symbolizes the ascending-descending benefit of coordination and unity, with resultant success. This is achieved through leaders and followers mutual respect, cooperation and support of one another. There is need and great benefit in further *I Ching* meditative consultation. Those who are troubled can be helped by carefully considering and promptly responding to these suggestions. This is a vision-logic consciousness expression of One's developmental tendency toward, and agency within, the transpersonal Reality of *Being's Pan-gnostic Transexistential Radiance*

Awareness, as seen from Onliness theory and perspective. See *Fires of Consciousness*, page 145.

```
-------      -------
-----------------
-------      -------
-------      -------
-------      -------
-------      -------
```

Christ-consciousness Self of Radiance

HEXAGRAM 20: TENDENCY TOWARD BEING'S TRANS-GNOSTIC TRANSEXISTENTIAL RADIANCE AWARENESS

You are not your conditioned and conditional social-cultural-historical self and consciousness. This is not Your True Nature and Condition. This is not Your *True Identity.* Only Self, which You now and ever are, is Real. In Self-realization, developmentally beyond (with the death of) conditional and conditioned body-mind centered compound personal-egoic self and consciousness, You are, in Truth, the Love, Wisdom and Compassion of uncreated, causeless, boundless, timeless and formless *Supreme Self Reality,* and non-other Than. Unfathomable, You are this birthless and deathless unassailable *Bliss-Divine Self* which is All and Each and None, Only and Completely. Awaken to, and *Be,* the Truth-consciousness of this ultimately unutterable and unqualifiable *Absolute Nondual Self Reality* that You always and already are. Transpersonally, within World-Soul Awareness's Consciousness Awakening, You are Multiplicity Meaning's *Configurative and Confluent Form of Mind-Psyche Nonduality,* this *Illuminative Bliss-Divine Realization Self-as-Self Awakening,* which is Seamless Self of Radiance. Personally, at the pre-transcendental developmental level of body-mind compound personal-egoic self and consciousness, this hexagram symbolizes the ascending-descending benefit of wise and compassionate instruction in the initial stage of One's course, gained through the offering of wisdom, compassion, and the transformative teachings of a Sage. With embracing acceptance, the Sage, looking down upon and witnessing the world, meditates and contemplates upon its suffering. However, these transforming Winds of change offered by the Sage must not only be Recognized, but *also* fully Realized by those who suffer in darkness and delusion. This is a vision-logic consciousness expression of One's developmental tendency toward, and agency within, the transpersonal Reality of *Being's Trans-gnostic Transexistential Radiance Awareness*, as seen from Onliness theory and perspective. See *Fires of Consciousness*, page 147.

```
------------------
------------------
-------   -------
-------   -------
-------   -------
-------   -------
```

Seamless Self of Radiance

HEXAGRAM 16: TENDENCY TOWARD NONBEING'S PAN-GNOSTIC ISTENTIAL EMPTINESS AWARENESS

You are not your reactionary ego-defensive and ego-guarded self and consciousness. This is not Your True Nature and Condition. This is not Your *True Identity*. Only Self, which You now and ever are, is Real. In Self-realization, developmentally beyond (with the death of) conditional and conditioned body-mind centered compound personal-egoic self and consciousness, You are, in Truth, the Love, Wisdom and Compassion of uncreated, causeless, boundless, timeless and formless *Supreme Self Reality*, and non-other Than. Unfathomable, You are this birthless and deathless unassailable *Bliss-Divine Self* which is All and Each and None, Only and Completely. Awaken to, and *Be,* the Truth-consciousness of this ultimately unutterable and unqualifable *Absolute Nondual Self Reality* that You always and already are. Transpersonally, within World-Soul Awareness's Consciousness Awakening, You are Multiplicity Meaning's *Fertile Mind-Psyche of Reflexivity*, this *Luminous Realization of Nowhere Vortex Vision*, this *Conception of Worlds Self-as-Self Revelation*, which is Formless Self of Emptiness. Personally, at the pre-transcendental developmental level of body-mind compound personal-egoic self and consciousness, this hexagram symbolizes the ascending-descending benefit gained through cooperative accomplishment of constructive and important action, based upon the calm confidence and repose of the *righteousness* of such action. In confident repose then, the firm, timely and swift movement and action of the Sage is in accord and harmony with Heaven (Wisdom and Truth) and Earth (Love and Compassion). This is a vision-logic consciousness expression of One's developmental tendency toward, and agency within, the transpersonal Reality of *Nonbeing's Pan-gnostic Istential Emptiness Awareness*, as seen from Onliness theory and perspective. See *Fires of Consciousness*, page 159.

```
-------      -------
-------      -------
------------------
-------      -------
-------      -------
-------      -------
```

Formless Self of Emptiness

HEXAGRAM 35: TENDENCY TOWARD NONBEING'S TRANS-GNOSTIC ISTENTIAL EMPTINESS AWARENESS

You are not your self-righteousness posturing self and consciousness. This is not Your True Nature and Condition. This is not Your *True Identity*. Only Self, which You now and ever are, is Real. In Self-realization, developmentally beyond (with the death of) conditional and conditioned body-mind centered compound personal-egoic self and consciousness, You are, in Truth, the Love, Wisdom and Compassion of uncreated, causeless, boundless, timeless and formless *Supreme Self Reality*, and non-other Than. Unfathomable, You are this birthless and deathless unassailable *Bliss-Divine Self* which is All and Each and None, Only and Completely. Awaken to, and *Be*, the Truth-consciousness of this ultimately unutterable and unqualifable *Absolute Nondual Self Reality* that You always and already are. Transpersonally, within World-Soul Awareness's Consciousness Awakening, You are Multiplicity Meaning's *Mind-Psyche of Omniscient Vision and Perception*, this *Configurative Conception and Germination of Seeing None Each-where Self-as-Self Recognition*, which is Boundless Self of Emptiness. Personally, at the pre-transcendental developmental level of body-mind compound personal-egoic self and consciousness, this hexagram symbolizes the ascending-descending benefit of progress, merit, accomplishment and recognition, through application of One's substantial talents and abilities. In this way, there can occur, and be recognized, the integration of glad acceptance, brilliance and beauty, with resultant progress toward beneficial achievements. This is a vision-logic consciousness expression of One's developmental tendency toward, and agency within, the transpersonal Reality of *Nonbeing's Trans-gnostic Istential Emptiness Awareness*, as seen from Onliness theory and perspective. See *Fires of Consciousness*, page 160.

```
------------------
-------     -------
------------------
-------     -------
-------     -------
-------     -------
```

Boundless Self of Emptiness

HEXAGRAM 61: TENDENCY TOWARD BEING'S TRANS-GNOSTIC TRANSEXISTENTIAL EMPTINESS EXPERIENCE

You are not your illusory separate-self-sense *subject* versus otherness-perceived *object* self and consciousness. This is not Your True Nature and Condition. This is not Your *True Identity*. Only Self, which You now and ever are, is Real. In Self-realization, developmentally beyond (with the death of) conditional and conditioned body-mind centered compound personal-egoic self and consciousness, You are, in Truth, the Love, Wisdom and Compassion of uncreated, causeless, boundless, timeless and formless *Supreme Self Reality*, and non-other Than. Unfathomable, You are this birthless and deathless unassailable *Bliss-Divine Self* which is All and Each and None, Only and Completely. Awaken to, and *Be,* the Truth-consciousness of this ultimately unutterable and unqualifable *Absolute Nondual Self Reality* that You always and already are. Transpersonally, within World-Soul Experience's Consciousness Awakening, You are Serenity Communion's *Perfect Emptiness Heart-Soul of Unreflexivity,* this *Transfiguring Bliss* of *Numinous Transparency and Unity Self-as-Self Awakening,* which is Divine Self of Emptiness. Personally, at the pre-transcendental developmental level of body-mind compound personal-egoic self and consciousness, this hexagram symbolizes the ascending-descending benefit of confidence, sincerity, great accomplishment and success, through flexible penetration of, and persistence in, a righteous course. Movement is advantageous now. Joyful and gentle confidence and persistence accords with Heaven (Wisdom and Truth), and can successfully accomplish whatever is sets before it. Cautious and deliberate thought needs to be taken before One acts. This is a vision-logic consciousness expression of One's developmental tendency toward, and agency within, the transpersonal Reality of *Being's Trans-gnostic*

Transexistential Emptiness Experience, as seen from Onliness theory and perspective. See *Fires of Consciousness,* page 163.

```
------------------
------------------
-------    -------
-------    -------
------------------
------------------
```

Divine Self of Emptiness

HEXAGRAM 60: TENDENCY TOWARD BEING'S PAN-GNOSTIC TRANSEXISTENTIAL EMPTINESS EXPERIENCE

You are not your guilt, remorse and shame self and consciousness. This is not Your True Nature and Condition. This is not Your *True Identity*. Only Self, which You now and ever are, is Real. In Self-realization, developmentally beyond (with the death of) conditional and conditioned body-mind centered compound personal-egoic self and consciousness, You are, in Truth, the Love, Wisdom and Compassion of uncreated, causeless, boundless, timeless and formless *Supreme Self Reality*, and non-other Than. Unfathomable, You are this birthless and deathless unassailable *Bliss-Divine Self* which is All and Each and None, Only and Completely. Awaken to, and *Be*, the Truth-consciousness of this ultimately unutterable and unqualifable *Absolute Nondual Self Reality* that You always and already are. Transpersonally, within World-Soul Experience's Consciousness Awakening, You are Serenity Communion's *Dispersive Heart-Soul of One All-where Omnipotence*, this *Inceptive Power of Transfigurative Embrace Self-as-Self Expression*, which is Reality Self of Emptiness. Personally, at the pre-transcendental developmental level of body-mind compound personal-egoic self and consciousness, this hexagram symbolizes the ascending-descending benefit of progress and accomplishment through cautious *restraint* (or non-action), as well as regulated and systematic calculation in the practice of virtue. However, carefully avoid *overly restrictive,* severe or prolonged conditions and regulations. There is joy in undertaking virtuous but difficult, and even dangerous, goals. This is a vision-logic consciousness expression of One's developmental tendency toward, and agency within, the transpersonal Reality of *Being's Pan-gnostic Transexistential Emptiness Experience*, as seen from Onliness theory and perspective. See *Fires of Consciousness*, page 165.

-------   -------

-------   -------
-------   -------

Reality Self of Emptiness

HEXAGRAM 45: TENDENCY TOWARD NONBEING'S PAN-GNOSTIC ANTISTENTIAL EMPTINESS AWARENESS

You are not your endless seeking, searching and grasping pursuit of pleasure and distraction self and consciousness. This is not Your True Nature and Condition. This is not Your *True Identity*. Only Self, which You now and ever are, is Real. In Self-realization, developmentally beyond (with the death of) conditional and conditioned body-mind centered compound personal-egoic self and consciousness, You are, in Truth, the Love, Wisdom and Compassion of uncreated, causeless, boundless, timeless and formless *Supreme Self Reality*, and non-other Than. Unfathomable, You are this birthless and deathless unassailable *Bliss-Divine Self* which is All and Each and None, Only and Completely. Awaken to, and *Be*, the Truth-consciousness of this ultimately unutterable and unqualifiable *Absolute Nondual Self Reality* that You always and already are. Transpersonally, within World-Soul Awareness's Consciousness Awakening, You are Multiplicity Meaning's *Boundless Gnostic Mind-Psyche of Vision and Realization*, this *Cohesive Form of Meaning's Conception and Genesis Self-as-Self Truth-consciousness*, which is Unmediated Self of Emptiness. Personally, at the pre-transcendental developmental level of body-mind compound personal-egoic self and consciousness, this hexagram symbolizes the ascending-descending benefit of gathering together to correct and put things in order, so as to prepare for the unforeseen. Accomplishment of this objective is achievable and can be successful, but will requires firm persistence in a righteous course, and consultation with a person of wisdom and good judgment. Difficult and important sacrifices will need to be made. By observing what each gathers unto itself, One comes to understand the *inner* nature of all things. This is a vision-logic consciousness expression of One's developmental tendency toward, and agency within, the transpersonal

Reality of *Nonbeing's Pan-gnostic Antistential Emptiness Awareness,* as seen from Onliness theory and perspective. See *Fires of Consciousness,* page 168.

```
-------     -------
-----------------
-----------------
-------     -------
-------     -------
-------     -------
```

Unmediated Self of Emptiness

HEXAGRAM 12: TENDENCY TOWARD NONBEING'S TRANS-GNOSTIC ANTISTENTIAL EMPTINESS AWARENESS

You are not your fears, dreads and terrors self and consciousness. This is not Your True Nature and Condition. This is not Your *True Identity*. Only Self, which You now and ever are, is Real. In Self-realization, developmentally beyond (with the death of) conditional and conditioned body-mind centered compound personal-egoic self and consciousness, You are, in Truth, the Love, Wisdom and Compassion of uncreated, causeless, boundless, timeless and formless *Supreme Self Reality*, and non-other Than. Unfathomable, You are this birthless and deathlesss unassailable *Bliss-Divine Self* which is All and Each and None, Only and Completely. Awaken to, and *Be,* the Truth-consciousness of this ultimately unutterable and unqualifable *Absolute Nondual Self Reality* that You always and already are. Transpersonally, within World-Soul Awareness's Consciousness Awakening, You are Multiplicity Meaning's *Comprehending Mind-Psyche Mirroring of Numinous Transparent Apparancy*, this *Confluence of Formlessness's Configurative None Each-where Root-Form Self-as-Self Revelation*, which is Ineffable Void Self of Emptiness. Personally, at the pre-transcendental developmental level of body-mind compound personal-egoic self and consciousness, this hexagram symbolizes the ascending-descending danger of stagnation and obstruction, due to evil-doers who are central and in ascendance now. The great and good at the fringe are in decline, due to lack of contact and interaction between Heaven (Wisdom and Truth) and Earth (Love and Compassion). Avoid this danger by continuing in righteous persistence and by looking inward into self. Avoid all temptation of honors or riches under these circumstances. This is a vision-logic consciousness expression of One's developmental tendency toward, and agency within, the transpersonal Reality of *Nonbeing's Trans-gnostic*

Antistential Emptiness Awareness, as seen from Onliness theory and perspective. See *Fires of Consciousness,* page 169.

```
------------------
------------------
------------------
-------      -------
-------      -------
-------      -------
```

Ineffable Void Self of Emptiness

HEXAGRAM 41: TENDENCY TOWARD BEING'S TRANS-GNOSTIC EXISTENTIAL EMPTINESS EXPERIENCE

You are not your painful, agonizing and suffering self and consciousness. This is not Your True Nature and Condition. This is not Your *True Identity*. Only Self, which You now and ever are, is Real. In Self-realization, developmentally beyond (with the death of) conditional and conditioned body-mind centered compound personal-egoic self and consciousness, You are, in Truth, the Love, Wisdom and Compassion of uncreated, causeless, boundless, timeless and formless *Supreme Self Reality*, and non-other Than. Unfathomable, You are this birthless and deathless unassailable *Bliss-Divine Self* which is All and Each and None, Only and Completely. Awaken to, and *Be,* the Truth-consciousness of this ultimately unutterable and unqualifable *Absolute Nondual Self Reality* that You always and already are. Transpersonally, within World-Soul Experience's Consciousness Awakening, You are Serenity Communion's *Gnostic Heart-Soul Form of Unconditionality and Unity*, this *Source and Creation of Worlds Self-as-Self Reality*, which is Preferenceless Self of Emptiness. Personally, at the pre-transcendental developmental level of body-mind compound personal-egoic self and consciousness, this hexagram symbolizes the ascending-descending benefit of advantage gained, and in freedom from error; good fortune. This is achieved through the process of loss, reduction or elimination, which is called for now. Confident in One's direction, it is necessary to keep anger and desire under control. Making use of what is readily at hand, it is important to develop a plan and to have a goal in mind. This is a vision-logic consciousness expression of One's developmental tendency toward, and agency within, the transpersonal Reality of *Being's Trans-gnostic Existential Emptiness Experience*, as seen from Onliness theory and perspective. See *Fires of Consciousness*, page 172.

```
------------------
-------    -------
-------    -------
-------    -------
------------------
------------------
```

Preferenceless Self of Emptiness

HEXAGRAM 19: TENDENCY TOWARD BEING'S PAN-GNOSTIC EXISTENTIAL EMPTINESS EXPERIENCE

You are not your blindness, ignorance and cavalier indifference to others suffering and injustice self and consciousness. This is not Your True Nature and Condition. This is not Your *True Identity*. Only Self, which You now and ever are, is Real. In Self-realization, developmentally beyond (with the death of) conditional and conditioned body-mind centered compound personal-egoic self and consciousness, You are, in Truth, the Love, Wisdom and Compassion of uncreated, causeless, boundless, timeless and formless *Supreme Self Reality*, and non-other Than. Unfathomable, You are this birthless and deathless unassailable *Bliss-Divine Self* which is All and Each and None, Only and Completely. Awaken to, and *Be,* the Truth-consciousness of this ultimately unutterable and unqualifiable *Absolute Nondual Self Reality* that You always and already are. Transpersonally, within World-Soul Experience's Consciousness Awakening, You are Serenity Communion's *Meditative Heart-Soul Potency of Numinous Apparent Transparency*, this *Apprehending Seed-Void of Perfect Emptiness Self-as-Self Awakening*, which is Enlightened Self of Emptiness. Personally, at the pre-transcendental developmental level of body-mind compound personal-egoic self and consciousness, this hexagram symbolizes the ascending-descending benefit of care, joyful acceptance, growth and progress (great success), using the way of approach and righteous persistence. This is accomplished through the nourishment and wisdom of One's teachings to, and abiding empathetic affection for, those in need, so as to correct and rectify their problems and confusion. Later, however, evil and misfortunate factors and circumstance will once again prevail. This is a vision-logic consciousness expression of One's developmental tendency toward, and agency within, the transpersonal Reality of *Being's Pan-gnostic Existential Emptiness Experience*, as seen from Onliness theory and perspective. See *Fires of Consciousness,* page 174.

-------   -------
-------   -------
-------   -------
-------   -------

Enlightened Self of Emptiness

HEXAGRAM 6: TENDENCY TOWARD NONBEING'S TRANS-GNOSTIC ANTISTENTIAL AWAKENING AWARENESS

You are not a person or personal self and consciousness. This is not Your True Nature and Condition. This is not Your *True Identity*. Only Self, which You now and ever are, is Real. In Self-realization, developmentally beyond (with the death of) conditional and conditioned body-mind centered compound personal-egoic self and consciousness, You are, in Truth, the Love, Wisdom and Compassion of uncreated, causeless, boundless, timeless and formless *Supreme Self Reality*, and non-other Than. Unfathomable, You are this birthless and deathless unassailable *Bliss-Divine Self* which is All and Each and None, Only and Completely. Awaken to, and *Be,* the Truth-consciousness of this ultimately unutterable and unqualifable *Absolute Nondual Self Reality* that You always and already are. Transpersonally, within World-Soul Awareness's Consciousness Awakening, You are Realization Knowledge's *Mind-Psyche of Boundless Understanding*, this *All All-where Trans-essent Silence of Worlds Self-as-Self Recognition*, which is All-pervading Self of Awakening. Personally, at the pre-transcendental developmental level of body-mind compound personal-egoic self and consciousness, this hexagram symbolizes the ascending-descending danger and peril of opposition, obstacles, strife, conflict, contention and dispute, which ultimately cannot be resolved and thus results in great disadvantage, and possibly disaster. It is important to seek wise counsel and advice, and then carefully and cautiously formulate One's plans before taking action. It is disadvantageous to initiate a journey at this time. This is a vision-logic consciousness expression of One's developmental tendency toward, and agency within, the transpersonal Reality of *Nonbeing's Trans-gnostic Antistential Awakening Awareness,* as seen from Onliness theory and perspective. See *Fires of Consciousness*, page 186.

```
------------------
------------------
------------------
-------      -------
------------------
-------      -------
```

All-pervading Self of Awakening

HEXAGRAM 47: TENDENCY TOWARD NONBEING'S PAN-GNOSTIC ANTISTENTIAL AWAKENING AWARENESS

You are not your relative compound personal-egoic self and consciousness. This is not Your True Nature and Condition. This is not Your *True Identity*. Only Self, which You now and ever are, is Real. In Self-realization, developmentally beyond (with the death of) conditional and conditioned body-mind centered compound personal-egoic self and consciousness, You are, in Truth, the Love, Wisdom and Compassion of uncreated, causeless, boundless, timeless and formless *Supreme Self Reality*, and non-other Than. Unfathomable, You are this birthless and deathless unassailable *Bliss-Divine Self* which is All and Each and None, Only and Completely. Awaken to, and *Be,* the Truth-consciousness of this ultimately unutterable and unqualifable *Absolute Nondual Self Reality* that You always and already are. Transpersonally, within World-Soul Awareness's Consciousness Awakening, You are Realization Knowledge's *Truth of Comprehending Numinous Transparent Apparancy*, this *Scient Mind-Psyche of Joy and Perception Self-as-Self Awakening*, which is Compassion (Sacred) Self of Awakening. Personally, at the pre-transcendental developmental level of body-mind compound personal-egoic self and consciousness, this hexagram symbolizes the ascending-descending potential benefit of progress, accomplishment and attainment of One's goal. That is, success and good fortune despite adversity, difficulty and weariness, but *only* through great and determined persistence in a righteous course; and perhaps at the risk of One's life. The adversity derives from something hidden. This is a vision-logic consciousness expression of One's developmental tendency toward, and agency within, the transpersonal Reality of *Nonbeing's Pan-gnostic Antistential Awakening Awareness*, as seen from Onliness theory and perspective. See *Fires of Consciousness*, page 187.

```
-------     -------
-----------------
-----------------
-------     -------
-----------------
-------     -------
```

Compassion (Sacred) Self of Awakening

HEXAGRAM 24: TENDENCY TOWARD BEING'S PAN-GNOSTIC EXISTENTIAL AWAKENING EXPERIENCE

You are not your endless clinging and attachment self and consciousness. This is not Your True Nature and Condition. This is not Your *True Identity*. Only Self, which You now and ever are, is Real. In Self-realization, developmentally beyond (with the death of) conditional and conditioned body-mind centered compound personal-egoic self and consciousness, You are, in Truth, the Love, Wisdom and Compassion of uncreated, causeless, boundless, timeless and formless *Supreme Self Reality*, and non-other Than. Unfathomable, You are this birthless and deathless unassailable *Bliss-Divine Self* which is All and Each and None, Only and Completely. Awaken to, and *Be*, the Truth-consciousness of this ultimately unutterable and unqualifable *Absolute Nondual Self Reality* that You always and already are. Transpersonally, within World-Soul Experience's Consciousness Awakening, You are Holiness Compassion's *Unconditional Gnostic Heart-Soul*, this *Each Each-where Attention and Loving Embodiment of Worlds Self-as-Self Expression*, which is Trans-manifest Self of Awakening. Personally, at the pre-transcendental developmental level of body-mind compound personal-egoic self and consciousness, this hexagram symbolizes the ascending-descending benefit of the cycle of return and completion. Thus, the freedom and advantage of the movement, growth and progress of a new cycle's successful beginnings. Strength is now increasing, so it is best to have a goal in view. At the end of a cycle, its purpose and reason become apparent. This is a vision-logic consciousness expression of One's developmental tendency toward, and agency within, the transpersonal Reality of *Being's Pan-gnostic Existential Awakening Experience*, as seen from Onliness theory and perspective. See *Fires of Consciousness*, page 190.

```
-------       -------
-------       -------
-------       -------
-------       -------
-------       -------
-------------------
```

Trans-manifest Self of Awakening

HEXAGRAM 27: TENDENCY TOWARD BEING'S TRANS-GNOSTIC EXISTENTIAL AWAKENING EXPERIENCE

You are not your illusory single and separately perceived individual self and consciousness. This is not Your True Nature and Condition. This is not Your *True Identity*. Only Self, which You now and ever are, is Real. In Self-realization, developmentally beyond (with the death of) conditional and conditioned body-mind centered compound personal-egoic self and consciousness, You are, in Truth, the Love, Wisdom and Compassion of uncreated, causeless, boundless, timeless and formless *Supreme Self Reality*, and non-other Than. Unfathomable, You are this birthless and deathless unassailable *Bliss-Divine Self* which is All and Each and None, Only and Completely. Awaken to, and *Be,* the Truth-consciousness of this ultimately unutterable and unqualifable *Absolute Nondual Self Reality* that You always and already are. Transpersonally, within World-Soul Experience's Consciousness Awakening, You are Holiness Compassion's *Now-Here Presence of Numinous Apparent Transparency*, this *Lucent Heart-Soul of Inception and Tranquility Self-as-Self Truth-consciousness*, which is Omnipresent Self of Awakening. Personally, at the pre-transcendental developmental level of body-mind compound personal-egoic self and consciousness, this hexagram symbolizes the ascending-descending benefit of nourishment, recovery and growth for those in need, as well as appropriate nourishment of One's self. This will require firm and righteous persistence, and timely application is critically important. Observe how beings nourish themselves and others. The Holy Sage, through Wisdom, Love and Compassion, nourishes all beings. This is a vision-logic consciousness expression of One's developmental tendency toward, and agency within, the transpersonal Reality of *Being's Trans-gnostic Existential Awakening Experience*, as seen from Onliness theory and perspective. See *Fires of Consciousness*, page 192.

```
------------------
-------    -------
-------    -------
-------    -------
-------    -------
------------------
```

Omnipresent Self of Awakening

HEXAGRAM 64: TENDENCY TOWARD NONBEING'S
TRANS-GNOSTIC ISTENTIAL AWAKENING AWARENESS
You are not your self-contracted, inaccessible and isolative self and
consciousness. This is not Your True Nature and Condition. This
is not Your *True Identity*. Only Self, which You now and ever are, is
Real. In Self-realization, developmentally beyond (with the death of)
conditional and conditioned body-mind centered compound personal-egoic self and consciousness, You are, in Truth, the Love, Wisdom
and Compassion of uncreated, causeless, boundless, timeless and
formless *Supreme Self Reality*, and non-other Than. Unfathomable,
You are this birthless and deathless unassailable *Bliss-Divine Self*
which is All and Each and None, Only and Completely. Awaken
to, and *Be,* the Truth-consciousness of this ultimately unutterable
and unqualifiable *Absolute Nondual Self Reality* that You always
and already are. Transpersonally, within World-Soul Awareness's
Consciousness Awakening, You are Realization Knowledge's *Mind
Psyche of Silent Omniscient Consciousness*, this *Gnostic Perception of
Reflexive Clarity Self-as-Self Reality*, which is Innate-nature Self of
Awakening. Personally, at the pre-transcendental developmental level
of body-mind compound personal-egoic self and consciousness, this
hexagram symbolizes the ascending-descending future benefit of
progress and success, but not at this point as this is the middle course
of One's as yet incomplete endeavors and efforts. First, there are en-
countered further challenges, difficulties and setbacks. No fixed or
specific goal is favorable now. It is important to carefully discrimi-
nate so as to assign things according to their inherent holonic order and arrangement. This is a vision-logic consciousness expression
of One's developmental tendency toward, and agency within, the
transpersonal Reality of *Nonbeing's Trans-gnostic Istential Awakening*

Awareness, as seen from Onliness theory and perspective. See *Fires of Consciousness,* page 195.

```
------------------

-------       -------

------------------

-------       -------

------------------

-------       -------
```

Innate-nature Self of Awakening

HEXAGRAM 40: TENDENCY TOWARD NONBEING'S PAN-GNOSTIC ISTENTIAL AWAKENING AWARENESS

You are not your educational, job titles, awards and accomplishments self and consciousness. This is not Your True Nature and Condition. This is not Your *True Identity*. Only Self, which You now and ever are, is Real. In Self-realization, developmentally beyond (with the death of) conditional and conditioned body-mind centered compound personal-egoic self and consciousness, You are, in Truth, the Love, Wisdom and Compassion of uncreated, causeless, boundless, timeless and formless *Supreme Self Reality*, and non-other Than. Unfathomable, You are this birthless and deathless unassailable *Bliss-Divine Self* which is All and Each and None, Only and Completely. Awaken to, and *Be,* the Truth-consciousness of this ultimately unutterable and unqualifable *Absolute Nondual Self Reality* that You always and already are. Transpersonally, within World-Soul Awareness's Consciousness Awakening, You are Realization Knowledge's *Conceiving Mind-Psyche of Configurative Truth*, this *Resplendence and Nonduality Self-as-Self Recognition*, which is Nonabiding Self of Awakening. Personally, at the pre-transcendental developmental level of body-mind compound personal-egoic self and consciousness, this hexagram symbolizes the ascending-descending possible benefit of resolution, release, growth and good outcomes, if prompt action is *now* taken of either: withdrawal and return, so as to find a middle course, if no goal is to be gained by moving forward, *or* prompt advance is now taken, if some goal is to be gained by moving forward. The south and west are favorable at this time. There is now immanent danger, so that action to avoid it finds release, growth and resolution. One needs to forgive and deal leniently with others. This is a vision-logic consciousness expression of One's developmental tendency toward, and agency within, the transpersonal Reality of

Nonbeing's Pan-gnostic Istential Awakening Awareness, as seen from Onliness theory and perspective. See *Fires of Consciousness,* page 196.

```
-------    -------
-------    -------
-----------------
-------    -------
-----------------
-------    -------
```

Non-abiding Self of Awakening

HEXAGRAM 3: TENDENCY TOWARD BEING'S PAN-GNOSTIC TRANSEXISTENTIAL AWAKENING EXPERIENCE

You are not your social-cultural, aesthetic, political and economic values and opinions self and consciousness. This is not Your True Nature and Condition. This is not Your *True Identity*. Only Self, which You now and ever are, is Real. In Self-realization, developmentally beyond (with the death of) conditional and conditioned body-mind centered compound personal-egoic self and consciousness, You are, in Truth, the Love, Wisdom and Compassion of uncreated, causeless, boundless, timeless and formless *Supreme Self Reality*, and non-other Than. Unfathomable, You are this birthless and deathless unassailable *Bliss-Divine Self* which is All and Each and None, Only and Completely. Awaken to, and *Be,* the Truth-consciousness of this ultimately unutterable and unqualifable *Absolute Nondual Self Reality* that You always and already are. Transpersonally, within World-Soul Experience's Consciousness Awakening, You are Holiness Compassion's *Omnipotence of Action and Attention*, this *Heart-Soul of Transformative Unreflexive Luminosity Self-as-Self Awakening*, which is Birthless, Deathless Self of Awakening. Personally, at the pre-transcendental developmental level of body-mind compound personal-egoic self and consciousness, this hexagram symbolizes the ascending-descending difficulty, adversity and struggle in the initial stages of growth and development, but with determined persistence in a righteous course and focus on consolidating present situations and circumstances, great ultimate progress, growth, accomplishment and success can be attained. One now needs to avoid seeking new goals, and work to set present difficulties in order. This is a vision-logic consciousness expression of One's developmental tendency toward, and agency within, the transpersonal Reality of *Being's Pan-gnostic*

Transexistential Awakening Experience, as seen from Onliness theory and perspective. See *Fires of Consciousness,* page 198.

```
-------     -------
------------------
-------     -------
-------     -------
-------     -------
------------------
```

Birthless, Deathless Self of Awakening

HEXAGRAM 42: TENDENCY TOWARD BEING'S TRANS-GNOSTIC TRANSEXISTENTIAL AWAKENING EXPERIENCE

You are not your controlling, dominating and manipulative self and consciousness. This is not Your True Nature and Condition. This is not Your *True Identity*. Only Self, which You now and ever are, is Real. In Self-realization, developmentally beyond (with the death of) conditional and conditioned body-mind centered compound personal-egoic self and consciousness, You are, in Truth, the Love, Wisdom and Compassion of uncreated, causeless, boundless, timeless and formless *Supreme Self Reality*, and non-other Than. Unfathomable, You are this birthless and deathless unassailable *Bliss-Divine Self* which is All and Each and None, Only and Completely. Awaken to, and *Be,* the Truth-consciousness of this ultimately unutterable and unqualifiable *Absolute Nondual Self Reality* that You always and already are. Transpersonally, within World-Soul Experience's Consciousness Awakening, You are Holiness Compassion's *Truth of Each Each-where Presence*, this *Heart-Soul Eternity and Inclusivity Self-as-Self Revelation*, which is Wisdom (Truth) Self of Awakening. Personally, at the pre-transcendental developmental level of body-mind compound personal-egoic self and consciousness, this hexagram symbolizes the ascending-descending benefit of progress, gain, advantage and accomplishment for the many, which are fruits of the integration of Heaven (Wisdom and Truth) and Earth (Love and Compassion). Progress and gain now smoothly and actively unfold. Having a goal in mind, and a ready willingness to move toward the good and away from that which is evil, are important now. This is a vision-logic consciousness expression of One's developmental tendency toward, and agency within, the transpersonal Reality of *Being's Trans-gnostic Transexistential Awakening Experience*, as seen from Onliness theory and perspective. See *Fires of Consciousness*, page 200.

```
------------------
------------------
-------    -------
-------    -------
-------    -------
------------------
```

Wisdom (Truth) Self of Awakening

HEXAGRAM 51: TENDENCY TOWARD NONBEING'S PAN-GNOSTIC ISTENTIAL MYSTERY EXPERIENCE

You are not your untruthful, deceptive, devious and evasive self and consciousness. This is not Your True Nature and Condition. This is not Your *True Identity.* Only Self, which You now and ever are, is Real. In Self-realization, developmentally beyond (with the death of) conditional and conditioned body-mind centered compound personal-egoic self and consciousness, You are, in Truth, the Love, Wisdom and Compassion of uncreated, causeless, boundless, timeless and formless *Supreme Self Reality,* and non-other Than. Unfathomable, You are this birthless and deathless unassailable *Bliss-Divine Self* which is All and Each and None, Only and Completely. Awaken to, and *Be,* the Truth-consciousness of this ultimately unutterable and unqualifiable *Absolute Nondual Self Reality* that You always and already are. Transpersonally, within World-Soul Experience's Consciousness Awakening, You are Holiness Compassion's *Inspired Heart-Soul of Unreflexive Energy,* this *Transfigurative Action and Grace of Form Self-as-Self Reality,* which is Consciousness Self of Mystery. Personally, at the pre-transcendental developmental level of body-mind compound personal-egoic self and consciousness, this hexagram symbolizes the ascending-descending benefit of growth, order, happiness and success. However, it is the sustained and powerful forces of movement and action, like continuous, loud and frightening thunder, that are the underlying source of such growth, order, happiness and success. One who remains balanced and steadfast in the face of such powerful manifest forces is indeed a leader to be followed. Fear can be a useful and important guide and mentor. This is a vision-logic consciousness expression of One's developmental tendency toward, and agency within, the transpersonal Reality of *Nonbeing's Pan-gnostic Istential*

Mystery Experience, as seen from Onliness theory and perspective. See *Fires of Consciousness,* page 213.

```
-------     -------
-------     -------
-----------------
-------     -------
-------     -------
-----------------
```

Consciousness Self of Mystery

HEXAGRAM 21: TENDENCY TOWARD NONBEING'S TRANS-GNOSTIC ISTENTIAL MYSTERY EXPERIENCE

You are not your envy, jealousy and possessiveness self and consciousness. This is not Your True Nature and Condition. This is not Your *True Identity*. Only Self, which You now and ever are, is Real. In Self-realization, developmentally beyond (with the death of) conditional and conditioned body-mind centered compound personal-egoic self and consciousness, You are, in Truth, the Love, Wisdom and Compassion of uncreated, causeless, boundless, timeless and formless *Supreme Self Reality*, and non-other Than. Unfathomable, You are this birthless and deathless unassailable *Bliss-Divine Self* which is All and Each and None, Only and Completely. Awaken to, and *Be*, the Truth-consciousness of this ultimately unutterable and unqualifable *Absolute Nondual Self Reality* that You always and already are. Transpersonally, within World-Soul Experience's Consciousness Awakening, You are Holiness Compassion's *Brilliance and Power of Trans-ceptive Boundlessness*, this *Heart-Soul Force and Vergency of Each Each-where Receptivity Self-as-Self Awakening*, which is Alpha and Omega Self of Mystery. Personally, at the pre-transcendental developmental level of body-mind compound personal-egoic self and consciousness, this hexagram symbolizes the ascending-descending benefit of progress, containment, strength, brilliance and success through complete deliberation, using clear and carefully defined legalistic reasoning and judgment, and then strong movement to act upon such deliberation. This outcome is like the moving sound of thunder and the brilliance of lightning in a powerful storm. This is a vision-logic consciousness expression of One's developmental tendency toward, and agency within, the transpersonal Reality of *Nonbeing's Trans-gnostic Istential Mystery Experience*, as seen from Onliness theory and perspective. See *Fires of Consciousness*, page 214.

-------   -------

-------   -------
-------   -------

Alpha and Omega Self of Mystery

HEXAGRAM 59: TENDENCY TOWARD BEING'S TRANS-GNOSTIC TRANSEXISTENTIAL MYSTERY AWARENESS

You are not your work, vocation or profession self and consciousness. This is not Your True Nature and Condition. This is not Your *True Identity*. Only Self, which You now and ever are, is Real. In Self-realization, developmentally beyond (with the death of) conditional and conditioned body-mind centered compound personal-egoic self and consciousness, You are, in Truth, the Love, Wisdom and Compassion of uncreated, causeless, boundless, timeless and formless *Supreme Self Reality*, and non-other Than. Unfathomable, You are this birthless and deathless unassailable *Bliss-Divine Self* which is All and Each and None, Only and Completely. Awaken to, and *Be*, the Truth-consciousness of this ultimately unutterable and unqualifable *Absolute Nondual Self Reality* that You always and already are. Transpersonally, within World-Soul Awareness's Consciousness Awakening, You are Realization Knowledge's *Comprehending Mind-Psyche of Reflexive Truth*, this *Understanding of Infinite Configurative Form Reality Self-as-Self Revelation*, which is Pathless Self of Mystery. Personally, at the pre-transcendental developmental level of body-mind compound personal-egoic self and consciousness, this hexagram symbolizes the ascending-descending ultimate benefit of progress, safety, concrete accomplishment and success, even in the face of disintegration, scattering, dispersion and danger, through willingness to move, and its related movement, so as to return to One's place of physical and spiritual refuge and peace. Persistence in a righteous course is advantageous. This is a vision-logic consciousness expression of One's developmental tendency toward, and agency within, the transpersonal Reality of *Being's Trans-gnostic Transexistential Mystery Awareness*, as seen from Onliness theory and perspective. See *Fires of Consciousness*, page 216.

```
------------------
------------------
-------   -------
-------   -------
------------------
-------   -------
```

Pathless Self of Mystery

HEXAGRAM 29: TENDENCY TOWARD BEING'S PAN-GNOSTIC TRANSEXISTENTIAL MYSTERY AWARENESS

You are not your illusory polarity-duality-perceived fragmented self and consciousness. This is not Your True Nature and Condition. This is not Your *True Identity*. Only Self, which You now and ever are, is Real. In Self-realization, developmentally beyond (with the death of) conditional and conditioned body-mind centered compound personal-egoic self and consciousness, You are, in Truth, the Love, Wisdom and Compassion of uncreated, causeless, boundless, timeless and formless *Supreme Self Reality*, and non-other Than. Unfathomable, You are this birthless and deathless unassailable *Bliss-Divine Self* which is All and Each and None, Only and Completely. Awaken to, and *Be,* the Truth-consciousness of this ultimately unutterable and unqualifable *Absolute Nondual Self Reality* that You always and already are. Transpersonally, within World-Soul Awareness's Consciousness Awakening, You are Realization Knowledge's *Mind-Psyche Vision and Understanding of Holo-ceptive Unconditionality*, this *Perception of Convergency and All Each-where Luminosity Self-as-Self Reality*, which is Liberated Self of Mystery. Personally, at the pre-transcendental developmental level of body-mind compound personal-egoic self and consciousness, this hexagram symbolizes the ascending-descending possibility of grave and sustained danger, but it may be possible to avoid this through integrity of conduct and careful monitoring and regulation of mind, in conjunction with skilled, penetrating, flexible and confident action. Virtuous action and the instruction of others in the conduct of life's activities, are important now. This is a vision-logic consciousness expression of One's developmental tendency toward, and agency within, the transpersonal Reality of *Being's Pan-gnostic Transexistential Mystery Awareness*, as seen from Onliness theory and perspective. See *Fires of Consciousness*, page 218.

```
-------      -------
-----------------
-------      -------
-------      -------
-----------------
-------      -------
```

Liberated Self of Mystery

HEXAGRAM 17: TENDENCY TOWARD NONBEING'S PAN-GNOSTIC ANTISTENTIAL MYSTERY EXPERIENCE

You are not your sexuality and sexual gender role, identity, fantasies and feelings self and consciousness. This is not Your True Nature and Condition. This is not Your *True Identity.* Only Self, which You now and ever are, is Real. In Self-realization, developmentally beyond (with the death of) conditional and conditioned body-mind centered compound personal-egoic self and consciousness, You are, in Truth, the Love, Wisdom and Compassion of uncreated, causeless, boundless, timeless and formless *Supreme Self Reality,* and non-other Than. Unfathomable, You are this birthless and deathless unassailable *Bliss-Divine Self* which is All and Each and None, Only and Completely. Awaken to, and *Be,* the Truth-consciousness of this ultimately unutterable and unqualifable *Absolute Nondual Self Reality* that You always and already are. Transpersonally, within World-Soul Experience's Consciousness Awakening, You are Holiness Compassion's *Heart-Soul Genesis of Attention and Creativity,* this *Presence and Apprehending Body of Love Self-as-Self Awakening,* which is Ecstatic Realization Self of Mystery. Personally, at the pre-transcendental developmental level of body-mind compound personal-egoic self and consciousness, this hexagram symbolizes the ascending-descending benefit of progress, joy, peace and great success, through the timely following of One who leads through righteous persistence which is in accord with goodness, beauty and truth. Responding to, and being in harmony with, the tenor of the times is now an important principle. When darkness descends, One needs to look inward to find peace and rest. This is a vision-logic consciousness expression of One's developmental tendency toward, and agency within, the transpersonal Reality of *Nonbeing's Pan-gnostic Antistential Mystery Experience,* as seen from Onliness theory and perspective. See *Fires of Consciousness,* page 221.

-------   -------

-------   -------
-------   -------

Ecstatic Realization Self of Mystery

HEXAGRAM 25: TENDENCY TOWARD NONBEING'S TRANS-GNOSTIC ANTISTENTIAL MYSTERY EXPERIENCE

You are not your cruelty, vindictiveness and pettiness self and consciousness. This is not Your True Nature and Condition. This is not Your *True Identity*. Only Self, which You now and ever are, is Real. In Self-realization, developmentally beyond (with the death of) conditional and conditioned body-mind centered compound personal-egoic self and consciousness, You are, in Truth, the Love, Wisdom and Compassion of uncreated, causeless, boundless, timeless and formless *Supreme Self Reality*, and non-other Than. Unfathomable, You are this birthless and deathless unassailable *Bliss-Divine Self* which is All and Each and None, Only and Completely. Awaken to, and *Be,* the Truth-consciousness of this ultimately unutterable and unqualifable *Absolute Nondual Self Reality* that You always and already are. Transpersonally, within World-Soul Experience's Consciousness Awakening, You are Holiness Compassion's *Perfect Void-Emptiness and Fullness of Eternity,* this *Transfigurative Heart-Soul of Receptivity and Grace Self-as-Self Truth-consciousness,* which is Universal Self of Mystery. Personally, at the pre-transcendental developmental level of body-mind compound personal-egoic self and consciousness, this hexagram symbolizes the ascending-descending benefit of progress, growth, movement, strength, accomplishment and success, realized through the action of righteous persistence with great integrity, sincerity and simplicity. Goals lacking in righteousness, integrity, sincerity and simplicity, and thus not in accord with Heaven (Love, Wisdom and Compassion), are to be avoided and will fail if undertaken. One needs to give generously so as to nourish all beings. This is a vision-logic consciousness expression of One's developmental tendency toward, and agency within, the transpersonal Reality of

Nonbeing's Trans-gnostic Antistential Mystery Experience, as seen from Onliness theory and perspective. See *Fires of Consciousness*, page 222.

```
------------------
------------------
------------------
-------   -------
-------   -------
------------------
```

Universal Self of Mystery

HEXAGRAM 4: TENDENCY TOWARD BEING'S TRANS-GNOSTIC EXISTENTIAL MYSTERY AWARENESS

You are not your sense of despairing, depressed and hopeless self and consciousness. This is not Your True Nature and Condition. This is not Your *True Identity*. Only Self, which You now and ever are, is Real. In Self-realization, developmentally beyond (with the death of) conditional and conditioned body-mind centered compound personal-egoic self and consciousness, You are, in Truth, the Love, Wisdom and Compassion of uncreated, causeless, boundless, timeless and formless *Supreme Self Reality*, and non-other Than. Unfathomable, You are this birthless and deathless unassailable *Bliss-Divine Self* which is All and Each and None, Only and Completely. Awaken to, and *Be,* the Truth-consciousness of this ultimately unutterable and unqualifable *Absolute Nondual Self Reality* that You always and already are. Transpersonally, within World-Soul Awareness's Consciousness Awakening, You are Realization Knowledge's *Mind-Psyche Morphosis of Understanding and Productivity*, this *Silent and Comprehending Vision-Seed Self-as-Self Recognition*, which is All-encompassing Self of Mystery. Personally, at the pre-transcendental developmental level of body-mind compound personal-egoic self and consciousness, this hexagram symbolizes the ascending-descending danger of judgment and action based on youthful immaturity, inexperience, ignorance and rashness; even though at times such rashness can succeed. If One who is immature is open to and earnestly seeks instruction, it is the duty of the mature, cultivated and experienced to instruct such a One. Those who sincerely seek instruction will progress and succeed. Good and resolute conduct will nurture One's virtue. This is a vision-logic consciousness expression of One's developmental tendency toward, and agency within, the transpersonal Reality of *Being's*

Trans-gnostic Existential Mystery Awareness, as seen from Onliness theory and perspective. See *Fires of Consciousness,* page 225.

```
------------------

-------      -------

-------      -------

-------      -------

------------------

-------      -------
```

All-encompassing Self of Mystery

HEXAGRAM 7: TENDENCY TOWARD BEING'S PAN-GNOSTIC EXISTENTIAL MYSTERY AWARENESS

You are not your narcissistic self-adulation, idolization and aggrandizement self and consciousness. This is not Your True Nature and Condition. This is not Your *True Identity*. Only Self, which You now and ever are, is Real. In Self-realization, developmentally beyond (with the death of) conditional and conditioned body-mind centered compound personal-egoic self and consciousness, You are, in Truth, the Love, Wisdom and Compassion of uncreated, causeless, boundless, timeless and formless *Supreme Self Reality*, and non-other Than. Unfathomable, You are this birthless and deathless unassailable *Bliss-Divine Self* which is All and Each and None, Only and Completely. Awaken to, and *Be,* the Truth-consciousness of this ultimately unutterable and unqualifable *Absolute Nondual Self Reality* that You always and already are. Transpersonally, within World-Soul Awareness's Consciousness Awakening, You are Realization Knowledge's *Perfect Form-Fullness and Emptiness of Nonduality,* this *Mind-Psyche of Stillness and Configurative Beauty Self-as-Self Expression,* which is Identity Self of Mystery. Personally, at the pre-transcendental developmental level of body-mind compound personal-egoic self and consciousness, this hexagram symbolizes the ascending-descending benefit of progress, accomplishment and success as an experienced leader of others under dangerous and difficult circumstances, realized through firm and correct persistence in a righteous course. It is important to teach and nourish those You lead, and to treat them with kindness and leniency. This is a vision-logic consciousness expression of One's developmental tendency toward, and agency within, the transpersonal Reality of *Being's Pan-gnostic Existential Mystery Awareness,* as seen from Onliness theory and perspective. See *Fires of Consciousness,* page 227.

```
-------      -------
-------      -------
-------      -------
-------      -------
-----------------
-------      -------
```

Identity Self of Mystery

HEXAGRAM 44: TENDENCY TOWARD NONBEING'S TRANS-GNOSTIC ANTISTENTIAL MIND AWARENESS

You are not your human being self and consciousness. This is not Your True Nature and Condition. This is not Your *True Identity*. Only Self, which You now and ever are, is Real. In Self-realization, developmentally beyond (with the death of) conditional and conditioned body-mind centered compound personal-egoic self and consciousness, You are, in Truth, the Love, Wisdom and Compassion of uncreated, causeless, boundless, timeless and formless *Supreme Self Reality*, and non-other Than. Unfathomable, You are this birthless and deathless unassailable *Bliss-Divine Self* which is All and Each and None, Only and Completely. Awaken to, and *Be,* the Truth-consciousness of this ultimately unutterable and unqualifable *Absolute Nondual Self Reality* that You always and already are. Transpersonally, within World-Soul Awareness's Consciousness Awakening, You are Intuition Knowledge's *Silent Mind-Psyche Form of Cognition and Perception Nonduality*, this *Holo-scient Understanding of Conforming and Configurative Fluidity Self-as-Self Expression*, which is Nameless, Not Even Self of Mind. Personally, at the pre-transcendental developmental level of body-mind compound personal-egoic self and consciousness, this hexagram symbolizes the ascending-descending *potential* benefit of contact, intercourse, meeting and communication, which is basic to the interactive mutual support of Love, Wisdom and Compassion from which the Good, Beautiful and True arise, *if* such intercourse and communication is boldly accomplished through the tranquil strength and power of open and all-encompassing *glad acceptance*. The widespread awareness and timely application of this principle is critically important. This is a vision-logic consciousness expression of One's developmental tendency toward, and agency within, the transpersonal Reality of *Nonbeing's Trans-gnostic*

Antistential Mind Awareness, as seen from Onliness theory and perspective. See *Fires of Consciousness,* page 241.

-------   -------

Nameless, Not Even Self of Mind

HEXAGRAM 28: TENDENCY TOWARD NONBEING'S PAN-GNOSTIC ANTISTENTIAL MIND AWARENESS

You are not your self-indulgent, self-absorbed, vain and superficial self and consciousness. This is not Your True Nature and Condition. This is not Your *True Identity*. Only Self, which You now and ever are, is Real. In Self-realization, developmentally beyond (with the death of) conditional and conditioned body-mind centered compound personal-egoic self and consciousness, You are, in Truth, the Love, Wisdom and Compassion of uncreated, causeless, boundless, timeless and formless *Supreme Self Reality*, and non-other Than. Unfathomable, You are this birthless and deathless unassailable *Bliss-Divine Self* which is All and Each and None, Only and Completely. Awaken to, and *Be,* the Truth-consciousness of this ultimately unutterable and unqualifiable *Absolute Nondual Self Reality* that You always and already are. Transpersonally, within World-Soul Awareness's Consciousness Awakening, You are Intuition Knowledge's *Mind-Psyche of Holo-ceptive Unconditionality*, this *Comprehending Morphosis and Throughness Reflexivity Self-as-Self Recognition*, which is Buddha-nature Self of Mind. Personally, at the pre-transcendental developmental level of body-mind compound personal-egoic self and consciousness, this hexagram symbolizes the ascending-descending benefit of accomplishment and success, through movement and flexibility with joy and gentleness acting in conjunction. It is important to have a goal or destination in view. However, there is a clear danger in relation to possible excess and strain upon the central supporting structures here involved, which must be carefully monitored. Without regret or fear, One must *stand alone* in this circumstance, withdrawing from the world. This is a vision-logic consciousness expression of One's developmental tendency toward, and agency within, the transpersonal Reality of *Nonbeing's Pan-gnostic Antistential Mind*

Awareness, as seen from Onliness theory and perspective. See *Fires of Consciousness*, page 242.

------- -------

------- -------

Buddha-nature Self of Mind

HEXAGRAM 36: TENDENCY TOWARD BEING'S PAN-GNOSTIC EXISTENTIAL MIND EXPERIENCE

You are not your bounded, restricted, contracted and contained self and consciousness. This is not Your True Nature and Condition. This is not Your *True Identity*. Only Self, which You now and ever are, is Real. In Self-realization, developmentally beyond (with the death of) conditional and conditioned body-mind centered compound personal-egoic self and consciousness, You are, in Truth, the Love, Wisdom and Compassion of uncreated, causeless, boundless, timeless and formless *Supreme Self Reality*, and non-other Than. Unfathomable, You are this birthless and deathless unassailable *Bliss-Divine Self* which is All and Each and None, Only and Completely. Awaken to, and *Be,* the Truth-consciousness of this ultimately unutterable and unqualifable *Absolute Nondual Self Reality* that You always and already are. Transpersonally, within World-Soul Experience's Consciousness Awakening, You are Righteousness Compassion's *Eternal Attention and Presence of Each Each-where Void-Emptiness*, this *Translucent Heart-Soul of Transfigurative Intensity Self-as-Self Revelation*, which is Abyss Self of Mind. Personally, at the pre-transcendental developmental level of body-mind compound personal-egoic self and consciousness, this hexagram symbolizes ascending-descending difficulty, darkening of the light, obscuration, injury and repression. Yet steadfast and righteous persistence, and awareness in the face of such circumstance, will bring advantage and reward. In such difficulty and obscuration, and despite One's internal fears and troubles, it is important to outwardly act with gentleness and willing acceptance, while concealing One's interior determination and brilliance of mind and character. A leader, though concealing One's light nevertheless shines. This is a vision-logic consciousness expression of One's developmental tendency toward, and agency within, the transpersonal Reality of *Being's Pan-gnostic Existential Mind Experience*, as seen from Onliness theory and perspective. See *Fires of Consciousness*, page 244.

```
-------      -------
-------      -------
-------      -------
------------------
-------      -------
------------------
```

Abyss Self of Mind

HEXAGRAM 22: TENDENCY TOWARD BEING'S TRANS-GNOSTIC EXISTENTIAL MIND EXPERIENCE

You are not your relative, conditional and contingent self and consciousness. This is not Your True Nature and Condition. This is not Your *True Identity*. Only Self, which You now and ever are, is Real. In Self-realization, developmentally beyond (with the death of) conditional and conditioned body-mind centered compound personal-egoic self and consciousness, You are, in Truth, the Love, Wisdom and Compassion of uncreated, causeless, boundless, timeless and formless *Supreme Self Reality*, and non-other Than. Unfathomable, You are this birthless and deathless unassailable *Bliss-Divine Self* which is All and Each and None, Only and Completely. Awaken to, and *Be*, the Truth-consciousness of this ultimately unutterable and unqualifable *Absolute Nondual Self Reality* that You always and already are. Transpersonally, within World-Soul Experience's Consciousness Awakening, You are Righteousness Compassion's *Power of Transceptive Boundless Genesis and Grace*, this *With-ness Heart-Soul of Unreflexivity Self-as-Self Reality*, which is Non-attaining, All-ness Self of Mind. Personally, at the pre-transcendental developmental level of body-mind compound personal-egoic self and consciousness, this hexagram symbolizes the ascending-descending benefit of elegance, learning and success through careful observation of varied processes and patterns, so as to have a constructive influence upon them. In contemplating the patterns and processes of Heaven (Love, Wisdom and Compassion) One comes to understand the nature of all things. Generally, beings attain and then remain at a certain level of cultural development. Decisions of serious and far reaching legalistic consequence need to be cautiously and extensively considered. This is a vision-logic consciousness expression of One's developmental tendency toward, and agency within, the transpersonal Reality of *Being's*

Trans-gnostic Existential Mind Experience, as seen from Onliness theory and perspective. See *Fires of Consciousness,* page 246.

```
------------------
-------     -------
-------     -------
------------------
-------     -------
------------------
```

Non-attaining, All-ness Self of Mind

HEXAGRAM 50: TENDENCY TOWARD NONBEING'S TRANS-GNOSTIC ISTENTIAL MIND AWARENESS

You are not your waking dream-based or dreaming relative mind of self and consciousness. This is not Your True Nature and Condition. This is not Your *True Identity*. Only Self, which You now and ever are, is Real. In Self-realization, developmentally beyond (with the death of) conditional and conditioned body-mind centered compound personal-egoic self and consciousness, You are, in Truth, the Love, Wisdom and Compassion of uncreated, causeless, boundless, timeless and formless *Supreme Self Reality*, and non-other Than. Unfathomable, You are this birthless and deathless unassailable *Bliss-Divine Self* which is All and Each and None, Only and Completely. Awaken to, and *Be,* the Truth-consciousness of this ultimately unutterable and unqualifiable *Absolute Nondual Self Reality* that You always and already are. Transpersonally, within World-Soul Awareness's Consciousness Awakening, You are Intuition Knowledge's *Scient Configurative Cognition of Worlds*, this *Omniscient Mind-Psyche of Whole Envisioning Self-as-Self Truth-consciousness*, which is Tao Self of Mind. Personally, at the pre-transcendental developmental level of body-mind compound personal-egoic self and consciousness, this hexagram symbolizes the ascending-descending benefit of righteous sacrifice, which leads to holy and virtuous progress of accomplishment and supreme success. It is important to maintain the way of righteousness, wisdom and compassion in this necessary and beneficial illuminating fire of sacrifice. One needs to sacrifice for, and thus nourish, those in need. This is a vision-logic consciousness expression of One's developmental tendency toward, and agency within, the transpersonal Reality of *Nonbeing's Trans-gnostic Istential Mind Awareness*, as seen from Onliness theory and perspective. See *Fires of Consciousness*, page 248.

```
------------------
-------    -------
------------------
------------------
------------------
-------    -------
```

Tao Self of Mind

HEXAGRAM 32: TENDENCY TOWARD NONBEING'S PAN-GNOSTIC ISTENTIAL MIND AWARENESS

You are not your mind's desires, dreams, goals and aspirations self and consciousness. This is not Your True Nature and Condition. This is not Your *True Identity*. Only Self, which You now and ever are, is Real. In Self-realization, developmentally beyond (with the death of) conditional and conditioned body-mind centered compound personal-egoic self and consciousness, You are, in Truth, the Love, Wisdom and Compassion of uncreated, causeless, boundless, timeless and formless *Supreme Self Reality*, and non-other Than. Unfathomable, You are this birthless and deathless unassailable *Bliss-Divine Self* which is All and Each and None, Only and Completely. Awaken to, and *Be,* the Truth-consciousness of this ultimately unutterable and unqualifiable *Absolute Nondual Self Reality* that You always and already are. Transpersonally, within World-Soul Awareness's Consciousness Awakening, You are Intuition Knowledge's *Silent Mind-Psyche of Reflexivity,* this *Perfect Fullness Joyful and Suffusive Understanding of Void-Emptiness Self-as-Self Awakening,* which is Absolute Self of Mind. Personally, at the pre-transcendental developmental level of body-mind compound personal-egoic self and consciousness, this hexagram symbolizes the ascending-descending benefit of progress, advantage, accomplishment, long endurance and sustained success, through the conjoined interaction of firmness and mildness in a course of righteous persistence and preservation. It is advantageous to have a goal in view. Such righteous persistence and steadfastness can indeed transform the world. This is a vision-logic consciousness expression of One's developmental tendency toward, and agency within, the transpersonal Reality of *Nonbeing's Pan-gnostic Istential Mind Awareness,* as seen from Onliness theory and perspective. See *Fires of Consciousness,* page 250.

```
-------      -------
-------      -------
-----------------
-----------------
-----------------
-------      -------
```

Absolute Self of Mind

HEXAGRAM 63: TENDENCY TOWARD BEING'S PAN-GNOSTIC TRANSEXISTENTIAL MIND EXPERIENCE

You are not your rationalization, excuses and self-justification self and consciousness. This is not Your True Nature and Condition. This is not Your *True Identity.* Only Self, which You now and ever are, is Real. In Self-realization, developmentally beyond (with the death of) conditional and conditioned body-mind centered compound personal-egoic self and consciousness, You are, in Truth, the Love, Wisdom and Compassion of uncreated, causeless, boundless, timeless and formless *Supreme Self Reality,* and non-other Than. Unfathomable, You are this birthless and deathless unassailable *Bliss-Divine Self* which is All and Each and None, Only and Completely. Awaken to, and *Be,* the Truth-consciousness of this ultimately unutterable and unqualifable *Absolute Nondual Self Reality* that You always and already are. Transpersonally, within World-Soul Experience's Consciousness Awakening, You are Righteousness Compassion's *Dispassionate Transfigurative Passion of Worlds,* this *Lucent and Inspired Omnipotent Heart-Soul of Action Self-as-Self Revelation,* which is Undivided Self of Mind. Personally, at the pre-transcendental developmental level of body-mind compound personal-egoic self and consciousness, this hexagram symbolizes the ascending-descending initial benefit of progress and success in small matters, and completion of One's undertaking. But after completion and initial success there can occur danger, stagnation and disorder. Careful advanced planning, preparation and persistence in a righteous course can greatly lessen such danger and disorder. This is a vision-logic consciousness expression of One's developmental tendency toward, and agency within, the transpersonal Reality of *Being's Pan-gnostic Transexistential Mind Experience,* as seen from Onliness theory and perspective. See *Fires of Consciousness,* page 253.

```
-------    -------
-----------------
-------    -------
-----------------
-------    -------
-----------------
```

Undivided Self of Mind

HEXAGRAM 37: TENDENCY TOWARD BEING'S TRANS-GNOSTIC TRANSEXISTENTIAL MIND EXPERIENCE

You are not your venal, aggressive, bullying and abusive self and consciousness. This is not Your True Nature and Condition. This is not Your *True Identity*. Only Self, which You now and ever are, is Real. In Self-realization, developmentally beyond (with the death of) conditional and conditioned body-mind centered compound personal-egoic self and consciousness, You are, in Truth, the Love, Wisdom and Compassion of uncreated, causeless, boundless, timeless and formless *Supreme Self Reality*, and non-other Than. Unfathomable, You are this birthless and deathless unassailable *Bliss-Divine Self* which is All and Each and None, Only and Completely. Awaken to, and *Be,* the Truth-consciousness of this ultimately unutterable and unqualifable *Absolute Nondual Self Reality* that You always and already are. Transpersonally, within World-Soul Experience's Consciousness Awakening, You are Righteousness Compassion's *Transforming Heart-Soul of Unreflexivity*, this *Intense and Infusive Void-Emptiness Illumination of Worlds Self-as-Self Awakening*, which is Non-clinging, Non-attachment Self of Mind. Personally, at the pre-transcendental developmental level of body-mind compound personal-egoic self and consciousness, this hexagram symbolizes the ascending-descending benefit of family strength and harmony, through coordination and integration of male and female strength and weakness functions and capacities within the family, so as to balance and mutually support one another; and in this way to strengthen, harmonize and stabilize the family. In turn, such family harmony and balance will greatly benefit the well being and stability of the whole world. Persistence, truth and consistency are especially emphasized in this circumstance and process. This is a vision-logic consciousness expression of One's developmental tendency toward, and agency within, the transpersonal Reality of *Being's Trans-gnostic Transexistential Mind Experience,* as seen from Onliness theory and perspective. See *Fires of Consciousness,* page 254.

```
------------------
------------------
-------     -------
------------------
-------     -------
------------------
```

Non-clinging, Non-attachment Self of Mind

HEXAGRAM 55: TENDENCY TOWARD NONBEING'S PAN-GNOSTIC ISTENTIAL ONLINESS EXPERIENCE

You are not your intellectualizing, abstracting and theorizing self and consciousness. This is not Your True Nature and Condition. This is not Your *True Identity*. Only Self, which You now and ever are, is Real. In Self-realization, developmentally beyond (with the death of) conditional and conditioned body-mind centered compound personal-egoic self and consciousness, You are, in Truth, the Love, Wisdom and Compassion of uncreated, causeless, boundless, timeless and formless *Supreme Self Reality*, and non-other Than. Unfathomable, You are this birthless and deathless unassailable *Bliss-Divine Self* which is All and Each and None, Only and Completely. Awaken to, and *Be,* the Truth-consciousness of this ultimately unutterable and unqualifiable *Absolute Nondual Self Reality* that You always and already are. Transpersonally, within World-Soul Experience's Consciousness Awakening, You are Righteousness Compassion's *Heart-Soul of Omnipotent Presence and Grace,* this *Intensity of Spirit's Germinating Form of Emptiness, this Searing Fire of Worlds Self-as-Self Revelation,* which is Uncreated Self of Onliness. Personally, at the pre-transcendental developmental level of body-mind compound personal-egoic self and consciousness, this hexagram symbolizes the ascending-descending benefit of abundance, progress, development and success, accomplished through the ebb and flow of change. At the same time, it is important to recognize and accept the *impermanence* of all phenomena, as well as the cyclic waxing and waning of all benefits. Now, movement motivated by brilliance predominates, with resultant progress, development, abundance and success. Legal decisions and penalty apportionments need to be carefully decided. This is a vision-logic consciousness expression of One's developmental tendency toward, and agency within, the transpersonal Reality of *Nonbeing's Pan-gnostic Istential Onliness Experience,* as seen from Onliness theory and perspective. See *Fires of Consciousness,* page 269.

```
-------    -------
-------    -------
------------------
------------------
-------    -------
------------------
```

Uncreated Self of Onliness

HEXAGRAM 30: TENDENCY TOWARD NONBEING'S TRANS-GNOSTIC ISTENTIAL ONLINESS EXPERIENCE

You are not your relative mind self and consciousness. This is not Your True Nature and Condition. This is not Your *True Identity*. Only Self, which You now and ever are, is Real. In Self-realization, developmentally beyond (with the death of) conditional and conditioned body-mind centered compound personal-egoic self and consciousness, You are, in Truth, the Love, Wisdom and Compassion of uncreated, causeless, boundless, timeless and formless *Supreme Self Reality*, and non-other Than. Unfathomable, You are this birthless and deathless unassailable *Bliss-Divine Self* which is All and Each and None, Only and Completely. Awaken to, and *Be,* the Truth-consciousness of this ultimately unutterable and unqualifable *Absolute Nondual Self Reality* that You always and already are. Transpersonally, within World-Soul Experience's Consciousness Awakening, You are Righteousness Compassion's *Transforming Heart-Soul of Genesis and Creativity*, this *Luminous Sight of Each Each-where Enfoldingness Attention Self-as-Self Truth-consciousness*, which is No-separation, Oneness Self of Onliness. Personally, at the pre-transcendental developmental level of body-mind compound personal-egoic self and consciousness, this hexagram symbolizes the ascending-descending benefit of interdependency, brilliance, beauty and success, through quiet firmness, clarity, righteous persistence, gentleness and docility. In this illuminating way, One can constructively transform the world. This is a vision-logic consciousness expression of One's developmental tendency toward, and agency within, the transpersonal Reality of *Nonbeing's Trans-gnostic Istential Onliness Experience*, as seen from Onliness theory and perspective. See *Fires of Consciousness*, page 270.

-------   -------

-------   -------

No-separation, Oneness Self of Onliness

HEXAGRAM 57: TENDENCY TOWARD BEING'S TRANS-GNOSTIC TRANSEXISTENTIAL ONLINESS AWARENESS

You are not your actions and behaviors. This is not Your True Nature and Condition. This is not Your *True Identity*. Only Self, which You now and ever are, is Real. In Self-realization, developmentally beyond (with the death of) conditional and conditioned body-mind-centered compound personal-egoic self and consciousness, You are, in Truth, the Love, Wisdom and Compassion of uncreated, causeless, boundless, timeless and formless *Supreme Self Reality*, and non-other Than. Unfathomable, You are this birthless and deathless unassailable *Bliss-Divine Self* which is All and Each and None, Only and Completely. Awaken to, and *Be,* the Truth-consciousness of this ultimately unutterable and unqualifable *Absolute Nondual Self Reality* that You always and already are. Transpersonally, within World-Soul Awareness's Consciousness Awakening, You are Intuition Knowledge's *Comprehending Mind-Psyche of Omniscient Insight and Truth,* this *Flowering Void-Emptiness Silence and Formlessness, this Creator and Destroyer of Worlds Self-as-Self Reality*, which is Timeless Self of Onliness. Personally, at the pre-transcendental developmental level of body-mind compound personal-egoic self and consciousness, this hexagram symbolizes the ascending-descending benefit of progress, achievement and success in lesser matters, through action in accord with Love, Wisdom and Compassion, which will require and involve penetration, flexibility, gentleness and especially willing submission. It is advantageous to have a goal in mind, and to consult a wise person in the matters at hand. This is a vision-logic consciousness expression of One's developmental tendency toward, and agency within, the transpersonal Reality of *Being's Trans-gnostic Transexistential Onliness Awareness*, as seen from Onliness theory and perspective. See *Fires of Consciousness*, page 272.

-------   -------

-------   -------

Timeless Self of Onliness

HEXAGRAM 48: TENDENCY TOWARD BEING'S PAN-GNOSTIC TRANSEXISTENTIAL ONLINESS AWARENESS

You are not your anguish, agonies and losses self and consciousness. This is not Your True Nature and Condition. This is not Your *True Identity*. Only Self, which You now and ever are, is Real. In Self-realization, developmentally beyond (with the death of) conditional and conditioned body-mind centered compound personal-egoic self and consciousness, You are, in Truth, the Love, Wisdom and Compassion of uncreated, causeless, boundless, timeless and formless *Supreme Self Reality*, and non-other Than. Unfathomable, You are this birthless and deathless unassailable *Bliss-Divine Self* which is All and Each and None, Only and Completely. Awaken to, and *Be,* the Truth-consciousness of this ultimately unutterable and unqualifable *Absolute Nondual Self Reality* that You always and already are. Transpersonally, within World-Soul Awareness's Consciousness Awakening, You are Intuition Knowledge's *Stillness Mind-Psyche of Morphosis and Productivity*, this *Insight Understanding and Knowledge of All All-where Boundlessness Self-as-Self Revelation*, which is Unfathomable Self of Onliness. Personally, at the pre-transcendental developmental level of body-mind compound personal-egoic self and consciousness, this hexagram symbolizes the ascending-descending benefit of the abundant nourishment and support readily available to us in nature so as to meet and sustain our fundamental needs, *if* we have the insight, ingenuity and foresight to attain such nourishment and support. Without such insight, ingenuity and foresight, failure in attainment of nature's nourishment and support will certainly occur. One needs to stimulate and encourage others with advise and assistance. This is a vision-logic consciousness expression of One's developmental tendency toward, and agency within, the transpersonal Reality of *Being's Pan-gnostic Transexistential Onliness Awareness*, as seen from Onliness theory and perspective. See *Fires of Consciousness*, page 274.

-------   -------

-------   -------

-------   -------

Unfathomable Self of Onliness

HEXAGRAM 49: TENDENCY TOWARD NONBEING'S PAN-GNOSTIC ANTISTENTIAL ONLINESS EXPERIENCE

You are neither your social-cultural nor your family roles, relationships and identities self and consciousness. This is not Your True Nature and Condition. This is not Your *True Identity*. Only Self, which You now and ever are, is Real. In Self-realization, developmentally beyond (with the death of) conditional and conditioned body-mind centered compound personal-egoic self and consciousness, You are, in Truth, the Love, Wisdom and Compassion of uncreated, causeless, boundless, timeless and formless *Supreme Self Reality*, and non-other Than. Unfathomable, You are this birthless and deathless unassailable *Bliss-Divine Self* which is All and Each and None, Only and Completely. Awaken to, and *Be,* the Truth-consciousness of this ultimately unutterable and unqualifiable *Absolute Nondual Self Reality* that You always and already are. Transpersonally, within World-Soul Experience's Consciousness Awakening, You are Righteousness Compassion's *Gnostic Heart-Soul of Unconditional Presence and Attention*, this *Transforming Grace and Apprehending Power of Love Self-as-Self Awakening*, which is Unspeakable Self of Onliness. Personally, at the pre-transcendental developmental level of body-mind compound personal-egoic self and consciousness, this hexagram symbolizes the ascending-descending benefit of necessary revolution, renovation and change, which brings progress, joy, accomplishment and great success through firm and determined efforts in a righteous course. This will not occur without conflict. Such profound change will be appreciated by others only after it has been fully accomplished. One must make clear to others the need and planned course of such revolutionary change, and to carefully plan and regulate its timing. This is a vision-logic consciousness expression of One's developmental tendency toward, and agency within, the transpersonal Reality of *Nonbeing's Pan-gnostic Antistential Onliness Experience,* as seen from Onliness theory and perspective. See *Fires of Consciousness,* page 277.

-------   -------

-------   -------

Unspeakable Self of Onliness

HEXAGRAM 13: TENDENCY TOWARD NONBEING'S TRANS-GNOSTIC ANTISTENTIAL ONLINESS EXPERIENCE

You are not your sense of helplessness, emptiness and worthlessness self and consciousness. This is not Your True Nature and Condition. This is not Your *True Identity*. Only Self, which You now and ever are, is Real. In Self-realization, developmentally beyond (with the death of) conditional and conditioned body-mind centered compound personal-egoic self and consciousness, You are, in Truth, the Love, Wisdom and Compassion of uncreated, causeless, boundless, timeless and formless *Supreme Self Reality*, and non-other Than. Unfathomable, You are this birthless and deathless unassailable *Bliss-Divine Self* which is All and Each and None, Only and Completely. Awaken to, and *Be,* the Truth-consciousness of this ultimately unutterable and unqualifable *Absolute Nondual Self Reality* that You always and already are. Transpersonally, within World-Soul Experience's Consciousness Awakening, You are Righteousness Compassion's *Infusive Heart-Soul of Numinous Apparent Transparency*, this *Fiery Force of Spirit's Conceptive Vitality and Passion Self-as-Self Recognition*, which is Ultimate Self of Onliness. Personally, at the pre-transcendental developmental level of body-mind compound personal-egoic self and consciousness, this hexagram symbolizes the ascending-descending benefit of creativity, brilliance, strength, progress and success, through righteous persistence within and through mutual support and cooperation. In this way, weakness and strength mutually respond to one another, as between lovers and friends. One needs to discern, and then respond to, the natures, talents and capacities of others. It is advantageous to journey. This is a vision-logic consciousness expression of One's developmental tendency toward, and agency within, the transpersonal Reality of *Nonbeing's Trans-gnostic*

Antistential Onliness Experience, as seen from Onliness theory and perspective. See *Fires of Consciousness,* page 278.

-------   -------

Ultimate Self of Onliness

HEXAGRAM 18: TENDENCY TOWARD BEING'S TRANS-GNOSTIC EXISTENTIAL ONLINESS AWARENESS

You are not your monetary riches and material possessions self and consciousness. This is not Your True Nature and Condition. This is not Your *True Identity*. Only Self, which You now and ever are, is Real. In Self-realization, developmentally beyond (with the death of) conditional and conditioned body-mind centered compound personal-egoic self and consciousness, You are, in Truth, the Love, Wisdom and Compassion of uncreated, causeless, boundless, timeless and formless *Supreme Self Reality*, and non-other Than. Unfathomable, You are this birthless and deathless unassailable *Bliss-Divine Self* which is All and Each and None, Only and Completely. Awaken to, and *Be,* the Truth-consciousness of this ultimately unutterable and unqualifiable *Absolute Nondual Self Reality* that You always and already are. Transpersonally, within World-Soul Awareness's Consciousness Awakening, You are Intuition Knowledge's *Gnostic Mind-Psyche of Boundless Truth and Understanding,* this *Intuitive Perception of Essence and Comprehending Harvest of Insight and Inspiration Self-as-Self Expression,* which is All-present, No-ness Self of Onliness. Personally, at the pre-transcendental developmental level of body-mind compound personal-egoic self and consciousness, this hexagram symbolizes the ascending-descending benefit of progress, accomplishment and success, through the effort of moving forward with carefully formulated plans so as to clear present decay and disorder, and to establish new order. This is the eternal cycle of phenomena impermanence. Here, gentleness and firmness are integrated and conjoined. This is a vision-logic consciousness expression of One's developmental tendency toward, and agency within, the transpersonal Reality of *Being's Trans-gnostic Existential Onliness Awareness,* as seen from Onliness theory and perspective. See *Fires of Consciousness,* page 280.

```
------------------
-------      -------
-------      -------
------------------
------------------
-------      -------
```

All-present, No-ness Self of Onliness

HEXAGRAM 46: TENDENCY TOWARD BEING'S PAN-GNOSTIC EXISTENTIAL ONLINESS AWARENESS

You are not your raging and vengefulness self and consciousness. This is not Your True Nature and Condition. This is not Your *True Identity*. Only Self, which You now and ever are, is Real. In Self-realization, developmentally beyond (with the death of) conditional and conditioned body-mind centered compound personal-egoic self and consciousness, You are, in Truth, the Love, Wisdom and Compassion of uncreated, causeless, boundless, timeless and formless *Supreme Self Reality*, and non-other Than. Unfathomable, You are this birthless and deathless unassailable *Bliss-Divine Self* which is All and Each and None, Only and Completely. Awaken to, and *Be,* the Truth-consciousness of this ultimately unutterable and unqualifable *Absolute Nondual Self Reality* that You always and already are. Transpersonally, within World-Soul Awareness's Consciousness Awakening, You are Intuition Knowledge's *Still and Silent Mind-Psyche of Numinous Transparent Apparency*, this *Prehending Cognition and Trans-ideation of Worlds Self-as-Self Awakening*, which is Supreme Self of Onliness. Personally, at the pre-transcendental developmental level of body-mind compound personal-egoic self and consciousness, this hexagram symbolizes the ascending-descending benefit of progress, ascension and accomplishment through virtuous action. However, because One's position is not strong One needs to take care in the timing of forward movement, but to nonetheless proceed. It is advantageous to consult a wise person. One must be *willing* to follow the ways of virtue so as to achieve *true* accomplishment and success. This is a vision-logic consciousness expression of One's developmental tendency toward, and agency within, the transpersonal Reality of *Being's Pan-gnostic Existential Onliness Awareness*, as seen from Onliness theory and perspective. See *Fires of Consciousness*, page 282.

```
-------      -------
-------      -------
-------      -------
------------------
------------------
-------      -------
```

Supreme Self of Onliness

REFERENCES

Adi Da Samraj (Da Free John) (1985). *The Dawn Horse Testament of Heart-Master Da Free John.* Middletown, CA: The Dawn Horse Press.

Blofeld, J. (Translator and Editor) (1968). *I Ching: The Book of Change.* New York: E. P. Dutton and Co.

Feng, G. and J. English (Translators) (1972). *Lao Tsu: Tao Te Ching.* New York: Vintage Books.

Friedrich, C. J. (Editor) (1954). *The Philosophy of Hegel.* New York: The Modern Library-Random House, Inc.

Huxley, A. (1944). *The Perennial Philosophy.* New York: Harper & Row.

Isherwood, C. (Editor) (1972). *Vedanta for Modern Man.* New York: The New American Library, Inc.

Kapleau, P. (Compiler) (1965). *The Three Pillars of Zen: Teaching Practice Enlightenment.* Boston: Beacon Press.

King James Version. *The Holy Bible*. New York: World Publishing Co.

Lama Surya Das (1997). *Awakening the Buddha Within*. New York: Broadway Books-Bantam Doubleday Dell Publishing Group, Inc.

Lau, D. C. (Translator) (1988). *Lao Tzu: Tao Te Ching*. New York: Penguin Books.

Legge, J. (Translator and Editor) (1964). *I Ching: Book of Changes*. New York: Bantam Books, Inc.

Mitchell, S. (Translator and Editor) (1991). *The Enlightened Mind: An Anthology of Sacred Prose*. New York: Harper.

Mitchell, S. (Translator) (1991). *Tao Te Ching: A New English Version*. New York: HarperCollins Publishers.

Reps, P. (Compiler and Editor) (1989). *Zen Flesh, Zen Bones: A Collection of Zen and pre-Zen Writings*. New York: Anchor Book-Doubleday.

Ross, N. (Compiler and Editor) (1960). *The World of Zen: An East-West Anthology*. New York: Vintage Books.

Sri Aurobindo (Compiled by P. B. Saint-Hilaire) (1995). *The Future Evolution of Man: The Divine Life upon Earth*. Pondicherry, India: Sri Aurobindo Ashram Publication Department.

Sri Nisargadatta Maharaj (Translated by M. Frydman) (2012). *I Am That: Talks with Sri Nisargadatta Maharaj*. Durham, North Carolina: The Acorn Press.

Sri Nisargadatta Maharaj (Edited by Jean Dunn) (2006). *Consciousness and the Absolute: The Final Talks of Sri Nisargadatta Maharaj*. Durham, North Carolina: The Acorn Press.

Sri Ramana Maharshi (Translated by T. M. P. Mahadevan) (2008). *Who Am I: The Teachings of Bhagavan Sri Ramana Maharshi*. Tiruvannamal 606 603 Tamil Nadu, India: V. S. Ramanan, President, Board of Trustees Sri Ramanasramam.

Sri Ramana Maharshi (2011). *A Talk with Sri Ramana Maharshi* (a video on youtube.com at Sri Ramana Maharshi). Cinefx Film Productions.

Sri Ramana Maharshi (Edited by Arthur Osborne) (1997). *The Collected Works of Ramana Maharshi*. York Beach, Maine: Samuel Weiser.

Suzuki. D. T. (Compiler and Editor) (1960). *Manual of Zen Buddhism*. New York: Grove Press, Inc.

Swami Prabhavananda and F. Manchester (Translators and Editors) (1957). *The Upanishads: Breath of the Eternal*. New York: The New American Library-Mentor Books.

Swami Prabhavananda and C. Isherwood (Translators) (1960). *The Song of God: Bhagavad-Gita.* New York: The New American Library-Mentor Books.

Treon, M. (1981a). "Organismic communicology: a prologue - dead leaves and living shadows moving in the wind." *Papers In Linguistics: International Journal of Human Communication,* 14 (1), 131-148.

Treon, M. (1981b). "Organismic communicology: a second prologue - reflection, shadow and illusion." *Papers In Linguistics: International Journal of Human Communication, 14 (3), 359-375.*

Treon, M. (1989). *The Tao of Onliness: An I Ching Cosmology - The Awakening Years.* Santa Barbara, CA: Fithian Press.

Treon, M. (1996). *Fires of Consciousness: The Tao of Onliness I Ching.* Goodyear, AZ: Auroral Skies Press.

Treon, M. (2009). *Uncreated Timeless Self of Radiant Emptiness-Onliness Consciousness and Commentaries: Formulations of a Post-metaphysical Integral Transpersonal Communicology.* Goodyear, AZ: Auroral Skies Press.

Treon, M. (2011). *Enlightenment Dialogues: A Journey of Post-metaphysical Onliness Awakening.* Goodyear, AZ: Auroral Skies Press.

Treon, M. (2015). *Enlightenment's Awakening: An Onliness Path of Truth-consciousness Realization.* Goodyear, AZ: Auroral Skies Press.

Whitehead, A. (1967). *Science and the Modern World.* New York: Macmillan.

Wilber, K. (1980). *The Atman Project: A Transpersonal View of Human Development.* Wheaton, IL: Quest.

Wilber, K. (1981). *Up From Eden: A Transpersonal View of Human Evolution.* New York: Doubleday-Anchor.

Wilber, K. (1983). *Eye to Eye: The Quest for the New Paradigm.* Boston: Shambhala Publications.

Wilber, K. (1984). *A Sociable God: Toward a New Understanding of Religion.* Boston: Shambhala Publications.)

Wilber, K. (1995). *Sex, Ecology, Spirituality: The Spirit of Evolution.* Boston: Shambhala Publications.

Wilber, K. (1996). *A Brief History of Everything.* Boston: Shambhala Publications.

Wilber, K. (1997). *The Eye of Spirit: An Integral Vision for a World Gone Slightly Mad.* Boston: Shambhala Publications.

Wilber, K. (1998). *The Marriage of Sense and Soul: Integrating Science and Religion.* New York: Random House, Inc.

Wilber, K. (2000). *One Taste: The Journals of Ken Wilber.* Boston: Shambhala Publications.

Wilber, K. (1999-2000). *The Collected Works of Ken Wilber*, Vol. 1-8. Boston: Shambhala Publications.

Wilber, K. (1999-2000, vol. 4). *Integral Psychology: Consciousness, Spirit, Psychology, Therapy.* (in *The Collected Works of Ken Wilber*, vol. 4). Boston: Shambhala Publications.

Wilber, K. (2004). *The Simple Feeling of Being: Embracing Your True Nature.* Boston: Shambhala Publications.

Wilber, K. (2007). *Integral Spirituality: A Startling New Role for Religion in the Modern and Postmodern World.* Boston: Integral Books-Shambhala Publications.

Wilber, K., J. Engler and D. P. Brown (1986). *Transformations of Consciousness: Conventional and Contemplative Perspectives on Development.* Boston: Shambhala Publications.

63806485R00165

Made in the USA
Charleston, SC
10 November 2016